INTRODUCTIONS
TO
ENGLISH LITERATURE

Edited by
BONAMY DOBRÉE

Volume III

AUGUSTANS AND ROMANTICS

AUGUSTANS AND ROMANTICS

1689—1830

by H. V. D. DYSON
Lecturer in English at the University of Reading

and JOHN BUTT
Lecturer in English at Bedford College, London

With Chapters on Art, Economics and Philosophy by
GEOFFREY WEBB, F. J. FISHER, and H. A. HODGES

THE CRESSET PRESS
LONDON

First Published 1940

Made and Printed by the Replika Process in Great Britain by
PERCY LUND, HUMPHRIES & CO. LTD.
London and Bradford

ACKNOWLEDGMENTS

WE owe a debt of apology and a debt of thanks: of apology, to the readers of other volumes in this series, who have been kept waiting for volume III by many forces beyond our control; of thanks, to those friends who have so generously given us their assistance and advice:—Professor F. M. Stenton, for his kindly endurance of what must have been for him a tedious evening; Professor R. Dewar, for Burns and encouragement; Mr. C. S. Lewis, for reading proofs and for very much else; Mr. and Mrs. Tillotson, for scrutinising much of the bibliography; Professor James R. Sutherland, for help with Defoe; Mr. F. W. Bateson for lending proof-sheets of the *Cambridge Bibliography of English Literature*; and Mr. D. W. Jefferson for his help in the compilation of the books on aesthetics.

H.V.D.D.
J.B.

CONTENTS

CONTENTS—*continued*

EDITOR'S PREFACE

IF there is a danger of literature becoming separated from life, and at times the danger becomes actuality, there is a still greater one of the same thing happening in the study of literature. For one thing, it is apt to become that most arid of studies, literary history, in which history is largely, and literature, in any real meaning of the word, entirely ignored. The literature of the past is only of value in so far as it has significance to-day, just as history is only of use if it can throw a light upon the contemporary scene. But in the same way as history becomes illuminating by study, by finding out not only what people did, but why they did it, what circumstances, thoughts and emotions brought them to act, so we enlarge the boundaries within which the literature of the past has value if we gain an insight into the circumstances, thoughts and feelings which produced not only the writers, but also the readers of any particular period.

People of different ages speak different languages; not that the words are necessarily different, but the implications are. We of the twentieth century mean very little when we speak of the "social virtues", whereas to an eighteenth-century writer the phrase implied a whole philosophy of civilisation. For us to understand what Donne meant when he wrote:

> On man heaven's influence works not so,
> But that it first imprints the ayre,
> Soe soule into the soule may flow. . . .

we have to be at least aware of a whole body of philosophic thought, we might say of philosophic apprehension, to which most of us are likely to be strangers, but which was common at the beginning of the seventeenth century. Thus one of the objects of literary study should be to enable us to translate the language of another day into that of our own, which we can only do if we realise that these divergencies of expression are not merely a question of literary allusion, but of what entered the minds of educated people every day, coloured the spectacles through which they looked at life, and moulded the form in which they uttered their feelings. Thus it is not altogether idle to ponder why Ben Jonson should have written:

> What beckoning ghost besprent with April dew
> Hails me so solemnly to yonder yew
> > (*Elegy on Lady Jane Pawlett*)

while Pope should have preferred:

> What beckoning ghost athwart the moonlit glade
> Invites my steps, and points to yonder shade
> > (*In Memory of an Unfortunate Lady*)

for there is a reason which lies deeper than personal idiosyncrasy.

It has become a platitude to say that an age is reflected in its literature, and like all platitudes the saying has ceased to have any force. Moreover, an age is often much better represented by what is no longer read, than by the works which we still take from our shelves. If, for instance, we try to reconstruct the Restoration period from the plays of the time, we shall get a view which is, to say the least of it, misleading: the age is far better represented by the turgid flood of pamphlets which issued from the inkpots of Penn and Muggleton, Thomas Hicks, John Faldo, and a dozen other forgotten and vituperative sectarians. We tend to read Dryden's plays, or certain of the satires, in preference to his other work, but he is far nearer his age in *Religio Laici* and *The Hind and the Panther* than in his now more popular writings. And if each age brings forth its own recognisable progeny, how is it that Milton and Etherege appeared together? or Thomas Hardy and Max Beerbohm? Each age has so many facets, that it is difficult to pitch on any as being

14

its outstanding mirror, though each age will have certain
peculiarities not shared by the others. But these peculiarities
are often merely the surface of fashion, accidental rather than
essential, and until we know something of the age, we cannot tell which peculiarity, when explained, can have any
significance for us.

Yet, if it is dangerous to regard literature as the looking-
glass of its time, every age has certain problems which seem to
it to be of major urgency. In the Shakespearian age it was to
incorporate the "new learning" into life; later in the seventeenth century, the politico-religious issue was the important
one; the eighteenth century, again, was lured by a vision of
civilised man. That is to say that each age has its philosophy, its scale of values. But philosophy, which to some extent conditions literature, is itself conditioned, partly by the
way people live, and partly by the influx of thought from
foreign countries, though it is as well to remember that such
thought will only penetrate or take root in a country already
prepared for it. Therefore, the way people live, their social
and political grouping, their economic formation, to some
extent determine the way they write. Much has lately been
made of the influence of economics: too much, for Marx cannot account for Milton, and it is as easy to argue that the
economic development of the eighteenth century was due to
the idea of the universe as defined by Newton, as that "Dutch
finance", commercialism, and the expansion of trade, gives a
clue to the philosophy of history which runs through Gibbon's
Decline and Fall. Yet economics have an effect on literature;
we can see it to some extent in *Piers Plowman*, and without
the rise of the middle classes at the end of the seventeenth
century we could not have had Defoe, Steele, or Addison;
the polite essayist could not have come into being, quite
apart from whether or not he preached the bourgeois
virtues.

The influence of foreign thought is a subject that has
loomed too large, perhaps, in most histories of literature,
mainly because literature has on the whole been treated as
separate from life. The influence of something on somebody
has been a favourite subject for theses, and the answers have

been as dubious as the theme has been ill-defined. Because Chaucer, having read Dante's

> Quali i fioretti di notturno gelo
> chinati e chiusi, poi che il sol gl'imbianca,
> si drizzen tutti aperti in loro stelo;
>
> tal mi fec' io. . . .
>
> <div align="right">(<i>Inferno</i> II, 127. . . .)</div>

or, more probably, the corresponding lines in the *Filostrato* of Boccaccio, proceeded to sing

> But right as floures, thorugh the colde of night
> Y-closed, stoupen on hir stalkes lowe,
> Redressen hem a-yein the sonne bright,
> And spreden on hir kinde cours by rowe:
> Right so gan. . . .
> . . . .Troilus. . . .
>
> <div align="right">(<i>Troilus and Criseyde</i>, II St. 139)</div>

that is not to say that Chaucer was influenced by Dante or by Boccaccio; indeed no prettier contrast to the *Divina Commedia* could be found than *The Canterbury Tales*, though it is clear that there is some connection between them and the *Decameron*. No one really familiar with the comedy of France and England in the seventeenth century, with an understanding of what they were up to, can believe that the English were influenced by the French to more than a superficial degree. Nevertheless, the thought of one country, or of one individual, can very profoundly affect a period, and the scepticism of Montaigne is apparent throughout the seventeenth century from Shakespeare to Halifax. In the same way, German thought obscured the clarity of Coleridge, and puffed the thought and style of Carlyle to an almost intolerable smokiness.

The writer, therefore, is, besides being a unique individual, the product of the forces of his time. However much we may regret it, we have to abandon Shelley's contention that "poets are the unacknowledged legislators of the world", though we need not altogether throw over the position; for though, no doubt, thought does sometimes influence action, it is more usually the successor of deeds, and it will not be denied that Locke is a child of the Revolution just as Hobbes was of the Great Rebellion. It is truer to say with Arnold that poetry is a criticism of life, though not quite true, for literature is, rather, a growth from life itself, a part of life, not its harvest only. We can go further and say that it is so ravelled with life that it can be described also as the soil and the seed. But that metaphor should lead to such confusion is enough to indicate how closely tangled with life literature is, how complex the relation between them, and how impossible it is to separate one from the other.

. . . .

The object of the Introductions in this series is to give the student some idea of the soil out of which the works of literature grew, so as to be able to grasp with fuller understanding the books mentioned in the Bibliographies. This, then, is not yet another History of English Literature, but rather, to exaggerate a little, a History of England in which not kings, battles, diplomatic or constitutional struggles, nor even economic development, are given pride of place, but literature. As is suitable to our age in which economics have come to be given a high place as determinants not only of our lives, but of our manner of thinking and feeling, and even of our religion, economics will be given more stress than they have hitherto been allowed in books on literature, but not, as some would no doubt wish, to the exclusion of everything else. For instance, though the question of the control of money no doubt played a larger part in the Great Rebellion than we were most of us brought up to believe, it would be absurd to neglect the religious elements in the struggle. Indeed, as Professor R. H. Tawney has shown, it was religion itself that largely determined the economic trend of the eighteenth century. The effect of religion on literature is more easily traceable; it begins with Beowulf and runs through the whole, most markedly in the periods where the Church to a large extent stamped the nature of society, or when controversy

17   B

raged high, as it did from the Reformation—or at least from the time of the *Marprelate Tracts*—to the foundation of the Bank of England. Philosophy also plays an important part, not only as being the matter of much admirable writing, but also in the general attitude towards life exhibited by writers who unconsciously, rather than in full awareness, absorbed the ideas of their time. But philosophy again is affected by economics, for no one can doubt that the individualism of the nineteenth century was largely the result of the Industrial Revolution, and that Carlyle's Cromwell must own as fore-bears Adam Smith and James Watt. Science also can affect literature, and without Huxley there would probably have been a different Hardy.

Another addition to the view of literature is made in these volumes by giving due place to the sister arts where they rose to any height, or seem to have importance with respect to writing. Thus music had an effect on poetry in the seventeenth century, while painting and architecture affected the poetry, and perhaps the prose, of the eighteenth. Wherever, in short, the literary "movement" of a time seems congruous with that of the other arts, they are included in the survey. Most important of all, however, is the social background, the changes of milieu indicated, say, by the decay of the guilds or the rise of nationalism; for these are the things which most affect the way people live, and therefore what they will most wish to write and to read.

The Bibliographies which form the major part of each volume are designed to give the reader a detailed view of the literature of each period; and being classified and commented will enable him to study or to enjoy either any special branch, or the whole literature of the period. Only the specialist can read everything; but the aim of this series is to enable anyone who so wishes, to get a clear idea of any one period by reading with a certain degree of fervour for a year, a clear notion not only of what was written, but, so to speak, of why and how, from what impulses, with what objects, and in what conditions morally speaking. It is hoped by this method to integrate literature with life, and so give the writings of the past that meaning without which to read is to be baffled, and to miss that greatest of all pleasures, a sense of unity of feeling with the writer of any work. Lacking this, literature is too far separated from living, and can have but little value.

The manner in which English literature has been split up in this series no doubt demands an explanation. There are many ways in which it can be split up. This has been done variously, sometimes rather arbitrarily, by centuries or other irrelevant measuring rods, more often by grouping it around great figures: The Age of Wordsworth and so on: or by literary movements: The Romantic Revival, for instance. These divisions have their uses, but for our purpose here they tend to subordinate life to literature. It is admitted that there is an element of arbitrariness in the present divisions also, but the object is to relate literature to life, disregarding movements, which may only be different aspects of the same thing. The divisions here correspond in the main with social sense; roughly indeed, with what reservations you will, and with contradictions of a rule which cannot be rigid, since human nature refuses to fit into compartments.

In the first period, after the Conquest, you can say with some plausibility (though it is in this period that our structure is weakest) that literature was much more diffused among different classes; it was written for no particular brand of person. Everyone would read *Piers Plowman*, or applaud the miracle plays. There is, it is true, much that is courtly about Chaucer, but there is much that is not. When we get to Spenser, say, we feel that literature is being written for an aristocracy: the drama still maintained its general appeal (though even as early as the moralities and interludes there is a shift away from the people), but it became more and more aristocratic, till under Charles II it was entirely courtly. This period, then, we can describe as the aristocratic period: Donne, Jeremy Taylor, Sir Thomas Browne, Milton, are writers for an aristocracy, and this social sense we may say was established by the Tudors, and exploited by the Stuarts, till it came to an end at the Revolution of 1688. Then, with great suddenness, there appeared a literature written by the middle class, of the middle class, and for the middle class:

19

the pamphleteers, the essayists, and soon Defoe and the novelists. Even the drama changed with startling rapidity, with the anti-aristocratic satire of Farquhar, and the sentimental comedy of Steele.

The ideas of the middle class, with its strong sense, as it then had, of an organised society, gave place in the last century to the idea of individualism, due partly to the French, and partly to the Industrial Revolution. It had been begun by the romantic poets, with their break-away from the idea of "society" so dear to the eighteenth century. It might grieve Shelley to think that he was the forerunner of the excellent Dr. Smiles, but so it is. At all events, individualism dominated literature until the War of 1914–18. But even before that it was breaking down (having somewhat oddly consorted with a blatant imperialism), as can be seen from the plays of Mr. Bernard Shaw, and still more, perhaps, from the novels of Mr. E. M. Forster. The post-War period had its own characteristics; a new twist was given to the human view by investigations into psychology, ethnology, physics, and by the Russian Revolution.

There are, of course, several objections to this sort of division: odd elements appear everywhere: you cannot, for instance, rank Bunyan among aristocratic writers. But some division has to be made along chronological lines. It may be objected that the first period needs at least two volumes: it is so long and so varied. That is true, but the number of works which remain which can be of interest to the general reader are comparatively few, and it was thought better to devote more space to our more recent heritages, as being both fuller of works we are likely to read, and as having a closer influence upon our present-day approach to living.

BONAMY DOBRÉE

AUGUSTANS AND ROMANTICS

1689-1830

CHAPTER I

INTRODUCTION

I

THE period with which this volume deals saw the rise of
this country to the status of an imperial power of the
first rank. Commerce and industry expanded prodigiously
and the national wealth was multiplied many times. The
union with Scotland (1707) formed Great Britain which,
after a similar fate had overtaken Ireland in 1801, became
the United Kingdom. This latter union lasted until 1922.
For a great part of the period we were engaged in wars in
the course of which we lost one empire and acquired another.
Marlborough is the most imposing figure of the Age of Anne;
Wellington of the Age of Reform. These two ages offer
some sharp contrasts.

Queen Anne has become one of our national legends and
has given her name to the civilisation of the early eighteenth
century. To her contemporaries she seems to have been a
popular and rather remote figure, honoured for her piety
and domestic misfortunes. To Swift and other Tories her
reign seemed a golden age, the memory of which contrasted
agreeably with the Walpole régime. We are equally tempted
to idealise the whole epoch, which in retrospect seems to
have been a time of tranquillity and contentment. Despite
wide-spread poverty, and a low standard of living for the

bulk of the population, there appears to have been no consciousness of pressing social problems. In most parts of the country the traditional community life of the village continued and the time-honoured distinctions of wealth and rank were unquestioned. The countryside was administered by squire and parson and the world of Sir Roger de Coverley is its delightful record. Addison was a sensitive spirit who concealed much of the misery and brutality of the time; no doubt a very different tale could have been told. Still, the picture was painted and contemporaries were pleased to accept it. Englishmen have always had a weakness for squires.

The London of Ned Ward's *London Spy* and Gay's *Trivia* was a great self-governing city of over half a million inhabitants. There in adjoining streets might be found extremes of wealth and poverty, of high civilisation and degrading brutality. The world of Congreve's plays and of the *Rape of the Lock* lived alongside Grub Street and Alsatia and shared some of their habits. The mob were turbulent and ready to riot on slight provocation, but there seems to have been a rude good-nature in their violence. Certainly there was no sign of strong class hostility: the riots were partly a manifestation of English "liberty" and partly a rough and dangerous kind of amusement.

The small educated class were homogeneous in their outlook; despite party and personal differences, their aims and ideals were extraordinarily uniform. They were proud of their political achievements and looked confidently forward to increased happiness and prosperity. The rapidly rising middle-class element desired to share the tastes and acquire the polish of the aristocracy; it was from them that the impulse which underlay the foundation of the various societies for the improvement of manners and morals chiefly came. Their betters were glad enough to share in the profits of middle-class commercial enterprise.

"Queen Anne" literature was a closer and fuller reflection of contemporary society than any that has appeared before or since. Writers, unless they had failed to rise from the submerged circles of Grub Street, held an assured place in an assured society. Addison and Steele, Pope and Swift, Prior and Gay, were not only the entertainers of the ruling aristocracy, but were admitted to their intimacy. Their world was secure and leisured, civilised enough to take delight not only in grace and eloquence and charm, but also in outspoken and frequently scathing, personal comment. The identity of outlook and interests shared by the governing class and intelligentsia is, perhaps, the most striking aspect of the age. Poets and wits were not only admitted to salon and drawing-room, but political and diplomatic careers of the highest distinction were open to them. Such careers, indeed, were only possible through the encouragement of those in whose hands the real power lay. Addison became a Secretary of State and married a countess; partly these were the rewards of his talents, partly of his anxious, unremitting exploitation of the patronage extended to him by the leaders of the Whig party. These leaders, Somers, Halifax, Wharton, required able pens at their service and Addison eagerly accepted the favours he was offered. Swift, a man of incomparably superior gifts, moral and intellectual, achieved even greater influence than his friend and rival. But his pride and honesty crippled his ambition and his party secured his services at a cheaper rate. But the wits of both sides, Kit-cat and Scriblerus alike, spoke to and for a society that understood them and their language. It was all in the family.

But their social and moral self-criticism rarely extended to the foundations on which the whole structure stood. Property and privilege were taken for granted, however savagely incidental abuses might be attacked. A thorough assault on the whole system of a hierarchical society, almost feudal in its nice sense of grades and orders, would have been less resented than neglected. A revolutionary point of view would have been considered rather stupid than wicked. The nation had tampered with such things during the Civil War and under the Commonwealth, and the outcome had been the rule of fanatics and soldiers. Henceforward the Church of Bishop Burnet and an annual Mutiny Act would be effectual safeguards against those excesses of piety and militarism that had rendered "the good old cause" so odious. With some misgivings about the present, but few fears for the future, Augustan writers found appropriate material in the contemplation of the life of their fellows. Man in society, his conduct and aspirations, the reform of morals and the refinement of manners were enough.

By the end of our period this apparent unity had disappeared. The old traditions were breaking down under the stress of an increasingly complex national economy. Whatever reality there had ever been in the apparent peace and contentment of the Augustan countryside had now disappeared. Estates became larger and in many places the peasantry lost such land as they had and became solely wage-earners. They were also rapidly losing their rights on the now almost completely enclosed commons. Domestic industries, once a valuable supplement to their earnings in many parts of the country, had been replaced by the factories or had become miserably unremunerative. Of course there had been enclosures on a considerable scale long before the eighteenth century, and the misery of the labourer of 1820 could have been matched a hundred years earlier, but there is no doubt that throughout this period the condition of the countryman steadily declined. Scientific farming and greed lowered his status. The large landlords became more and more powerful as fields and men passed increasingly under their control. Rents rose, and in many cases the development of minerals under their property added to their wealth. There were fewer yeoman freeholders and more rent-paying farmers. Between the dates of Defoe's *Tour* and Cobbett's *Rural Rides* the relations between men and between classes had gravely deteriorated.

In the new towns of the north and midlands conditions were still more obviously insupportable. The roses round the door of an old and leaky cottage, the beauty of many of the wretched villages, the amenities of country life might seem to the passer-by to offer some consolations to the starving and rheumatic labourer. In the new towns no such illusions were possible. It was clear that change must come and that the day of the amateur in administration had

24

begun to wane. The era of factory acts and blue-books was beginning. Conditions were tense and difficult everywhere. The upper classes seemed to face a future of violence and revolution, and for many of the poor any sort of change must have appeared to offer better hopes than their present state. The period that had opened with the triumphs of 1688 appeared to be ending in disaster and confusion. In actual fact the middle class were about to enter upon their now matured inheritance and the Victorian Age was being born. But there were many to whom that prospect, could they have foreseen it, would have brought very little comfort.

Writers now ceased to speak on behalf of a whole community or even to be intelligible to all their readers. They seem rather to have spoken for particular elements, for certain political or philosophical ideas, often only for themselves and their friends. The sense of widely shared purpose, of belonging to an ordered and comprehensive community, had been lost, and literature had become sectarian. A much larger reading public, loss of contact between its different elements, the weakening of common religious and moral beliefs, political and social confusion, in part account for these changes. There was a fuller, if vaguer, sense of the possibilities of life. Poetry became more exciting, often more exalted; experiments multiplied, and there was a wider range of achievement: but few of the Romantic poets seem to offer us a complete presentation of what they see. There is something fragmentary about their achievements. Some died too young, others too old. The Augustans finished their work, but the Romantics—let that unsatisfactory term serve to describe the typical writers of the early nineteenth century—could not. Wordsworth's great poem was never completed, although in one form or another he managed to say all that he wished. Shelley, for all his reading and intelligence, never knew enough to control his longer poems. Keats died just as he had learnt to write greatly. *Don Juan* is incomplete and we feel would have remained so had Byron doubled the number of its cantos; still hell or marriage would have been denied the hero.

Running through all is the assertion that man is no longer at home in the society he has shaped. The figure of man in society is replaced by that of man over against a society that has discarded him or that he has abandoned The commonest characters in poetry are solitaries; haunted like the Ancient Mariner; self-exiled like Childe Harold; like Endymion bewildered seekers after beauty, or like Alastor steering a strange course to death. Wordsworth's reliance cn his past and its memories is embodied in his Wanderer and Solitary; all his typical figures are lonely; beggars, forsaken women, remote shepherds, strong, lost creatures. Society is seen as something alien, unfriendly, remote from the hopes and fears of the individual. There is no common background of faith and aspiration; a world is in pieces. Men spoke for groups which had little knowledge of one another, and no group found a voice that could speak on its behalf with full authority. Wordsworth wrote nobly about countrymen but he did not write for them; no party ever endorsed Shelley's programme.

But these different groups—the competent Augustans and the aspiring Romantics—have been too dramatically contrasted. There were, in fact, many elements in life and letters which were common to the whole period 1689–1830, but it is difficult to avoid emphasising the obvious differences at a first approach. Augustans and Romantics, by their work and manifestoes, compel us to consider them as more alien to one another than they really were.

A social historian would probably find in the steady development of the power and influence of a trading, and later also a manufacturing, middle class, the most significant feature of the entire period. It must be remembered that this development took place while an essentially aristocratic system prevailed in politics. In time the middle classes were to take a big share of political power, still later to absorb it almost completely and to impose their ideals upon the whole nation. But this was not yet.

An admirable example of the typical outlook of trade and dissent early in our period is to be found in *Robinson Crusoe* (1719). Adventure and piety are well combined in

the story. Hardship, slavery, perils, shipwreck and sickness
teach Crusoe many lessons. He is as respectable, shrewd and
God-fearing on his island as ever merchant in the City.
His misfortunes turn his thoughts to religion and he prospers
exceedingly in soul and body. Living in a kind of patriarchal
celibacy, he is as careful of the decencies of his clothes and
person as any chapel-goer. A little hairy about the face
and literally armed to the teeth, sheltered by his umbrella,
guarded by his dog, echoed by his parrot, he is the very
soul of industrious and sober England—he values his rum
chiefly for medicinal purposes—in a rather dry and dangerous place. He reads his Bible, prays, meditates on the ways
of God and his own sinfulness, observes the Sabbath and
grows rich. He tames the wild goats and induces them to
multiply, grows corn and fortifies his dwelling. He even
converts and clothes the heathen who arrives so providen-
tially to break his loneliness and exercise his virtue. Other
less convenient and no less naked heathen are suitably
shot to pieces, and their Christian prisoners are rescued.
Crusoe shows sympathy for Catholic Spaniards. A hundred
years later and it is doubtful whether he would have counted
a Spaniard as his "even Christian". It was not that Spaniards
grew worse but that Dissent as it triumphed grew more
exclusive. Friday's father also is rescued from death and the
appetites of his enemies, and reunited to his affectionate
son: some share of Crusoe's prosperity and good fortune
attends his servant.

The *Farther Adventures* sustains Crusoe's character. He is
still the adventurous trader who will travel all the seas of
the world for a fair return on his capital. Reason and religion guide his conduct: he avoids trouble when he can
and fights hard when he must; imperturbable and resource-
ful in crisis and humbly and devoutly thankful when delivered from peril, he is alike ready to do a good stroke of
business or to aim a blow at the devil. He is a very typical
hero of commonplace dissenting England.

The literature of the *whole* period affords abundant evidence of the importance and development of the middle-
class outlook. Congreve, in his life-time the most admired of

English writers, belonged to a freer age of experiment un-
controlled by public opinion. His intelligence is as free as
the life he depicted: no aristocracy have ever employed their
leisure quite so aristocratically as to be altogether worthy
of him. In the days of Addison he did not really fit in; he
did little good work after 1700. For Addison wrote for
people who wanted to get on, to be improved, to be instructed—an ordinary but talented mind writing for other
ordinary minds. Congreve and his audience—always suppos-
ing that such an audience could have been found—did not
want to get on or to be improved or to be instructed. They
wanted to find out, to know and to enjoy. Addison was
critical, but it was with a ready-made criticism; Congreve
represented the spirit of free, critical inquiry which despises
a faked answer to its questions, and counts wit a form
of wisdom and not a kind of social insurance against
excess. A comparison of the work of the two will afford
excellent examples of all that the good bourgeois is and is
not.

Ordinary men with ordinary outlooks came into their
own. Addison and Steele, Fielding and Richardson, Johnson
and Wordsworth write about, if not always for, the commonplace, everyday world. Reason and common sense are their
controls. The heroes are gone or survive only in the mock-
heroism of Pope or Fielding, whose heroes are diminished
by the very fact of their stature. They are partly revived
for a while in the mythologies of Shelley and the fictions of
Byron. In some way or other most of the greater writers
from Addison to Shelley are moralists who do not conceal
their intentions to improve, correct, and reform. Even Blake,
who revived the prophetic tradition that had slept since
Milton, was as hearty a moralist as Addison. Of course it was
not Addison's morality that he expounded.

The association between a particular morality and the
middle classes is commonly taken for granted. It is certainly
true that traders are singularly vulnerable to public opinion,
and are more under the necessity of "keeping up appear-
ances" than a landed aristocracy or a propertyless proletariat. One thing is said to lead to another, and a grocer

who seeks too persistently the company of his neighbour's wife may well also mix sand with his sugar.

The following piece from Goldsmith's *Bee* (1759) may afford an illustration:

OF THE PRIDE AND LUXURY OF THE MIDDLING CLASS OF PEOPLE

Of all the follies and absurdities which this great metropolis labours under, there is not one, I believe, at present, appears in a more glaring and ridiculous light than the pride and luxury of the middling class of people; their eager desire of being seen in a sphere far above their capacities and circumstances, is daily—nay hourly—instanced by the prodigious numbers of mechanics, who flock to the races, and gaming-tables, brothels, and all public diversions this fashionable town affords.

You shall see a grocer or a tallow-chandler sneak from behind the counter, clap on a laced coat and a bag, fly to the E.O. table, throw away fifty pieces with some sharping man of quality, while his industrious wife is selling a pennyworth of sugar, or a pound of candles, to support her fashionable spouse in his extravagance.

I was led into this reflection by an odd adventure, which happened to me the other day at Epsom races, where I went, not through any desire, I do assure you, of laying bets, or winning thousands; but at the earnest request of a friend who had long indulged the curiosity of seeing the sport, very natural for an Englishman. When we had arrived at the course, and had taken several turns to observe the different objects that made up this whimsical group, a figure suddenly darted by us, mounted and dressed in all the elegance of those polite gentry who come to show you they have a little money, and rather than pay their just debts at home, generously come abroad to bestow it on gamblers and pickpockets. As I had not an opportunity of viewing his face till his return, I gently walked after him, and met him as he came back, when, to my no small surprise, I beheld, in this gay Narcissus, the visage of Jack Varnish, a humble vender of prints. Disgusted at the sight, I pulled my friend by the sleeve, pressed him to return home, telling him all the way, that I was so enraged at the fellow's impudence, I was resolved never to lay out another penny with him.

And now, pray, sir, let me beg of you to give this a place in your paper, that Mr. Varnish may understand he mistakes the thing quite, if he imagines horse-racing commendable in a tradesman; and that he who is revelling every night in the arms of a common strumpet (though blessed with an indulgent wife) when he ought to be minding his business, will never thrive in this world. He will find himself soon mistaken, his finances decrease, his friends shun him, customers fall off, and himself thrown into a jail. I would earnestly recommend this adage to every mechanic in London, "Keep your shop, and your shop will keep you". A strict observance of these words will, I am sure, in time, gain them estates. Industry is the road to wealth, and honesty to happiness; and he who strenuously endeavours to pursue them both, may never fear the critic's lash, or the sharp cries of penury and want.

So the trader tends to avoid the more dramatic and talk-provoking vices and to indulge rather in the meaner weaknesses of hypocrisy and hard bargaining. A nation of shopkeepers is likely to have hypocrisy for its national failing. But this is all very doubtful. Statistical inquiry has yet to show the prevalence of vice amongst grocers and indeed the figures would be hard to arrive at. It is certainly true that for those in some trades and in some professions the appearance of evil is more damaging than for others; but about private practice it is impossible to generalise. Middle-class morality is largely a myth just as the excesses of the upper classes in any age have received more attention than they deserve. But both are admirable publicity.

The primary needs of a developing commercial community are security and freedom: security so that long-term policies may mature; and freedom for a man to do what he will with his own. The age we are considering saw the steady development of both these essential conditions.

It is evident also that in these years there was a marked increase in sheer good-will as displayed in many humanitarian movements. In various ways, from the time of the establishment of the Societies for the Reformation of Manners and for the Propagation of Christian Knowledge to that of Howard and Wilberforce, man's attitude towards his neighbour became more tolerant and more kindly. The confusion and unhappiness of the early nineteenth century were largely due to ignorance: where men could see clearly they usually acted rightly. But knowledge came slowly in a world that to many seemed fuller of threats than of promises.

II

POLITICS AND PEOPLE

Two great constitutional changes almost exactly mark the beginning and end of the period. 1689 saw the consummation of the great Revolution which substituted privilege for prerogative as the strongest force in our politics. The influence of the landed aristocracy henceforth effectively restricted the exercise of the royal prerogative. The principles of the Revolution are operative to this day and it was by virtue of them that in 1830 a Whig government took office, pledged to bring about another far-reaching change and once again to modify the balance of political forces. After 1832 the power and influence of the middle classes steadily increased and very slowly, almost imperceptibly, the importance of the aristocracy lessened and their character changed.

Although both the great parties in the state combined to effect the Revolution of 1688, it was in essence a Whig affair. In supporting it the Tories had to abandon their stricter views of divine right and non-resistance, otherwise they could not have acknowledged the validity of the change. But the bland insistency of James II's attempts to establish a despotism above the laws of the land had carried him beyond even the acquiescence of his own High Tory ministers and had made him impossible as a ruler. His attempt to betray the Church of England, for which his father had died, outraged all save the handful whom bigotry or self-interest kept at his side. He was deserted even by members of his own family. So Tories as well as Whigs signed the invitation which brought over William of Orange.

In future the Judicature was free from the threat of royal interference, the House of Commons not only voted supplies but voted them for specific purposes, and whoever ruled England could only do so through Parliament. Increasingly the powers of the Crown became at the disposal of ministers in office. The strongest governments were those in which Crown, Parliament and people were in agreement as to the main objectives. Crown and people together could overturn a ministry and win an election as in 1710, or Crown and Parliament together could rule in defiance of public opinion by means of subservient ministers, as was the case for many years during George III's reign: but no king ever again attempted to set himself and his prerogatives above the law.

On the whole the Whigs were in most respects the more progressive party throughout this period. They held 1688 in proud and happy memory; they had changed the balance of the constitution when change was inevitable. It was natural when the pressure of public opinion again compelled a change—this time in the shape of parliamentary reform—that it should be effected under the auspices of a Whig ministry. But in many ways they were extremely reactionary. Little as they cared for the interests of an hereditary monarchy, they fervently believed that their own great families were the natural rulers of England. These families, Cavendishes, Russells, Fitzroys, Pelhams, Spencers, Lennoxes, were truly "princes in the land". Their power was firmly based on acres, the rent-roll from which increased steadily, control of Parliamentary boroughs, the dissenting vote and, until the 1780's, the support of the financial and commercial interests. When they were also backed, as between 1714 and 1760 they usually were, by the Crown, they were impregnable, and governments were overthrown rather by the intrigues of various family groups in their own party than by the action of the Tories; the latter, during these years, were only one element, by no means always the most important, of the opposition. To their own great influence was added that of the Crown which disposed of a mass of boroughs and a huge number of "places", many of them of great profit and little responsibility, both on the English and Irish establishments. Titles, decorations, sinecures, financial jobs were at the disposal of the most firmly established system that this country has known.

The Tory party, who between 1690 and 1714 were frequently in power, were handicapped by weaker organisation, divided leadership and the fact that their right wing were, not unjustly, suspected of Jacobitism. The nation's fear of a counter-revolution and civil war was a serious handicap to Tory ambitions. Dr. Johnson described a Tory as "one who adheres to the ancient constitution of the State, and the apostolic hierarchy of the Church of England". Certainly the chief permanent difference between them and the Whigs lay in their professed championship of the Church of England. Their voting strength was mainly amongst the country squires and clergy; few of the greater landowners supported them. During the reigns of William and Mary and Anne they were, on the whole, opposed to extensive foreign commitments, to the new Whig finance which involved a permanent national debt, and to standing armies. They were jealous of any encroachments by the commercial interests on those of the Land and by the Dissenters on the privileges of the Established Church. They reached the height of their power towards the close of Anne's reign, when they passed the Occasional Conformity and Schism Acts and made it a necessary qualification for membership of Parliament that a man should possess land worth £300 a year. Their foreign policy lost them the Duke of Marlborough and their Anglicanism gained them Swift.

After George I's accession, fear of their supposed Jacobite sympathies—which the conduct of such of their leaders as Bolingbroke, Ormonde and Atterbury did nothing to allay—kept them in the wilderness for nearly fifty years. At the end of that time a new king with new ideas—he wished to transform politics by freeing himself from the control of the great families and to rule through a party of his own—

C

found that their traditions made them the obvious supporters for his new type of royalism. Henceforth, except for a few short intervals, a Tory government of some sort was in power until the end of our period. In some respects they were not less progressive than the Whigs. It was a Tory ministry that had put through the Act of Settlement in 1701 which consolidated the Revolution settlement by establishing the crown in the Hanoverian dynasty; while a hundred and thirty-three years later Peel's Tamworth manifesto accepted the new order of which the Reform Bill was the substantial symbol. It is perhaps worth noting that both Bolingbroke and the younger Pitt took steps towards freer foreign trade and, most surprising of all, it was a Tory government which, in 1828, at the high cost of splitting their own party, repealed the religious tests for civil and military office. Both parties alike could bow to obvious necessities.

But it is not easy to speak of politics in definite party terms. Our modern stricter loyalties had not yet come and government often divided allegiance with party. During the Whig supremacy, 1714–60, under Walpole and the Pelhams, conflicts were mainly between groups of rival family interests in the same party. Whiggery in some form or other was safe enough under a Hanoverian king, while the least chance of a Stuart restoration remained. The long-expected change on the fall of Walpole, 1741–2, was a change rather of men, than of policy. As a contemporary wit complained:

With *W - - - - le's* Politicks the Year began;
But soon th'indignant Patriots chang'd the *Man;*
With Statesmen *new* the Nation hop'd *new* Schemes,
Saw *Glorious Visions*, and dreamt *Golden Dreams:*

When from a Trance of six Months they awoke,
They found *Truth* chang'd their fancy'd *Joy* to *Joke.*
Still the same Fate on *B - - t - - n's* Isle attends,
And wisely, as the Year *began*, it *ends.*[1]

[1] *The Foundling Hospital for Wit*, 1743, No. 1, p. 52.

The "Patriots", when they came into power, behaved very much as their predecessors, some of whom still remained in office, and it was not until the Seven Years War that the cleansing genius of Pitt had real scope.

The various administrations through which George III ruled during his first twenty years were certainly referred to as Tory by their opponents, although they were rarely supported by the successors of the Church and Crown squires of Bolingbroke's days. They were usually kept in power by a mass of placemen, pensioners and nominees to royal boroughs and were largely recruited from two Whig groups, the Grenvilles, and the "Bloomsbury Gang" headed by Bedford, Sandwich and Weymouth. The Grenvilles readily adhered to any government which they thought might support their claims to promotion to higher ranks in the peerage, and on the "Bloomsbury Gang" political and other ties sat loosely.

From the beginning there were Whig elements in the younger Pitt's first ministry and after the accession of the Portland Whigs in 1794, he was at the head of what was virtually a national government. Pitt never called himself a Tory. Even at the very end of our period, party government in the modern sense was rare: during most of the time it was an affair of connections. Between the Revolution and the Reform Bill the structure of English politics was aristocratic. Privilege was supreme. But although the country was governed by a single powerful class who controlled both Houses of Parliament, this class never became a closed caste, although it might possibly have done so had the Peerage Bill of 1719 become law. There was continual recruitment from below. Rich tradesmen and manufacturers bought estates, boroughs, and advowsons. In a generation or two they had been assimilated by the county families amongst whom they had settled. Money, sporting tastes and, towards the end of the period, education at a public school, overcame plebeian origin. Moreover, and this is truer of the beginning than the end of the period, younger sons of county families entered business houses or were apprenticed to a trade. Witwoud in *The Way of the World* before he

35

became a fop, had narrowly escaped being "bound Prentice to a Felt-maker in Shrewsbury".

New money came into the country; first mainly through commerce, later also from manufactures. The West Indies enriched Chatham's friend, Beckford, father of him who built Fonthill Abbey and wrote *Vathek*; the Pitts themselves derived most of their fortune from the East Indies. The "great Pitts", Chatham's grandfather, had had a Robinson Crusoe kind of career—all but the shipwreck and the piety—and, at first as "interloper", and later as a distinguished servant of the East India Company, prospered exceedingly. The landed gentry were not a very difficult class to join if one had the money. The Peels were in cotton, and beer nearly gave Whitbread the leadership of the Whigs. Trade was not utterly despised in this country at any time, unless those who practised it also talked of it. If a man were content not to hurry matters, in time he might go very far; at least as far as Pope's unfortunate Sir Balaam.

It would be a mistake to believe that the class that monopolised the functions and rewards of government were not subject to the pressure of popular opinion. In times of particular stress and urgency their opinion made itself manifest in several ways. Despite rotten boroughs and government influence and organised bribery, Parliament was never a body which merely registered ministerial decrees. The knights of the shire—county members—who sat booted and spurred to indicate their status, were sometimes really representative of the views of the forty-shilling freeholders who formed the bulk of their constituents and who were, perhaps, the most independent portion of the electorate. It is true that as time went on, and in many districts the freeholders tended to be replaced by tenant-farmers who paid rent to the great landlords, their independence diminished. But to the end of the period the knight of the shire was held in especial honour and his vote meant more than that of a member for a close borough. Many boroughs too, e.g., Westminster, Bristol, York, Norwich at various times, enjoyed a liberal franchise and an independent tradition. The voting in such places could and did indicate the atittude of considerable sections of the community towards important questions. During times of real tension, general elections, such as those of 1784 and 1831, showed unmistakably the wishes of the country. Moreover, the fact that speech inside the House of Commons was genuinely free kept politics alive. In the days of the Combination Acts and other reactionary wartime legislation of the younger Pitt's ministry, Fox and Grey and their handful of left-wing Whig . followers provided an intermittent and sometimes brilliant opposition, and kept progressive ideas before Parliament. The country reaped the reward of their casual but staunch constitutional opposition in the peaceful reforms of 1832–4.

Of equal importance with this freedom of speech was the almost complete freedom of the press. Some control was still exercised over dramatic performances: the acting of Gay's *Polly* was forbidden and Fielding's *Pasquin* and *The Annual Register for 1736* resulted in an Act for the stricter licensing of plays and for reducing the number of theatres in London. But from 1695 onwards the press was really free. After publication an action could be brought by the government for libel, blasphemy, or sedition, and heavy penalties might be exacted, but a man who was prepared to take the risk could print what he chose. Swift is, perhaps, our greatest political pamphleteer, Cobbett the most lovable. During the years of George III's personal rule Junius relentlessly attacked the government in prose, and Charles Churchill less brilliantly in verse, while the efforts of Wilkes also brightened that most drearily inglorious phase of our history. Wilkes and America between them drove home the fact that an irresponsible king was as great a menace to liberty and good government when he exercised his authority through a packed Parliament as when he claimed to set himself above the law.

Mention has been made of mobs. Most Londoners may have had no votes but they recorded their opinions in unmistakable, if not strictly constitutional, fashion. They rioted on every sort of occasion. They rioted against Roman Catholics under James II, against Catholics and Dissenters

37

alternately under Anne, excise concerned them under Walpole, and the suggested control of gin-drinking under Pelham. They demonstrated when the calendar was reformed and, when Bute was Prime Minister, against the Scots. Sometimes Guy Fawkes celebrations were a sufficient incentive, sometimes the anniversary of a sovereign's birthday; the fall of an old government or the formation of a new alike exacted a heavy toll of shattered windows and broken heads. In 1780 the Gordon Riots achieved the proportions, though not the impulse, of a revolution. In the early days of the French Revolution there had been riots in support of the established order, most memorably in Birmingham. In all parts of the country there were more serious disturbances in connection with the post-war hardships that followed Waterloo and, later, in support of parliamentary reform. In 1829, when Peel's new police replaced the older ill-organised bodies, which in times of great emergency had to be supplemented by the employment of regular troops, a new era of public order began.

Finally, a lavish use was made of the right of addressing petitions to the King in Parliament, framed often in the most robust and uncompromising terms. The people of England spoke with many voices.

This period is sufficiently near to us in time to be familiar, and sufficiently remote for us to regard it with detachment. Augustans and Romantics alike are really dead. We still find the Victorians disturbing and we share some of their troubles; their fears still shake us and we are a little worried by their doubts. Mr. Gladstone's memory is still toasted to-day, and not all churchmen are completely happy about Darwin. We incline to look back at the Victorian Age with either anger or nostalgia: it is so very close to us and so many Victorians still survive. With their predecessors the case is different; we may, if we will, freely enjoy their intimacy and, if we find them disappointing, they will not haunt us.

There is something rather John Bullish—the character was invented by Arbuthnot in Anne's reign—about the eighteenth and early nineteenth century. For all the culture and polish, picture-galleries and great libraries, there is an atmosphere of beef and pudding and beer that frequently invades our nostrils. High and low, a certain brutal individuality is found in all classes of society. Their savage punishments and cruel sports comment oddly on the cult of sentiment that ran from Steele to Byron. To the tough man the world offered ample room to bustle about in, and the courage and industry shown are sometimes terrifying. William Hutton of Birmingham was such a man. A runaway apprentice, by frugality and extreme hard work he achieved wealth and position. At eighty-five he would walk thirty miles a day and perform the most alarming feats of early rising and attention to business. His autobiography is almost inhuman in its tale of sheer endurance and triumph over circumstances. A more lovable figure, but no less staunch, is that of the poet Crabbe. His *Life* by his son, the Rev. George Crabbe the second, is an admirable commentary on the truth and fidelity of his poetry. For Crabbe endured, modestly and confidently, years of the drabbest kind of poverty, and seems to have been kept alive by sheer courage. Then suddenly, through the help and sympathy of Edmund Burke, his fortunes changed, and with equal modesty and confidence Crabbe entered upon a happy and honoured career. The tale of virtue rewarded was never told more agreeably. Many aspects of eighteenth-century life are illustrated in this biography.

But for quiet men there were quiet places, and it is unlikely that shy spirits like Cowper, or querulous recluses like Gray would have found greater happiness had they lived at any other time. Our sense of the rich variety of character and interest is due to the acute consciousness which recorded it. For the first time a large-scale world, inhabited by ordinary men, is depicted for us by essayist, poet and novelist. It is doubtful whether there is such a being as the "typical Englishman", but it is tempting to suggest that he flourished most abundantly in these years. When we think of our own race in terms of individuals we are likely to choose figures like Walpole, Dr. Johnson, Coke of Norfolk or Cobbett as being in some special way representative.

Foreigners might select Byron or Wellington. *Sally in our Alley*, *Rule Britannia*, *God Save the King*, fox-hunting and a serious attitude towards cricket are amongst the legacies of the age.

But for all the abundant normality, there is much of wild eccentricity and strangeness. It is dangerous to generalise, and there is good reason for stressing the oddity and extravagance that meets us everywhere. The period produced the profoundest English satirist in Swift, who conceals his full horror at what he sees by the simplicity of his statements; the most perverse sentimentalist in Sterne, who tells us so often that he's only fooling that we begin to believe him; Blake, whose sense of prophecy was so powerful that he invented a new mythology in which to restate ancient traditions; Shelley, the last poet to sing of redemption by suffering. The Wesleyan movement is contemporary with Chesterfield and Horace Walpole. As always, there is paradox and contradiction. With ingenuity and show of learning we emphasise one aspect of life and our omissions rise at a later date to mock our complacent conclusions. The peace of the English Augustans was more of a hope than a fact: the rural misery sung by Stephen Duck anticipated the later relentlessness of Crabbe's *Village*, and the company of his fellows found Swift as ill at ease as Byron. The later confusion and more obvious misery of the years of the industrial revolution coincided with more honourable matters. The patriotic sonnets of Wordsworth are perhaps the best record of the spirit of resistance to tyranny that saved this country and gave European liberty a chance of survival. Wellington and Castlereagh have never been favourites with progressive-minded writers, but between them they laid the foundations of a peace that endured longer than any other that we have known.

CHAPTER II

AUGUSTANS

I

POETRY is always renewing itself: every poet in one way or another proclaims a fresh return to nature. There is continual resistance to settled convention.

In 1697, before the Augustans had really begun to be Augustan, while "knowing Walsh" was breathing "correctness" over our numbers and preparing himself for his future rôle of tutor to Pope, we have the following protest against a too strict formalism. It occurs in the preface to *Poems on Affairs of State*, a collection mainly of political satires. After declaring that "what is now publish'd" is "a Collection of those vaulable (*sic* for valuable) Pieces, which several great Men have produc'd, no less inspir'd by the injur'd Genius of their Country, than by the Muses," it goes on, "I am sensible, that should we consult our superficial Hypocriticks, they would often be apt to arraign the Numbers; for there are a sort of Men, who having little other merit, than a happy chime, would fain fix the Excellence of Poetry in the smoothness of the Versification, allowing but little to the more Essential Qualities of a Poet, great Images, good Sense, etc. Nay they have so blind a Passion for what they Excell in, that they will exclude all variety of Numbers from *English* Poetry, when they allow none but *Iambics*, which must by an identy (*sic* for identity) of sound bring a very unpleasing satiety upon the Reader. I must own that I am of opinion that a great many rough Cadencies that are to be found in these Poems, and in the admirable *Paradise Lost*, are so far from Faults that they are

41

Beauties, and contribute by their variety to the prolonging the pleasure of the Readers." This ill-printed, interesting protest against those who "made poetry a mere mechanic art" ante-dates Pope's first appearance in print by eight years. It seems that there was already, in the bad sense, a school of Pope; a race of poets capable of nothing but a metrical tune, who were contented with their verses if "no harshness gives offence" and cared not at all whether or no there were any sense for the sound to echo.

In 1726 Thomson writes in the preface to the second edition of *Winter*

> "I know no subject more elevating, more amusing; more ready to awake the poetical enthusiasm, the philosophical reflection, and the moral sentiment, than the works of Nature. Where can we meet with such variety, such beauty, such magnificence? All that enlarges and transports the soul! What more inspiring than a calm, wide survey of them? In every dress nature is greatly charming—whether she puts on the crimson robes of the morning, the strong effulgence of noon, the sober suit of the evening, or the deep sables of blackness and tempest! How gay looks the Spring! how glorious the Summer! how pleasing the Autumn! and how venerable the Winter!—But there is no thinking of these things without breaking out into poetry; which is, by-the-by, a plain and undeniable argument of their superior excellence.
>
> For this reason the best, both ancient, and modern, Poets have been passionately fond of retirement, and solitude. The wild romantic country was their delight. And they seem never to have been more happy, than when, lost in unfrequented fields, far from the little busy world, they were at leisure, to meditate, and sing the Works of Nature.
>
> The Book of Job, that noble and ancient poem, which, even, strikes so forcibly through a mangling translation, is crowned with a description of the grand Works of Nature; and that, too, from the mouth of their Almighty Author."

Pope, who had already "stooped to truth, and moralised his song" and was in a few years to announce that "the proper study of Mankind is Man", approved of *The Seasons*, and we owe some of its most familiar passages to his revising hand.

It is less surprising to find Joseph Warton twenty years after *Winter* issuing a definite protest against overmuch didacticism: this is his Advertisement to *Odes on Various Subjects*.

"The Public has been so much accustom'd of late to didactic Poetry alone, and Essays on moral Subjects, that any work where the imagination is much indulged, will perhaps not be relished or regarded. The author therefore of these pieces is in some pain lest certain austere critics should think them too fanciful and descriptive. But as he is convinced that the fashion of moralising in verse has been carried too far, and as he looks upon Invention and Imagination to be the chief faculties of a Poet, so he will be happy if the following Odes may be look'd upon as an attempt to bring back Poetry into its right channel."

But man never ceased to be amongst the proper studies of poets and at the height of the romantic "return to nature" Wordsworth rediscovered "the great and universal passions of men" in a fresh setting.

Perhaps the most attractive quality of Augustan writing is its adequacy. The Augustans were masters of style and valued highly taste, elegance, and temperateness of expression. Whether we are examining the work of Defoe, Addison, Steele, Pope or Swift we cannot help noticing how seldom their range exceeds their grasp. Defoe, who well deserves to be named in this company, is certainly no great stylist and his manner has not the high polish of the others, but how clearly he sees what he is describing; and how clearly he makes us see it too.

Addison and Steele have never lacked readers or their due praise. Steele has at command the more lively style and the stronger feelings: some of the personal reminiscences he gives us foreshadow Charles Lamb. He has something of romantic extravagance both in his life and work, and mingles whimsicality with earnestness. There are gleams of a faint—slightly repellent—charm in all Addison's writing. Well-read, well-bred, and infinitely urbane, he is

an authority alike on Virgil and the niceties of feminine
deportment; unwilling to take any sort of risk, he snatches
no graces beyond the reach of art; he is always a somewhat
superior person. He unites the clear explanatory power of
a first-class extension lecturer with the experienced and
slightly patronising sentimentality of a writer for the heart-
and-home columns of our illustrated daily newspapers. A
brilliant journalist, he anticipated the public taste by a
careful study of prevailing tendencies. He had the great
gift of persuading his readers into a kind of intimacy with
him: it was assumed that both parties were anxious about
the same things, and that when Mr. Spectator had provided
the clear illumination of his knowledge and intelligence,
both would be found on the same side—the right side.
He enlisted contributors at times from amongst his readers
and was appropriately sensitive to their opinions. His
immense influence, though out of all proportion to his
abilities, was not undeserved. He was one of the great
shaping forces in the moral life of the times and his power
has only waned with that of the ideals of the middle-class
which he did so much to make articulate.

Pope's fine tribute was well-earned:

> "In all Charles's days,
> Roscommon only boasts unspotted bays;
> And in our own (excuse some Courtly stains)
> No whiter page than Addison remains.
> He, from the taste obscene reclaims our Youth,
> And sets the Passions on the side of Truth,
> Forms the soft bosom with the gentlest art,
> And pours each human Virtue in the heart."

His most stimulating work is to be found in his essays on
the Imagination; his greatest charm in those dealing with
Sir Roger de Coverley, where he developed and concluded
what had been begun by Steele. As a critic he is persuasive,
moderate and scholarly; his analysis of *Paradise Lost* is an
admirable example in its own kind. He was able to speak
to and for the educated classes in a manner that gave a new

definition to their aims and tastes. In him the more conventional Augustans saw themselves in a light that was at once amusingly critical and delicâtely flattering. Dr Johnson has praised his style once and for all:

"His prose is the model of the middle style; on grave subjects not formal, on light occasions not groveling; pure without scrupulosity, and exact without apparent elaboration; always equable, and always easy, without glowing words or pointed sentences. Addison never deviates from his track to snatch a grace; he seeks no ambitious ornaments, and tries no hazardous innovations. His page is always luminous, but never blazes in unexpected splendour.

"It was apparently his principal endeavour to avoid all harshness and severity of diction; he is therefore sometimes verbose in his transitions and connexions, and sometimes descends too much to the language of conversation; yet if his language had been less idiomatical, it might have lost somewhat of its genuine Anglicism. What he attempted, he performed; he is never feeble, and he did not wish to be energetic; he is never rapid, and he never stagnates. His sentences have neither studied amplitude, nor affected brevity: his periods, though not diligently rounded, are voluble and easy. Whoever wishes to attain an English style, familiar but not coarse, and elegant but not ostentatious, must give his days and nights to the volumes of Addison."

The art of the Augustans did not die with them: the sweetest tunes played on Pope's great instrument we owe to Goldsmith; and Crabbe, employing the same measure, followed Nature to a sterner goal. Goldsmith, too, is one of the final justifications of Addison: the measured flexible harmony of *The Spectator*'s prose is handled with a reviving freshness and an even more delicate certainty in *The Bee* and *Citizen of the World*.

There is an interesting, perhaps not too fanciful, parallel between the changes of fashion in literature and those in domestic architecture and gardening. In both we find movements, unsteady, digressive, and experimental, towards greater variety and picturesqueness.

In the reign of William III and the early part of the eighteenth century the so-called Queen Anne houses achieved their characteristic perfection. Dignified and harmonious, with their symmetrical well-balanced façades, and ample comfort within doors, they announce something of the same sound taste and security as Addison's essays: they seem appropriate dwellings for either Tory fox-hunters or retired merchants. At the same time Vanbrugh's huge baroque structures, such as Blenheim and Castle Howard, are admirable though less beautiful symbols of the way of life of the grandee patron, the cultured Whig land-owner. Meanwhile the lovely Stuart and Dutch formal gardens were giving place to elaborately modelled parks, with regular patterns of avenues, woods and water. Civilisation, stepping out from the walls and parterres of the enclosed garden, triumphantly imposed itself over a wider range of nature. Mankind, settling down to a long period of peace, was turning the countryside, where he could afford to do so, into a series of views. Nature was methodised indeed. At its best this super landscape gardening was magnificent: as at Boughton or Stowe where the princely owners had both the taste and fortune to:

Consult the Genius of the Place in all;
That tells the Waters or to rise, or fall;
Or helps th' ambitious Hill the heavens to scale,
Or scoops in circling theatres the Vale;
Calls in the Country, catches op'ning glades,
Joins willing woods, and varies shades from shades;
Now breaks, or now directs, th' intending Lines;
Paints as you plant, and, as you work, designs.

Presently purpose wavered and vistas wriggled. As Kent and "Capability" Brown entered into their kingdoms, some loss of definition and uncertainty of purpose appeared. Gardens were tucked away into corners and nature was no longer controlled and formalised but imitated in her unspecialised wildness. Parks began to look like wildernesses and man pretended to abdicate. An unconvincing wildness

46

was spread before the windows of the great Palladian palaces that asserted to the world the power and wealth of their owners. Towards the end of the century both houses and grounds became more eclectic and more curious. There was more experiment and a good deal of fumbling. The most lasting of the new fashions was the Gothic; the delicate turrets of Strawberry Hill, Fonthill so massively but precariously built, the towers of the new Belvoir Castle, bore witness to the revival of an interest in a feudal past. There was a distinctly baronial movement amongst the English upper-class. Other *motifs* were provided by Egypt, China, India, and Morocco; even when a classical tradition was maintained there was a tendency for English houses to appear unsuitably disguised as Greek temples. Many of the experiments were by no means unpleasing, and in some districts, notably the Cotswolds, the old ways of building, perfected in the seventeenth century, continued almost unaffected by the new styles.

Parks and gardens too began to show signs of importation and revival. Artificial ruins, old English cottages, hermitages and mossy cells emerged from shrubberies and added a new kind of variety to the empaled landscape. Greenery no longer was supreme and gardens imitated from a by-gone age began to appear. Like literature, gardening and architecture found new models and inspirations from earlier times and remoter places and, like literature, they suffered some loss. But in this new confusion there was at least as much gain as loss.

II

Neither Swift nor Pope was in any sense revolutionary, but neither was able to share Addison's complacency and satisfaction with the new age.

Swift was in sympathy with many Whig ideals. To him, who had attained his majority in 1688, the Revolution of that year was a plain necessity. At no time afterwards would he have contemplated the restoration of a Roman Catholic monarch. But the Whigs cared too little about the

47

Church of Ireland, and Harley was a skilful flatterer, so he turned his back on the political tradition in which he had been bred by Sir William Temple, and for the rest of his life, whether in the brief years of power or during the long hopeless time of opposition, he was the most formidable of Tory controversialists.

It is not always easy to see him as a zealous clergyman. The Church offered him when poor and uncertain of his prospects—though not of his genius—a career in a secure and established hierarchy, guaranteed him the moral order for which his heart craved, and sustained this order by ample sanctions. To the born controversialist was given a cause and the strength to maintain it. Not one of the masters of the contemplative life, he had, nevertheless, a genuine capacity for devotion, and the prayers that he wrote for various personal occasions show us a side of his character which he was at some pains to hide from the world.

Swift was a political genius of rare quality. His pen was the most persuasive since Dryden's, and like Dryden, he was, for his time, a moderate man. In the days of his power, when he was Harley's great master of moderate Tory propaganda, he showed equal capacity for persuading opponents that the government was right, and for showing friends that it was staunch. In the *Conduct of the Allies* he prepared the whole country for the peace that was finally signed at Utrecht; in his *Letter to the October Club* he reproved the root-and-branch instincts of the extreme Tories. His *Free Thoughts upon the Present State of Affairs* shows that he had worked out the possibilities of a permanent Tory government which might be maintained even by Hanoverians. His advice, if it could have been offered and accepted in time, might well have kept his friends in power for years. But Whig money and organisation were too strong for the disunited Tories, despite the numerical advantage which the latter seem to have had in the country. The feud between Bolingbroke and Harley, the former's inability to time his moves correctly, and the weakness and laziness of the latter, were proof against all the passion and logic of their great supporter. Swift's *History of the Four Last Years of the Queen* and *Enquiry*

48

into the Behaviour of the Queen's Last Ministry give us the politics of the time as he saw them.

His political genius was not that of Burke. He was rather a tactician than a strategist, and had not Burke's sense of history as the record of necessary changes carried out with reference to a known and understood past; the record of human efforts . to found, establish, and develop societies. The voting of a borough, the political tradition of a great family, the rules of debate in the House of Commons, these were significant fragments of a great organic whole, and in the fragments Burke saw the whole reflected. This clairvoyant vision of history was never Swift's. We scarcely ever feel that he rises clear above party and speaks for a whole community. Even in *The Drapier Letters*, though we endorse his intention, we take leave to doubt his facts. With Burke at his best, in his great American speeches for instance, we feel that he speaks for both sides, for all possible sides. He may not win the votes of his opponents but he has their minds. His speeches have something of the cleansing effect of great tragedy. They are perhaps the nearest thing to tragedy, in their comprehensiveness and manifested necessity, that the age produced, as Gibbon's *Decline and Fall* is nearest in order and in majesty of spirit to the epic poem.

Many of Swift's friends seem to have regarded him with misgivings, and since his death this attitude has been common amongst his readers. He had too much temper and independence for his own party leaders to feel able to offer him the natural rewards of his prowess, and, after his death, his greatest book for many years was found too disturbing in its implications to be taken with complete seriousness. *Gulliver's Travels* achieved its fame as a nursery classic because a full interpretation would have been too disturbing to "children of a larger growth." Its sheer quality in any case guaranteed it a mass of readers, and by pretending that it was mainly brilliant entertainment the world continued for a while to preserve its withers unwrung. Even to-day we sometimes pretend that its chief interest is political and that its concern is chiefly with a world now dead. But

Swift was not writing mainly for children nor are politics as such its main theme.

Gulliver's Travels is a survey of human pretensions and a commentary on human pride: it is the most uncompromising dissertation on the virtue of humility that has been written. We are well accustomed to consider the uncertainty and unhappiness of our lot and to wonder at the overplus of our misfortunes. Swift asserts that we deserve even less than we have, and that our misery is the measure of our selfish greed and arrogance. We are happier than we deserve. Swift's physical disability combined with his gifts developed in him a sense of solitude even in the midst of society. His claims to privileged treatment in his relations with others are a mark of this sense. Unlike Pope, he could never quite forget, in the company of friends, or in the use of his own powers, the terrible strangeness of the world and its great capacity for inflicting injury. This strangeness runs through *Gulliver's Travels*, which has for one of its recurrent *motifs* that of exile. Contrast it with *Robinson Crusoe*. Crusoe, even on his island, is a member of a community and as such he behaves. He is a wanderer or there would be no story, in peril and difficulties or the story would be dull, but his wanderings bring him home at the end and his dangers confirm his faith and secure his salvation. With Gulliver it is different. In the first book he is shipwrecked and is the sole survivor; in the second his companions desert him in their fear of the pursuing giant; in the third he is the victim of pirates; in the last book he comes to the land of the Houyhnhnms as a result of the mutiny of his own crew. The effect is cumulative. At the end he is insensible of human kindness and charity and can only see his own family as Yahoos; judgment has fled to brutish beasts.

His experiences have finally sundered him from his kind; the love of his family and the charity of the Portuguese captain meet with no acknowledgment. He can appreciate that human beings are capable of virtue but he is outside its operation. His solitude is that of Timon, not of Crusoe.

He has been in Lilliput amongst delicate-limbed pigmies and his sanity and honesty have received the reward which a petty world bestows upon plain dealing. His only friend amongst them is distinguished from his enemies in that he would have substituted blindness and a lingering death for the prompter execution they had proposed. Policy has made of friendship an ironic horror. In the second book the meanness of all Lilliput is concentrated in Gulliver's person: presumptuous corruption offers free tuition to the monsters, plain in mind and body, amongst whom fortune has placed the wanderer, and receives in return a bitterly different lesson.

There is high drama in the last book when Gulliver realises that he himself and his kin belong to the same species as the accursed Yahoos.

"The master horse ordered a sorrel nag, one of his servants, to untie the largest of these animals, and take him into the yard. The beast and I were brought close together, and our countenances diligently compared, both by master and servant, who thereupon repeated several times the word *Yahoo*. My horror and astonishment are not to be described, when I observed, in this abominable animal, a perfect human figure: the face of it indeed was flat and broad, the nose depressed, the lips large, and the mouth wide. But these differences are common to all savage nations, where the lineaments of the countenance are distorted by the natives suffering their infants to lie grovelling on the earth, or by carrying them on their backs, nuzzling with their face against the mother's shoulders. The fore-feet of the *Yahoo* differed from my hands in nothing else but the length of the nails, the coarseness and brownness of the palms, and the hairiness on the backs. There was the same resemblance between our feet, with the same differences, which I knew very well, though the horses did not, because of my shoes and stockings; the same in every part of our bodies, except as to hairiness and colour, which I have already described."

This is indeed to be shipwrecked, and all the artistry in style and narrative cannot conceal the enormous madness which the tale discovers. The madness is not Swift's, but that of a world that lives without sense or charity. Here and there—in some of the early parts of the first, second and fourth books; in Gulliver's relations with his big child-nurse; in his friendship with the sorrel nag, his fellow-servant—are touches of grace and charm. The nursery appeal is plain enough, if the main theme be disregarded, and so too are those close and illuminating references to politics which have been worked out for us by the late Sir Charles Firth.

Swift must not be identified with Gulliver too closely. His letters record for us a man, who though often troubled and bitter, took his full share of social life. In his own way he had a genius for friendship, and his loyalty to those he cared for when they were disgraced and in danger was un-qualified and devoted. But the early part of his life saw his hopes continuously deferred and, after the brief glory of 1710–14, his later years were spent, almost entirely, in em-bittered exile.

The *Tale of a Tub*, written almost thirty years before the publication of *Gulliver*, has never claimed as many readers. Its references are more remote, its form more wilful and perverse. Its offence to Swift's more orthodox contemporaries lay not in the vehemence of its expressions—ecclesiastical controversialists like the ridiculous Dr. Sacheverell employed even less clerkly language than Swift—but in the disturbing carelessness with which he used his powers. True, he did not apply to Martin what he applied to Peter and Jack, but there was an unintentional invitation to others to do so. Perhaps one day he might not notice which coat Martin was wearing, or even change his own.   This

> . . . clergyman of special note
> For shunning those of his own coat

might well be suspected, however unjustly, of an insufficient reverence for traditional garments and for wearing his own with indifference. It was not thus that the Church of England should be defended in an age of reason; a pious queen and Whig episcopate were unlikely to agree in promoting a man whose sense of the ludicrous carried him so far, and who wielded his sharp weapons so casually. The *Tale of a Tub* is hardly less comprehensive than its more familiar successor in its satiric survey. Humbug, literary and religious, fraud and pretence are its special targets. It was more immediately provocative than *Gulliver* and by no possibility could it be treated as a nursery fable.

At times Swift's irony seems more disturbing than the evils which it exposes, and the strength of his own sufferings at the spectacle of human unwisdom overpowers his readers so that his object is forgotten. The cold fury of the *Modest Proposal* and the mad heat of the *Legion Club* show rather a victim than a moralist.

This is all that can be said in this place of Swift except by way of briefest summary. His character is the most provocative of the whole age and in his writings we find the age's profoundest commentary on itself. The changes he wished for were not social in any limited sense. The system under which he lived would serve as well as any. That intelligence and disinterestedness which he found to be lacking would, if men lived in their light, effect without violence any necessary reforms. But he lived in a time of singular complacency when society was perhaps more tolerant than usual of its own weaknesses. His indignation was the measure of the futility of his task, that of persuading mankind to enter into their inheritance of sweetness and light to which, as beings capable of reason, they had been born.

III

Pope was the poet in whom his own age took most delight; he lost favour as the respect accorded to Augustan ideals diminished. Many of the controversies associated with his name are now still and the question is no longer raised as to whether or no he is a true poet. We may be content to leave the answer to Johnson or Hazlitt and to allow Joseph Warton to allot him his place in the ranks of the poetic hierarchy.

All his life he was a keen combatant. He fought for his own fame and honour, for the reputation of English poetry, and for human virtue. Probably this order represents their relative importance in his eyes.

He was enormously self-conscious. He had a cripple's vivid awareness of his difference from other men, and his aggressive technique was in part a compensation for his physical frailty. His sense of isolation was reinforced by the fact that he was a Roman Catholic; as such he was not a fully enfranchised Englishman and was liable to the payment of double taxes. The traditional university education was not available for him, and during periods of political tension, e.g., in 1715 and 1722, his real or supposed Jacobite sympathies strengthened the hands of his enemies. Moreover, he was of middle-class origin, and was taken up by the ruling group as their acknowledged poet. He had pride and courage enough to avoid becoming dependent on a patron, and, by the prodigious exertions he made in translating Homer, he established his financial security. The severe strain of this work may have sharpened his dislike of the strident poverty of Grub Street.

He was devoted to his art, and extremely sensitive both to good and bad poetry. The best poets among his contemporaries he regarded with genuine admiration. He assisted Gay with his *Beggar's Opera* and Thomson with his *Seasons*. Swift, whose verse, if not great poetry, is brilliant writing, was his intimate friend, and he was on good terms with Young and Prior. Savage was his pensioner. But his satiric energy was as readily released by bad writing as by personal attack; often indeed the two were combined. *The Dunciad* is not a generous poem; neither is it simply poetic persecution. Pope was attempting a defence of humane culture against the inroads of stupidity, pedantry, ignorance and dullness. There are structural weaknesses—Pope's writing and revision of this poem cover a period of nearly twenty years—and the substitution of Cibber for Theobald as the hero in the later versions was a stupid and malicious error; but there is ample evidence of Pope's sense of the very real threats which the enemies of enlightenment offered to an ordered and traditional civilisation. These perils are permanent and the conflict is a genuine one, but unhappily Pope struck at too many insignificant individuals whom it would have been wiser to ignore and more honourable to spare. The result was that the "dunces" received advertisement and *The Dunciad* is to-day unread.

Pope was a moralist. He had no well-reasoned system of ethics, but he was quite entitled to claim that he "stoop'd to Truth, and moralis'd his song". His satire was a weapon against those whom his success and disabilities infuriated, and his enemies seem usually to have begun the game—

> Satire's my weapon, but I'm too discreet
> To run amuck, and tilt at all I meet;
> I only wear it in a land of Hectors,
> Thieves, Supercargoes, Sharpers, and Directors.

If he chastened fools beyond their deserts and upon trivial occasion—

> Whoe'er offends, at some unlucky time
> Slides into verse, and hitches in a rhyme,
> Sacred to Ridicule his whole life long,
> And the sad burthen of some merry song,

and
> Fools rush into my head, and so I write—

he also hated and scourged corruption in high places and struck as hard at the rulers of the land as at the pitiful poverty of Grub Street. He was never afraid to

> Brand the bold front of shameless guilty men;
> Dash the proud Gamester in his gilded Car;
> Bare the mean Heart that lurks beneath a *Star*.

His pride in his power was not all wantonness.

> F. You're strangely proud.
> P.   So proud, I am no Slave:
> So impudent, I own myself no Knave:
> So odd, my Country's Ruin makes me grave.
> Yes, I am proud; I must be proud to see

Men not afraid of God, afraid of me:
Safe from the Bar, the Pulpit, and the Throne,
Yet touch'd and sham'd by *Ridicule* alone.
O sacred Weapon! left for Truth's defence,
Sole Dread of Folly, Vice, and Insolence!
To all but Heav'n-directed hands deny'd,
The Muse may give thee, but the Gods must guide:
Rev'rent I touch thee! but with honest zeal;
To rouse the Watchmen of the Public Weal,
To Virtue's Work provoke the tardy Hall,
And goad the Prelate slum'bring in his Stall.

"Unplac'd, unpension'd, no man's heir, or slave," he made no terms with what he found evil and, in a world of placemen, kept his independence.

Pope's position was in many ways more favourable than that of his great predecessor and master, Dryden. The latter was still at work during the first ten years of our period, and Pope, as a boy of twelve, is said to have seen him at Will's Coffee House shortly before his death.

Dryden in his great satiric years, 1681–7, when he produced his political and religious verse satires, was on the defensive. He was defending good order and tradition in Church and State against his main dread, innovation. "Innovation," he declared, "is a blow of fate." To his mind, full of the memory of the Civil War, continuity and the exercise of traditional authority seemed the most effective guarantees against the threat of violent revolution. Hence his opposition to Shaftesbury whom he admired and respected. After the political miracle of 1688 had happened, and a bloodless revolution had brought into being a new order and new political groupings, Dryden, unchanged though his convictions were, was honoured as an Elder Statesman of the republic of letters, and withdrew from public affairs. He set himself to earn a living under an alien dispensation by his translations and adaptations; defending when attacked—most notably in the Preface to his *Fables* —his art and his character. But he was never altogether at home in the England of William of Orange. Poverty and

Ronrey loch ?

the cold face of authority were to a slight extent mitigated by the kindness of friends and patrons but he was in some sense a survivor, a great voice speaking to a changed world.

Pope had known no other order of things than that of his maturity; whatever his private sympathies, his Pan lamented no Jacobite Syrinx, and he was comfortable enough as the laureate of a constitutional opposition. But his moral awareness was keener and more profound than Dryden's, and he attacked the new finance and the new politics largely on moral grounds. In "blest paper credit" he saw corruption more efficiently mobilised; in Walpole's political system a bloodless but paralysing tyranny. His account of the rise and ruin of Sir Balaam in the *Epistle to Bathurst* is not all satire and mockery. In it perhaps Pope reaches the nearest to tragic pity that his poetry could attain. Balaam is not only keen and frugal, lucky and unscrupulous, not only an up-to-date Mr. Badman; he is, both inside and outside the fable, a damned soul. There are evils abroad beyond the cure of Parliament or the touch of a king. A rage for money-making possesses the land and menaces our old ways of living.

> Statesman and Patriot ply alike the stocks,
> Peeress and Butler share alike the Box,
> And Judges job, and Bishops bite the town,
> And mighty Dukes pack Cards for half-a-crown.

Even in the account of Timon's villa, Pope's most abused piece of satiric description, there is pity mingled with his scorn. The soulless magnificence of Timon banishes humanity and exhibits the master of a petty principality as "A puny insect, shivering at a breeze!"

Perhaps Pope's greatest intellectual weakness was his too facile acceptance of an obvious order in things. Really the *Essay on Man* is half-falsified before it is well begun. The difficulty Pope tries to meet and, for all his fine and sensitive verse, does not meet, is just that the kind of apparent, purposeful order which he asserts can equally well be presented either as chaos or as cruel indifference. He does not really face the difficulties; he tries to charm them away.

Similarly he makes play with the plausible doctrine of the "ruling passion", but in his search for consistency in the inconsistent he does not go deep enough.

But he had knowledge as well as art and diagnosed relentlessly and sanely the dangers and weaknesses of his time. His powers of observation were by no means confined to men and manners; when he chooses he can give us natural beauty well enough. Like Swift, he set great store by friendship and kindliness and his friends repaid his affection. His stately compliments were part of the currency of the world in which he lived and were elicited by sincere admiration. No poet has more adequately spoken for the civilisation in which he had his part; his elaborately varied couplets chime the limitations and splendour of a stable, ordered, and proudly self-conscious way of living.

The best of the lesser Augustan poets show sufficient independence to refute the view that there was at any time a tyranny of Pope. Much admired and imitated as he was, his influence on other poetry was healthy and encouraged his contemporaries rather to pursue their own particular interests than to echo him.

We may perhaps get a fair view of the range and variety of Augustan literature if we look briefly at some of the work which appeared during the years 1725–30. These years saw the publication of *Gulliver* and *The Dunciad*, but they saw also some very different achievements. The closest in spirit and technique to Pope himself were Young, who was later to win fame, which time has changed to notoriety, with his *Night Thoughts*, and Savage, the subject of Johnson's earliest and most intimate *Life*. Young's *Love of Fame*, published in 1725, was inspired by Pope's satiric and metrical technique. But in some respects it anticipated Pope's most popular accomplishments and may well have offered models for some of his characters in the Moral Essay *On Women*. Young has a good eye for types and a good ear. He cannot sustain his verse at such length as Pope and his touch is less sure. But these satires are the real thing, and, in this kind, Pope was the one who followed.

In *The Bastard*, 1728, Savage's best known poem, there

is a personal quality of acrid disillusion. Unlike Pope, he shows his strong sense of isolation from society; he is a plaintive and observant Ishmael. Proud to claim, it is believed erroneously, noble but illegitimate parentage, he was the medium for some of Pope's contacts with the underworld, and the companion of Johnson in his Grub Street days.

In 1726 was published Dyer's *Grongar Hill* in David Lewis's *Miscellany*. *Grongar Hill*, in octosyllabic couplets which echo some of the music of *Il Penseroso*, is a charming piece of descriptive writing, shot through with moral and social commentary. The sense of society is there, but in the background, and Dyer steadily keeps his eye on the landscape which he is describing.

The earliest versions of Thomson's *Seasons* were published 1726–30, and were greatly amplified in subsequent years. Here pure description nearly takes the place of sense. The sensibilities are pleased and the mind is not troubled. Thomson had not the typical Augustan sense of economy in the use of his materials, nor their knowledge that when one has finished a poem it is a pity to go on writing it. His vocabulary is partly Miltonic, partly, as has recently been shown by Professor Nichol Smith, the traditional vocabulary of the Scottish graduate. His *Castle of Indolence*, written many years later, is commented on in a later section.

1728 saw the production and publication of Gay's *Beggar's Opera*, his best known work. Gay's association with Pope and Swift dated from the last years of Anne, when they were fellow-members of the Scriblerus Club, and sworn enemies of humbug, pedantry and dullness. *Gulliver's Travels*, *The Dunciad* and *The Beggar's Opera* in their different ways record the ideals which had first been formulated in the days of "glorious Anne".

Some mention must be made of Prior, who had died in 1721. In many ways he was the most independent of the Augustan poets. One of the most courtly and witty of writers, he has at times a fine and graceful commonness which characterises those of his poems which are chiefly read to-day.

CHAPTER III

THE AGE OF JOHNSON AND THE CLOSE OF THE EIGHTEENTH CENTURY

I

THE English novel was born and came to its first heady maturity in the lifetime of Johnson. Between 1740 and 1771 a new art-form came into being. Johnson's *Rasselas* has no place in this story. Whatever it may be called it is not a novel. The quest for happiness is largely conducted by means of solid, heavy conversation. Plot, character, action are not Johnson's business. It is an essay on the limitations of the human lot and the "conclusion in which nothing is concluded" might have begun instead of ending it. It is a noble exercise in virtue and wisdom; a perpetual reminder to our forgetfulness and a reproof to our unquenchable desire for a security which time and occasion cannot touch. It is the kind of reminder of our nature and destiny that only a prophet can offer.

There is nothing prophetic about the work of Richardson, Fielding, Smollett or Sterne. They are all in their different ways masters of characterisation, relentless depicters of how human beings behave. Man's larger hopes are nothing to them, and their morality, though serious, is inclined to be superficial. The first three allow a large tether to their heroes, and their presentation of evil is cramped and cut-and-dried. Bunyan's sense of the narrow line that divides the good man from the bad, his insistence that all are alike exposed to temptation, and that there is a way to Hell from the very gate of Heaven, has gone. To Bunyan all men are in error, and their state is precarious. The later writers, interested above all in the art of story-telling, seek sympathy for certain characters at the expense of others. The larger metaphysical context is gone. Justice has become more poetic, and characters suffer in accordance with their deserts. The prosperous career of Mr. Badman, happy and untroubled, is foreign to a utilitarian, middle-class morality which demands some kind of a dividend in return for the expenditure of righteous effort, and wishes to signify its sense of the folly of being on the wrong side. Bunyan, heir to a richer tradition, condemns Ignorance and allows Mr. Badman to prosper. His prosperity is the measure of his damnation.

Richardson's strength is recognised to be in minute psychological analysis of mood and motive. The epistolary method of his novels is well suited to such analysis and, once the initial improbability is got over, is no disadvantage. Like Fielding and Smollett, he has no large-scale heroic figures. In fact, the eighteenth-century novel is distinctly anti-heroic in tendency. The proportions are those of ordinary life. That tragic stature which lingered, not wholly seriously, on the stage, in the persons of Dryden's heroic protagonists, is gone. Even where an attempt is made to idealise, as in the case of Sir Charles Grandison, this is so. Sir Charles is a paragon, but no hero. Richardson's morality is utilitarian, sententious and bourgeois. It is rather an ethic of success than of virtue. Pamela's attitude to her situation illustrates this. Mr. B. plays one game, she another, and she imposes her will upon him and wins on her own terms.

Clarissa Harlowe is within hailing distance of real tragedy. The writing is in places extraordinarily strong, and Clarissa's actions are made reasonable by the relentlessly portrayed setting of the early part of the book. She is a victim, not so much of Lovelace, as of her family of petty persecutors. There is an almost Gallic realism in the portrayal of her relations. To the end, despite Richardson's incessant clamour, she remains a living person. Lovelace ruins her, not Richardson, although there are moments when he comes near to doing so. Normally Richardson's style is irritatingly vulgar, but he has something of Fielding's and Hogarth's strength in depicting the house of ill-fame to which Clarissa is taken. His improper persons are always clearly drawn. Clarissa's death is on the largest scale and the edification is imposing. Lovelace repents but is not allowed to live. He dies, however, like a gentleman, to the accompaniment of an appropriate gesture. But Richardson talks too much about gentlemen ever to portray a real one. Some of his characters, e.g., Miss Howe and Miss Grandison, show a sense of proportion and a graceful competence which would not have shamed Jane Austen.

In some ways, in his subtle allusiveness, in his infinite winding about of circumstance, in his sense of the importance of the insignificant, he anticipates Henry James. But whereas the latter's sensitiveness will never let him come quite to the point and keeps him for ever beautifully hinting, the sensitiveness of Richardson never lets him leave us in the slightest doubt as to what exactly is happening, has happened, and will happen. He leaves nothing to the reader to imagine; he is for ever picking at some sore place or other. The American is slightly over-bred, the Englishman distinctly under-bred. But his self-consciousness and interest in intricacies of motive were of a kind which our literature had not seen since *Troilus and Criseyde*.

Fielding's genius is stronger and bolder. He came to the novel after much experience of journalistic and dramatic writing. Already he was a master of burlesque. His life had been more varied and adventurous than that of the quiet printer who was his rival. His reading was wide and his sense of form powerful. His great gift to the novel was the power to move freely in space and time. The adventures of Tom Jones are numerous and often improbable, but they fit into a pattern consonant with that of our common experience. Richardson moves freely enough inside the minds of his characters. Fielding's freedom is that of the world of action. His ironic mind confers upon him a detachment which Richardson, being entangled in the web of his own sensibilities, seldom shows. He seems less conventional than Richardson, but the truth is really that his conventions are different. Richardson accepts nominal virtue and vice as the reality, and makes play with the names of moral qualities rather than the qualities themselves. Fielding is more rebellious and more popular. He pleads for the stout and the generous heart, the good but ordinary chap, who means no harm whatever he may do. A little weak perhaps, but what does that matter if his intentions are good? The cheerful giver may be forgiven if here and there he trespasses on the preserves of another. What he does matters less than what he is. It is commonplace, worldly morality with the balance tilted heavily in favour of virtues that the world has never found difficulty in admiring.

Presentation of characters is one of Fielding's highest accomplishments. They are presented in and by their speech and action. He is less the pure describer than Smollett and his great follower Dickens. Their method is rather that of the reporter, Fielding's of the dramatist. Boots and buttons, tricks of speech and oddities of countenance matter much less to him. There is an inwardness about Jones and Partridge and Booth that Smollett's characters lack. One sees the men before the details: remove the details from a Smollett character and the affair collapses. In some ways that is Smollett's strength. There is the less offence in his often highly disagreeable figures because they have no insides. They do not abide our judgment. Roderick Random is only a bustling noisy husk. Moreover Smollett moves with extraordinary speed. We have no time to raise objections. Fielding, in both plot and character, invites analysis: Smollett puts it by, and his books are in our memories rather as sensations than as stories. One must except from this suggestion Smollett's final masterpiece, *Humphry Clinker*, which is both more leisurely and more solid.

With Fielding we are never far from a Shakespearian tolerance and love of life. Even in *Jonathan Wild*, one of the most ironical works in the language, there is a kind of joy in the breadth and effrontery of life's underworld. After all, its inhabitants are no worse than their so-called betters, and one "great man" achieves greatness in much the same way as another. One achieves a noose and the other a Garter, but both are rooks in a world of gulls. In *Amelia* he

achieves moments of real tenderness. His insight into character is instinctive and not the result of deep speculation.
What the man in the street sees, he sees also; his mastery is
in manipulation and presentation. Fielding was, in his novels
at least, no reformer. Or rather he is a reformer of the school
of Dickens. He appeals to our sense of the ridiculous and
to our sympathies. He does not directly tell us what should
be done; having read his books, we should know.

His theory of the comic epic for long gave tone and
tendency to the novel. Not until Scott's *Bride of Lammermoor*,
do we get tragedy, professed and inescapable, in this form.
Even *Clarissa Harlowe* is not a tragedy, so much as a successful and absorbing cheat. Clarissa would have been saved if
Richardson had respected her as much as the other characters in the book do. Hers is a compelled death, imposed
from outside the story.

Smollett never recovered from a kind of angry perversity
that fills his novels like an unholy odour. The naval expedition to Cartagena in which he took part may have made
him an artist, but it also enslaved him. His work is curative,
like that of a surgeon, but he is a surgeon with unwashed
hands, who at times reminds us of a hangman. He worked
off much of this hankering after the loathsome in *Ferdinand,
Count Fathom*, a grim, dullish, tale of villainy, and in the
regrettable *Adventures of an Atom*, but he never quite out-
grew the medical student.

He has a good eye and is an excellent reporter of travel.
Travels through France and Italy is full of interesting judgments
and admirably recorded incident. He has a historian's sense
of people and places as well as a feeling for natural beauty
that reminds us that he was a contemporary of Gray. His
novels are admirable "source-books"; *Humphry Clinker* tells
us more about the everyday life, tastes and habits of ordinary
people than any other single book of the century. From him,
and from Fielding too, we can learn what manner of people
inhabited this country in the days of William Pitt.

Sterne is, it may be supposed, an ancestor of the surrealists.
But his technique is more like that of *A Tale of a Tub*. *Tristram Shandy* begins in the middle and the real, or at any

rate professed beginning, does not occur until the book is far gone. The end is impudence. And not the end only. A newcomer to Sterne should read *The Sentimental Journey* before *Tristram Shandy*, which latter should be approached with caution. The essence of Sterne's cult of feeling is in the shorter book. Bird in a cage, dead ass, traveller in distress, all excite their disproportionate response of sensibility. Here too the end is impudence. Impudence in the dark, a groping gesture, and the rest is silence. The impudence tones down and otherwise qualifies the emotional excess. It is Sterne's own feelings, not we, who are affronted by it.

Sterne was well read and his books are full. They allude to a complicated and varied world; story, incident, episode, lacuna, crowd one upon another. Perhaps the unity is in the main a unity of style. A style highly flexible, with soft winding beginnings and abrupt endings. His dialogues are incomparable and give us a strange sensation of a kind of double time—of infinitely quick wits and the slow development of themes. He develops a queer logic of the feelings which suits our own age well enough. He is the most poetical of the eighteenth-century novelists. Without Fielding's beautiful sense of articulate structure, he exhibits an imaginative mastery of a vast, private, blind world of which he seems sometimes a little afraid. He dares tell everything but not right out. We have to draw our own conclusions, for in anything like real conclusions Sterne does not traffic. He is our greatest master of extravaganza. The word "aside" might be printed as a kind of stage-direction before his works.

His morality is curious and not all contemptible. My uncle Toby could not have been created, except by one who had some intimate knowledge of plain goodness. He shares with Goldsmith's Dr. Primrose a divine simplicity. Sterne's very prurience mocks itself and is a kind of reproof to the secret thoughts of the world.

The Vicar of Wakefield can be enjoyed more easily than it can be criticised. The gentlest analysis pulls it to pieces to be set up again, whole and alive, at the next re-reading. Only a bad man will dislike it. It treats as much of folly as of goodness and they are not always separable. It has no place in a literary history of the novel, but it enlarges our experience. Goldsmith cares here little enough about improbability and takes the grossest liberties, but his tale is easier to believe for all that.

These writers gave prose fiction a place alongside great poetry.

II

Johnson has given his name to the literary epoch that stretches from the early forties until his own death in 1784. To some of the most important developments of that time he contributed little or nothing, and towards others he was suspicious and unfriendly, but his personal supremacy— pre-eminence as man and writer—cannot be abated. It is a superficial view that sees him as a reactionary Augustan maintaining in one age the prejudices of the last. True he cared for order and respected authority, but it was such order as his own intelligence had tested, and an authority that carried ample credentials. Like other critics he had his preferences and his blindnesses. No one else has written so well or so appreciatively of Dryden or Pope: he practised the same art as they and shared their dislike of the factiousness and greed that threaten the stability and good order of society. At the same time his own spirit was more profound than theirs. He had none of the moral vulgarity of Dryden, or the nervous savagery of Pope. His diagnosis of the ills of humanity was more searching.

His distinguishing quality can perhaps be called piety. Pious in the religious sense he certainly was, and in association with this he had a feeling for human dignity that his awareness of the ills that attend mortality only reinforced. Though his only tragedy was unsuccessful, his view of experience has in it something of the tragic. Both in *The Vanity of Human Wishes* and in *Rasselas* there is to be found a strong feeling of the futility of human aims, but it is not a futility that degrades, it is rather one that explains and interprets for us the fact of failure. Not the flesh but the world is the will o' the wisp for which men give their eternal

jewel. Neither action nor reason can redeem man from his
fate but neither is condemned. We ask the wrong things
and they are given to us, and we find ourselves as we were
before. The Christian and humanist traditions meet in
Johnson and he draws his strength from both.

More good scholars are at work on him and on his biographer Boswell than ever before and his status among literary
critics is an exalted one. But the ordinary reader to-day
does not find him attractive. His *Ramblers* have a massive
solemnity and an elaborate sententiousness that an age
accustomed to a different tempo finds tedious: his *Idlers*
belie their title. He is perhaps best approached through
the late Sir Walter Raleigh's *Six Essays on Johnson* which
is a landmark in wise and thoughtful criticism and has won
Johnson many readers. Boswell's *Life* has never lacked popularity but we do not necessarily turn from a study of it
with a strong desire to read what Johnson himself wrote.
Rather do we turn to other biographies, for the great
quality of Boswell is that he tells us so much of his subject
and yet makes us feel that Johnson was very much greater
than even Boswell knew. We turn to Mrs. Piozzi, to the
heavy-handed Sir John Hawkins, to Fanny Burney and half
a dozen others, and realise that the full truth about a man
can never be told. Had it been possible Boswell would have
done it. As it is, we are admitted to intimacy with Johnson
but the sense of the mystery of human personality is increased, as it increases with our knowledge of our own
friends.

It is almost a platitude to say that Johnson taught Boswell
his craft. His genius certainly he did not give him, nor his
overwhelmingly adequate technique. But all his life Johnson practised biography, in three or four of his essays he
expounded the art, and his sense of the inseparability of a
man and his work makes him the first of our Romantic
critics.

Johnson's scholarship and his morality are barriers between his work and our own quick and disillusioned wits,
but we can appreciate him in action and in society as his
biographers give him to us. His stern virtues, born of a

full knowledge of his own frailty and his strong discipline and control, we may recover in a more stable age. At present most readers will be inclined to confuse his aphorisms and enunciations on human conduct with the nursery copy-book maxims that distress our childhood and amuse our adolescence. It is possible to read the *Ramblers* so carefully that their apparent triteness is seen to be the recovery of a traditional morality that Johnson had proved upon his own rebellious pulses, but to do so is uncommon.

He introduces himself best to us perhaps in his *Life of Savage*, written soon after his friend's death in 1744 and later reprinted in his *Lives of the Poets*. Johnson's sweetness and charity and loyalty make a tiny epic of this tale of a dishonest but not untalented adventurer. Ungrateful, rather bogus, as we might now say, Savage survives in good company for ever because Johnson cared for him and gladly bore testimony to the difficulties and degradations that encompassed a man who, had he been luckier had perhaps been better. "Nor will any wise man presume to say, 'Had I been in Savage's condition, I should have lived or written better than Savage.' "

Johnson's most remarkable accomplishment is his *Dictionary* wherein the erudition is relieved by the surprising movements of a massive wit: his most brilliant is the *Preface* to his edition of Shakespeare. Some of his judgments on Shakespeare are astonishingly unlike our own, some of his prejudices almost perverse, but he rises greatly to his great occasion and there is no piece of general criticism on the same scale that approaches it. He exhibits the excellence of Shakespeare in its fullness and grandeur. Perhaps his preference for the comedies, which no modern critic would endorse, might well have been echoed by Shakespeare himself in certain moods.

The *Lives of the Poets*, the work of Johnson's old age, is a remarkable series of moral and critical judgments. Some of us to-day set high store on research, on the discovery and presentation of new facts. With such an attitude Johnson has little in common. Values interest him, and it is values that he gives us. His years of research were behind him and, if he wrote at the request of the booksellers, he wrote in a fashion that pleased himself. He is at his best in writing of Dryden and Pope, whose age he understood and whose work he greatly admired, and of Cowley and Waller, men whose reputation was high in the days of Dryden and waning slowly in those of Pope. Addison, whom he knew well enough when and how to praise, had perhaps too many reservations to win Johnson's full sympathy. Swift he never understood, and the politics of Milton, as well as his religion, he found displeasing. The querulous note in Gray angered him, and the rawness evident in Collins made him less generous as a critic than he had been as a friend. Yet where he can see his way he gives full measure. *Paradise Lost* and the *Elegy* are praised reasonably and well, if in a fashion that we find a trifle sententious.

The *Lives* is almost a treatise on certain phases of English poetry and certain aspects of English life. Like its author it is often contradictory and often provoking, but it adds depth and dignity to the English critical tradition. Perhaps in so brief a memorandum of Johnson as this, dignity is a good word on which to end.

But it is not easy to cease from writing or talking about him. Wisdom is a word that is lightly used and often misapplied. In Johnson's life and work it is abundant. But that life and work, to be fully appreciated, must be seen as a whole. Often an eccentric judgment in one place is corrected by a more measured statement elsewhere. For example, his condemnation of the pastoral form of *Lycidas* is well known. In the *Life of Milton* Johnson fears, and shows that he fears, the new fashion in poetry which seemed to him a revival, fruitless because limited by its models and having in it no principle of life, of the less desirable characteristics of some of Milton's poetry. He did not welcome the odes which were in his lifetime once more becoming fashionable. What he disliked in Gray, Warton, and Collins he attributed to the use of unsuitable models. He admired Milton but distrusted his influence on the living poetry of his own day. And many of us too feel that of all our great poetic traditions those of Milton both in his minor poems and in his epic, are the most dubious in their effects upon a young poet. Johnson knew well enough the charm of pastoral:

> "The satisfaction received from this kind of writing not only begins early, but lasts long; we do not, as we advance into the intellectual world, throw it away among other childish amusements and pastimes, but willingly return to it in any hour of indolence and relaxation. The images of true pastoral have always the power of exciting delight; because the works of nature, from which they are drawn, have always the same order and beauty, and continue to force themselves upon our thoughts, being at once obvious to the most careless regard, and more than adequate to the strongest reason, and severest contemplation."[1]

Elsewhere[2] he says: "That they (the Pastorals) exhibit a mode of life which does not exist, nor ever existed, is not to be objected; the supposition of such a state is allowed to Pastoral".

In these and in other passages Johnson shows his interest in the form which he characterised in connection with *Lycidas* as "easy, vulgar, and therefore disgusting". He thought indeed that there was much bad pastoral poetry in his own day, and was afraid that indifferent poetry was sheltering itself behind the reputations of the mighty dead. So he hit out. But in other moods and in other contexts he can praise what here he disliked and he has written nobly on the pastoral poems of Virgil, perhaps his favourite in this kind.

Similarly, despite misgivings, often quoted, about the use of blank verse he can say of *The Seasons:*

"His is one of the works in which blank verse seems properly used; Thomson's wide expansion of general views, and his enumeration of circumstantial varieties, would have been obstructed and embarrassed by the frequent inter-section of the sense, which are the necessary effects of rhyme." Johnson never put forth all his strength into one sentence and he can be quoted against himself to his own great advantage. Similarly we must remember that in

---

[1] *The Rambler, No.* 36.
[2] *Life of Ambrose Philips.*

Boswell's *Life* we have not only an objective account of facts but also a detailed record of Johnson's response to Boswell's probing questions. The biographer was always manœuvring his idol into positions which he thought appropriate, and a good deal of the book is concerned less with Johnson's reactions to experience in general than his reactions to Boswell. This detracts nothing from its value, but we must remember that with Boswell Johnson was not quite the same man as when he was in less assiduous company.

III

The seventeen-forties are important in the history of literary development. Poetry began once again to aspire and imagination to assume for itself more exalted functions. It is the time of the revival of the ode. The great names are those of Collins and Gray, but Akenside and Collins's friend and fellow Wykehamist, Joseph Warton, have earned a place in the story.

Collins's thin, badly-printed volume of odes dated 1746 is an important poetical landmark. Shakespeare, Milton, and the Greeks were the main influences, but he has too a personal contribution. His interest in form is not matched by his mastery but he tries many kinds. Indeed his formal range is wider than that of Keats, whom in his odes he is not altogether unlike. At least it has been found that after reading Keats it is often easier to appreciate Collins. His emotional range is limited. *The Passions, an Ode for Music*, is a spirited, vivid irregular piece, varied with skill and artistry; but there is little enough of passion about it. He is careless, casual and raw, but there is no more genuine lyric gift than his. Critics have never found him hard to undervalue nor lovers of poetry to enjoy. The truth is that he appeals rather to our instinct for poetry than to our considered experience, and crams our ears with musical promise. Associated in life with Johnson and in fame with Gray, he has suffered somewhat in relation to both. The points in poetry which Johnson was accustomed to evaluate and praise he did not find in Collins and the fresh lyrical impulses of the poems escaped him. In comparison with Gray, Collins's versification for all the wide variety of his experimentation is that of an amateur; and his notes, though sweeter and fresher, are less sure. Gray had the better ear, Collins the better voice. But both are nearly faultless in the latter's best work.

> How sleep the Brave, who sink to Rest,
> By all their Country's Wishes blest!
> When *Spring*, with dewy Fingers cold,
> Returns to deck their hallow'd Mold,
> She there shall dress a sweeter Sod,
> Than *Fancy's* Feet have ever trod.
>
> By Fairy Hands their Knell is rung,
> By Forms unseen their Dirge is sung;
> There *Honour* comes, a Pilgrim grey,
> To bless the Turf that wraps their Clay,
> And *Freedom* shall a-while repair,
> To dwell a weeping Hermit there!

The *Elegy wrote in a Country Church Yard* has become one of the "set books" of the English people. Its images and rhythms have stolen into their imagination. Perhaps the elegiac stanza has been put out of commission by this poem, wherein it has so consummately fulfilled itself. Subject and poem are indistinguishable; a quiet fountain of dusky images playing melodiously as the peaceful evening darkens. Less adventurous than Collins's *Ode*, it has a greater unity. Gray polished it with his usual care, admitting no stanza on its own merits, and carefully subduing all the details to the total effect. In spite of the personal note—the least happy part of the poem —there is a touch of anonymity about it. Almost any poet could have written the *Elegy* provided only that he were good enough. It is without fear and without pity, a solemn nocturne played by a great virtuoso. Its melancholy and touches of sententiousness are of the time; the abiding English countryside that coffins the uninteresting dead might have stirred any poet at any time. Perhaps Gray himself is betrayed by an occasional gentle fussiness— "Approach and read (for thou can'st read) the lay." The poetic imagination is stirring, is growing less content to comment and depict; it is beginning to create the thing it contemplates.

Of his regular Pindaric odes, *The Bard* and *The Progress of Poesy*, the latter is the more successful; it has much less of the "cumbrous splendour that we wish away." The revival of the major ode in English verse is a triumphant achievement, and the historical details do not interfere with the free movement of the noble measure. Neither poem could ever be popular. Gray wrote with a small cultured audience in mind, and that audience he tried to assist by his footnotes. To those readers who appreciate a display of learning in their poetry and who can enjoy the skilful handling and discreet parade of erudition these odes make their chief appeal. His self-parody, *Ode on the Death of a favourite Cat*, and the *Ode on a Distant Prospect of Eton College*, with its finely sustained note of plangency, are perhaps the most obviously pleasing of his other poems.

With Gray and Collins and some of their lesser contemporaries, the Wartons, Akenside and West, English poetry became aware of the far range of its varied inheritance and began to shape itself for new and greater tasks.

It is not really true that Gray "never spoke out". Probably he said in his poetry all that his poetry could have said, and the extreme care which is so apparent, seems less to be the result of an impulse to restrain his utterance than an attempt to achieve a standard worthy of the noblest tradition. All the same there are times when we could wish that his art had concealed itself a little more.

His freest, fullest utterances are to be found in his letters. In an age that made of letter-writing a notable art-form Gray's need fear no comparison. His prose is easier than his verse and much of it has the run and sparkle of good conversation. His range of interests is wide and he wears his learning with grace and good-breeding. The classics, fashion, architecture, contemporary poetry, politics and

scandal, travels and natural beauty are amongst the subjects touched on. He was not free from the scientific interests
of his age and plants and insects were among his delights.
Some of his letters to his Swiss friend Bonstetten show a
wealth of friendship and affection that we should not have
expected from the writer of the poems. Friendship, literary
criticism, and his comments on scenery, particularly that
amongst the English lakes, in the appreciation of which he
was a pioneer, occasion his best writing. We receive the
impression of a learned and wise scholar, moving gently
and wittily through life, not expecting too much in the way
of fortune or happiness, but with a great capacity for the
enjoyment of many kinds of experience. Probably some who
are unable to read his poetry would find pleasure in his
letters.

His friendship with Horace Walpole, himself a great
letter-writer, kept him in touch with the world of politics
and high life on which he commented in a strain of polished
sophistication worthy of his correspondent.

Others in Gray's lifetime were moved by antiquarian
interests and the sense of the past. The controversy in connection with James Macpherson's "Ossianic poems" is an old
story. From the first their authenticity was doubted and the
defenders of their author's pretensions as an editor rapidly
dwindled. But they were widely read and enjoyed and their
strange atmosphere of remote melancholy has not yet lost
all appeal. Macpherson kept alive in these strange fakes
ancient Celtic traditions, and founded a new European
fashion. In 1765 Dr. Thomas Percy published his *Reliques
of Ancient English Poetry* and brought into public notice a mass
of songs, ballads and romances: his ideas of the amount of
liberty that any editor may take with his text need not be
discussed here, and his controversy with Ritson is of mainly
academic interest.

During the seventeen-sixties poetry extended its range and
interests: as the forties tuned our numbers afresh, so the later
decade loaded them with new material. Smart's *Song to
David* recaptures the Hebrew psalmist's sense of the dynamic
aspect of nature as a manifestation of God's majesty.

> Of beasts . . . the beaver plods his task;
> While the sleek tygers roll'and bask,
>   Nor yet the shades arouse:
> Her cave the mining coney scoops;
> Where o'er the mead the mountain stoops,
>   The kids exult and brouse.
>
> Of gems . . . their virtue and their price,
> Which hid in earth from man's device,
>   Their darts of lustre sheathe;
> The jasper of the master's stamp,
> The topaz blazing like a lamp
>   Among the mines beneath.

Something of Blake's innocent, relentless eye and full-mouthed prophesying speech is here, something too of Browning's sense of diffused divinity.

Thomas Chatterton, who read old poems in an old city and became a poet and "perished in his pride", cared greatly for metre—with which he experimented brilliantly—and atmosphere. Although he disguised his voice at times and perpetrated a mass of harmless and fascinating "forgeries", his quality and variety of achievement are at times astonishing. He died before his eighteenth birthday, and it is impossible to do more than guess at what his later developments might have been. The world of the *Rowley Poems* is not a sham world, though much of the language and prosody is poorly contrived. It has been intensely imagined and vividly seen. Chaucer and some of his successors, Spenser and certain Elizabethan lyrics, made enduring patterns in his mind and set him chanting snatches of old tunes.

> Come, with acorn-cup and thorn,
> Drain my heart's blood all away;
> Life and all its good I scorn,
> Dance by night, or feast by day.
>   My love is dead,
>   Gone to his death-bed,
>   All under the willow-tree.

At the same time Goldsmith's *Traveller* and *Deserted Village* were drawing fresh music from Pope's great measure.

During the seventies James Beattie's *Minstrel* was the nearest thing to great poetry that appeared. There is here something of Wordsworth's view on the education that nature provides for her children and an anticipation of the voice of *Childe Harold* is heard at one point. The poem is interesting, with little touches of charm here and there. It is written in the Spenserian stanza which had been employed with increasing seriousness throughout the century. Earlier it had been used for burlesque and comic effects—there is indeed something about it that invites mockery—but there was a gradual realisation of its more serious possibilities as time went on.

Pope's *Alley*, a dirty little poem, had interested Shenstone, who is more celebrated as the owner of The Leasowes than as the choice minor poet that he often shows himself to be. In the successive versions of *The Schoolmistress*—1738–48—he showed the possibilities of this stanza for delicate and not unkindly poetic banter. With Thomson's *Castle of Indolence*, published in the same year as the final version of *The Schoolmistress*, the Spenserian measure became once more a thing of enchantment. The two cantos are very unequal in quality, the second being often painstakingly pedestrian in its moralising. But Thomson, despite his view that one ought in using this stanza to employ an archaic diction that borders on the ludicrous, achieved a masterpiece in the first canto, which includes perhaps the best-known single stanza of this kind that ever was written.

> As when a shepherd of the Hebrid Isles,
> Placed far amid the melancholy main,
> (Whether it be lone fancy him beguiles,
> Or that aerial beings sometimes deign
> To stand embodied to our senses plain)
> Sees on the naked hill, or valley low,
> The whilst in ocean Phoebus dips his wain,
> A vast assembly moving to and fro;
> Then all at once in air dissolves the wondrous show.

These poets preserved and enriched this stanza for the later poets of our period: for Scott in his *Vision of Don Roderick*, for Byron in *Childe Harold*, for Shelley in *The Revolt of Islam* and *Adonais*, for Keats in *The Eve of St. Agnes*.

IV

The great poetic names in the seventeen-eighties are those of Crabbe, Cowper, Burns, and Blake, three of whom exploited with a difference existing traditions, while the fourth had neither predecessors nor followers.

The years of Crabbe's work extend from 1783 until the end of our period. Crabbe is one of those who serve to remind us of the interlocking of fashions and the overlapping of styles. In an age essentially romantic, he retains some of the astringency and directness of the Augustans. A born story-teller and describer of exteriors, he is capable of excursions into the realm of dream and fantasy, and to the end of his career his couplets and imagination grow richer and he attains completer mastery of his medium. But it is not always easy to see why he writes in verse.

Cowper mingled gentleness with exquisite good breeding. Like so many on whom life presses with unusual severity he has at command a playful humour and can take a quiet delight in the incongruous. The author of the *Castaway* delighted our childhood with *John Gilpin*. Alike in his short poems, in *The Task*, and in his letters, his love of nature and quiet scenery, the changes of the seasons, the habits of animals—particularly his own pets—testifies to the alertness of his observation. *Yardley Oak* has no superior as an example of imaginative exploitation of the theme of growth and decay. It is unfinished and it looks as though Cowper had intended to "moralise his song", but the introduction of a human subject led nowhere. It is easy to underrate Cowper, who made small claim for his own poetry. His satires are not now much read, but in the modest kingdom where he reigns he is a true king.

Even in the eighteenth century, so rich in excellent letters,

77

Cowper's correspondence is remarkable. Much of it is gentle, entertaining gossip. As in his verse, he has admirable descriptions of quiet life within and without doors, and he has the trick of investing the commonplace with significance. Some of his letters record the measureless distress which afflicts sufferers from his malady. No man regarded his own troubles with a steadier gaze, or drew fairer light from the darkest places in human experience.

Robert Burns, a working farmer and excise officer, had a vital, warm and forthright personality, and a natural gift for vivid and witty speech. The schooling he had—principally in English writers—did something to develop this gift: but, by a happy chance, he never was able to say his say in English with anything like the distinction and ease he could command in his own native Scots. His first book, the *Poems*, published at Kilmarnock in 1786, though meant primarily to appeal to the folk of the neighbourhood, very soon carried the poet's name over the whole country. Instead of emigrating to seek his fortune in Jamaica, he found himself in Edinburgh, the favourite of society there for a season while supervising the new edition of his *Poems* of 1787. Later editions issued in Burns's lifetime were filled out more with English than with Scottish verse: indeed, save for *Tam o' Shanter* and a few shorter pieces, the best of Burns's poems as distinct from songs in the vernacular are contained in the 1787 volume. These poems paint the manners, life and ideas of the Scottish people among whom Burns had been brought up. A few are serious and moralising in tone; but the greater number, and the most pleasing and characteristic, are full of a rollicking humour, bespeaking an unconquerable, almost Falstaffian enjoyment of life. Even the touches of satire, both here and in poems (like *Holy Willie's Prayer*) not published till after the poet's death, are so obviously inspired by the love of being alive that laughter drowns most part of their bitterness and they rather read like song gone wrong than like satire proper. And indeed song is Burns's natural voice. He commenced poet in his fifteenth year from a desire to set words to the favourite dance tune of his first love, his companion in the harvest field. And the most important result of the Edinburgh visit was his connection with James Johnson and *The Scots Musical Museum*, of which Burns became practically literary editor from 1787 till his death. To this work and to a later, more staid venture of the same kind that invited his aid—George Thomson's *Select Scotish Airs*—Burns contributed the many songs that have established his fame. Some of these were original. But most were brilliant refurbishings of ancient Scottish numbers: for Burns as song-wright, preferring the life and world he knew best, turned again to the folk-airs and dance tunes that first guided his pen and—as the best service he could render his country—set about repairing and cleansing the frayed and often lewd verses that use had attached to these, and that threatened their continuance in esteem. His sure sense of the music that was his starting-point in each case, and his still surer instinct for the right word, have made him one of the greatest of artists in folk-song, and have been the means of securing for Scotland a body of popular music and song as good as any and better than most.

William Blake was something of a portent and just what he portended is not altogether clear. In his study of the Eliza-bethan drama, of Spenser and of Milton, he was in line with his age. Some of the lyrics in *Poetical Sketches*, his earliest volume, are exquisite. "How sweet I roam'd from field to field," "My silks and fine array", "Memory, hither come" are jewels in our national treasury. Already something of Blake's difference from other men and his strong sense of that differ-ence is apparent.

> Like a fiend in a cloud
>   With howling woe,
> After night I do croud
>   And with night will go;
> I turn my back to the east,
>   From whence comforts have increas'd;
> For light doth seize my brain
>   With frantic pain.

79

All his life he

> travel'd thro' a Land of Men,
> A Land of Men and Women too;
> And heard and saw such dreadful things
> As cold Earth-wanderers never knew,

and he was aware continually of this strangeness of himself in the world in which he travelled—

> O why was I born with a different face?
> Why was I not born like the rest of my race?

A stern asserter of orthodoxy, he turned round the ordinary orthodoxies of faith and experience, finding prison where others asserted they knew freedom, and death in what they declared was life—

> The Vision of Christ that thou dost see
> Is my Vision's Greatest Enemy.
>
> . . . . . .
>
> Thine loves the same world that mine hates;
> Thy heaven doors are my Hell Gates.

In his vindication of the claims of the imagination and distrust of reason he has affinities with the romantic poets, and something, too, of the romantic disharmony is his. His intuitions were in part corrupted by Swedenborg, and his execution—in his drawings certainly—suffers from his submission to a vicious High Renaissance geometric formula. But some of his engravings are powerful and relentless, and some of his minor decorations have great beauty.

The prophetic books call for—and have received—detailed examination and interpretation. On the whole, perhaps, it may be said that they represent an attempt to restate traditional Christianity in terms of Blake's mythological view of history. Paradox abounds and the accepted teaching of the churches is reversed.

Blake in his private life was friendly, simple, virtuous. As poet and artist he suffered from an enormous ignorance, and insufficient interest in his medium of expression. Prodi-

giously industrious, he never managed to achieve the fundamental, necessary brain work. All the poems are to some
extent Songs of Innocence: his is the "innocent eye" which
beholds all things, good and evil, with little reference to any
experience other than its own. Yet his horrified protest at
some of the more obvious contemporary suffering is vigorous,
if at times imperfectly sustained.

> Is this a holy thing to see
> In a rich and fruitful land,
> Babes reduc'd to misery,
> Fed with cold and usurous hand?

Or, more powerfully, as in the magnificent dark *London*;

> I wander thro' each charter'd street,
> Near where the charter'd Thames does flow,
> And mark in every face I meet
> Marks of weakness, marks of woe.

> In every cry of every Man,
> In every Infant's cry of fear,
> In every voice, in every ban,
> The mind-forg'd manacles I hear.
>
> .   .   .   .   .   .
>
> But most thro' midnight streets I hear
> How the youthful Harlot's curse
> Blasts the new born Infant's tear,
> And blights with plagues the Marriage hearse.

Some of his poems, like *The Tyger*, seem beyond criticism.
For all the complication of his mythologies, his imagination
never lost the simplicity and directness of childhood. Reason,
which he hated, never gave him pause. What he saw, in whatever world, he set down according to his own strange
formulae. He neither questioned nor criticised his visions,
and he never doubted himself.

The period that opened with the establishment of great

modern prose by Dryden remained true to its early promise. The last thirty or forty years of the eighteenth century succeed fittingly to the age of Addison and Swift and of the first great English novelists. They are the years of the great prose masters Johnson, Goldsmith, Burke and Gibbon. Goldsmith is perhaps the freest of these writers, if the least profound. There is no risk that he will be mastered by his subjects. In his casual, intimate writings he anticipates to a certain extent the more mannered, richer confidences of Lamb. His sensibilities are mobile rather than deep, and his admirable prose is the perfect vehicle for his detached, yet sympathetic, observations. In his comedies, *The Good Natur'd Man* and *She Stoops to Conquer*, he shows a sense of powerful, if not very subtle, stage situation, and in the latter play at least, he gives plenty of opportunities to his actors. Had he found the material and opportunity to write a third comedy, it might well have been a masterpiece. His great output of varied work, much of it hard food-winning toil, never staled his freshness nor tarnished his good-will.

Burke and Gibbon in many ways bring the pre-revolutionary age to a close. Burke introduced into politics a new moral fervour and sense of responsibility. No less practical and realistic than Machiavelli himself, he related politics to human needs and aspirations in a way that added a new chapter to the story of enlightened humanism. His belief in the perfection of the balanced constitutional arrangement of 1688 seems to us excessive; it had probably never worked as perfectly as he thought. But it might well have done so had England's leaders seen with his eyes and laboured with his spirit. In a most brilliant Parliamentary age, the age of Chatham, Pitt, Fox and Sheridan, he sometimes seems to be the only trained professional in a world of eloquent amateurs. In the art of persuasion he had his superiors, but his was the only prophetic voice that spoke with full knowledge of the deepest English traditions. He was alert to defend the constitution alike from the encroachments of royal influence and the assault of the new revolutionary doctrines of his later years. He was the first to develop a doctrine of political conservatism which could be said to conserve values rather than safeguard interests. His wisdom is perhaps most conspicuous in his American speeches, his command of picturesque eloquence in his speech *On the Nabob of Arcot's Debts*, his power of destructive apologetic in the *Letter to a Noble Lord*. It is doubtful whether any other political thinker has had a clearer view of the permanent interests of this country.

There is significance in Gibbon's choice of subject. *The History of the Decline and Fall of the Roman Empire* was written in the decline of an age of authority based on tradition and the past. Our Augustan phase was now ending and opinion was stirring uneasily. The apparent peace was over and the time of reformer and revolutionary, theorist and experimenter, was at hand. Gibbon celebrated the decline of the longest period of stable government that the Western world had known while the briefer and more delusive peace of our eighteenth century was coming to an end. The pace was quickening and Gibbon's long history reflected the long leisure and long reflection of an easier time.

The work is epic in scale and epic in its planning. Gibbon's control of his subject is unrivalled. Unrivalled too is the matching of the style to the various movements that he chronicled. Gibbon was a natural historian, careful and seemly in his attitude to his material. Modern research has corrected many of his conclusions but has left his panorama unimpaired. A modulated massiveness characterises the whole; a cool and reserved irony plays over those religious and metaphysical disputes the inwardness of which escaped Gibbon's detached mind; a wealth of colour illuminates the marches and counter-marches of armies and nations; it has something of the ordered majesty of the Roman Empire itself. *The Memoirs of the Life of Edward Gibbon* is a revealing commentary on himself and his attitude towards experience. It is good reading.

:

CHAPTER IV

ROMANTICS

I

THE Romantic Movement in this country was part of a much wider humanistic movement. All over Europe efforts were being made to reassert the existence of human values.

In the days of our Augustans there was still an international culture, shallow and precarious but still real. By the end of the century the traditions on which it had been based had lost their authority and failed to abide the questions of the time. The Romantics tried to find in the nature of man, in his longings, aspirations and uncertainties, above all in his imaginative life, some basis for a common culture, for a new set of sustaining beliefs. In England the chief part in the new quest for enlightenment fell to the poets, in whom the spirit of man once again went exploring and who achieved in their work, for all its frequent indiscipline, a new comprehensiveness and a new intensity.

It is customary to describe the chief literary activities between the years 1798 and 1830 by the term Romantic Revival. As has been noted in earlier sections of this essay much reviving had happened a good deal earlier. Interest in our older poets had never died, although some of them for a time had fallen out of favour. Throughout most of the eighteenth century the direct influence of Milton and Spenser was at least as great as that of Pope: indirectly of course they affected writers through. Pope himself who admitted to his friend Joseph Spence that Spenser was his original, and whose admiration for Milton is clear to any reader of

The Dunciad. After about 1730 the heroic couplet ceased to be the favourite English measure. A glance through Dodsley's oft reprinted and expanded *Collection of Poems by Several Hands* (1st and 2nd editions 1748) will confirm the truth of this statement. Blank verse was used throughout the century from John Philips's *Splendid Shilling* (1701) to Cowper's *Task* (1785). Among the notable poems in which blank verse was employed had been Thomson's *Seasons*, Somervile's *Chase*, Young's *Night Thoughts*, Blair's *Grave*, Dyer's *Fleece* and *Ruins of Rome*, Smart's *Hop-Garden*, Grainger's *Sugar-Cane*. As we have already seen there were important experiments in new or revived verse forms during the seventeen-forties, in the seventeen-sixties new themes were developed, and new material, much of it more or less antiquarian, appeared in our poetry, while the seventeen-eighties was a time of vigour and originality. Some years before the minor sonnet-fashion of Bowles, Thomas Warton, amongst others, had shown interest in this form, dead, save for a single sonnet by Gray, since Milton. The eighteenth century was full of revivals and many of them were romantic, but it was less self-conscious and less excited about them than the age we are now considering.

"Romantic" is an unsatisfactory term but everyone has some idea of what it means. It is evocative rather than descriptive. All poems, all works of imaginative literature, are both romantic and classic. It is a romantic thing to write a poem at all, to explore by means of words the uniqueness and universality of one's own experience, to communicate, as memorably as may be, moments that seem of high significance, to record one's solitary musings or ecstasies. To labour so that such record, such communication may achieve high and abiding excellence, that the statement may be final and finished, this is to seek the classical ideal. The romantic is the seeking for form, the classic its attainment. In so far as poems communicate the unique awareness of a single exploring consciousness they are romantic, in so far as this communication attains a stable and successful form they may be called classic. Perhaps one may be permitted to play yet another variation on this theme and suggest that the poet seeking immortality is romantic, the poem which achieves it is classic. But we crack the wind of these poor words running them thus.

The first thing to be said of this period is that it produced an immense variety of work of the highest quality, both prose and verse. It was particularly rich in poetry. The imagination was exalted. No longer was it looked upon as a commentator scribbling in the margin of experience. The very basis of experience itself was seen to consist of acts involving imagination. It operated in close and intimate alliance with reason, sometimes indeed it was the dominant partner. A transcendental attitude to experience replaced, not in philosophy alone, one that had hitherto been mainly empirical. The massive scholarship of the preceding age —the age of Malone, Tyrwhitt, Percy and Ritson—was at the service of the new literature. The historians, too, offered material that poets and novelists were quick to transform for their own use. It seemed as though the senses were quickened and the power of enjoyment increased. The poets made more far-reaching claims for themselves, as moralists, as prophets, as interpreters. They were very Antonies in their prodigality and bounty.

When their work is weak it tends to be so in discipline. In both good and bad senses the romantic writers were individualists. Good, in that they trusted their own integrity and intuitions and tried to set down faithfully what they themselves saw and felt; bad, in that they all show some loss of the disciplining sense of a community, of a society the existence and desirability of which could at all times be taken for granted. The discipline imposed by a common set of accepted values was lacking. Some, like Wordsworth, fought back against odds to recover their social heritage, some, like Shelley, never clearly defined their objectives and lived in a world of personal mythology.

In criticism, as well as in creative writing, the imagination, the power of seeing and sympathising, became a powerful instrument. On the whole the great English critics from Dryden to Johnson conceived of their function as *in the main* a judicial one. Coleridge, Lamb, Hazlitt, De Quincey, generally speaking, are rather interpreters than judges. The importance of judgments of value is not forgotten but the method is changed. The romantic critics share lavishly the pleasure they receive from the works they are discussing: the communication of pleasure is hardly less their function than that of the poets themselves. They are perhaps less disinterested than their predecessors.

At the same time classical ideals and classical models were never forgotten. One of the most characteristic features of the Romantic Revival was its rediscovery of the charm and power of the Greek elements in the old pagan civilisation.

If the Augustans looked back towards the Rome of Maecenas, Virgil and Horace, the Romantics looked further back still. A Greek spirit has been claimed for some of Keats's poems: Shelley was a genuine classical scholar whose thought was much influenced by what he knew of Plato, and who, in his most celebrated work, rehandled a fable which had been treated by Æschylus. Elegy, ode, tragedy and, in some sort, epic in which the age was prolific, looked back to greater traditions than the satires and Horatian imitations which were characteristic of the so-called classical Augustans. Nor were these minor classical forms neglected; Canning and the *Anti-Jacobin* writers and Byron kept alive the tradition of social and political criticism in verse. In the same year that *Lyrical Ballads* was published Landor's *Gebir*, beautifully over-written though it is, heralded a new development of strict formal perfection. Landor's austerity, clarity of outline, restrained delicacy of perception, enriched the classical tradition of English poetry throughout his long life which extended over two literary epochs. For the purpose of this essay it may be sufficient to recall that his *Imaginary Conversations* which, together with the thickly-sown jewellery of his epigrams, are the most familiar of his writings to present-day readers, added a further glory to the decade— the eighteen-twenties—which saw the publication of Lamb's "Elia" essays, Hazlitt's *Table-Talk* and *Spirit of the Age* and, in their earliest form, de Quincey's *Confessions of an English Opium Eater*. Peacock, master of caricature and travesty,

87

who had too his own delicate and playful romanticism not untouched by sentiment, still delights the connoisseur of choice literary vintages. While the "official" reviews, *The Edinburgh*, *The Quarterly*, and *Blackwoods* remained faithful to the judicial type of criticism, and corrected, often with severity, the taste of the time.

II

The greatest and most durable poet was William Wordsworth, who is for all seasons and for all weathers. He was both versatile and original, an interesting critic both of his own and other men's work; master of ode and sonnet, narrative poem and poem of meditation. Both moralist and seer, he was romantic in his transcendental view of the poetic imagination, classic in his stern rectitude. He found in his own experience during the most difficult and distressing period of his life as well as in the joyful abundance of the simple pleasures of his youth, themes which inspired his best work and most profound reflections.

The publication of *Lyrical Ballads* in 1798 is commonly and rightly hailed as a literary event of the first importance. It was perhaps the most important publication since Shakespeare. At least the volumes of 1798, 1800 and 1807 offer an enlargement of the possibilities of poetry which it is difficult to parallel (except by bringing in Shakespeare.)

In one way Wordsworth was the culmination of the whole imaginative effort of a hundred years. The age of reason, of moral instruction, of emotional sensibility had found at last a full voice and a comprehensive vision.

In another way he had no predecessors. The commonly invoked so-called heralds of the Romantic revival, Lady Winchilsea, Parnell, Thomson, Crabbe and Cowper, offered, no doubt, example and instruction. The very best moments of Thomson, Cowper's *Yardley Oak*, hint at the quality of the Wordsworth that is to come, as Greene, Peele and that lot hint at Shakespeare. But the disproportion in achievement is as great.

The chief interest of *Lyrical Ballads* is of course not in

88

language but in subject. For the first time, not common ordinary people merely—the eighteenth century had dealt well enough with them—but people of total insignificance, the outcast, the maimed, the betrayed, the solitary, the defective are fully enfranchised. Many of the poems in the first collection are not very good, but nearly all of them have a touch of greatness.

The anti-heroic tendency which has marked the whole period has reached its culmination; the heroes are dead. But heroism remains. Wordsworth was the first poet for many years to see that the world of human oddities and relics is a real one. Real by virtue of the love and loyalty that the members of it bear to one another. The relationship between Betty Foy and her son is as valid as that between Coriolanus and his mother. The poem truly is a poor one but it could only have been written at that time by a very great poet. We are accustomed to-day to speak and think of proletarian masses. Wordsworth was struck by the *solitude* of the very poor: those whom time and casualty have placed beyond the reach of relief have little feeling of a "collective". The leech-gatherer is almost as lonely as the dead, but his courage refreshes the brooding poet. For those who are desolate "there is a comfort in the strength of love", perhaps in the mere memory of the love that once made them strong. Wordsworth has a full share of the emotional sensibility of his predecessors in prose and verse, but the discipline of his art raises it to a higher power. Solitude he understood. In the account of his personal crisis which he gives us in *The Prelude* we realise that when the full impact of disaster struck him he was alone. No man can make a decision for another; to encounter a moral or intellectual crisis is to be alone. What saved Wordsworth was probably not so much Coleridge or his sister or "the Nature that never did forsake the heart that loved her" as the realisation that he was a great poet. With timely utterances he relieved his heart, if at first to an audience of one. The prophetic sense which as an undergraduate he had had of his high destiny was fulfilled for him in a very dark hour. In the light of this experience of desolation he became the poet of solitude.

His weakness is lack of dramatic sense. His poetry is rather that of the inspired commentator and contemplative than that of the full sharer in the life he is portraying. He has in his less happy pieces, too much of the technique of the interviewer.

There are two aspects of Wordsworth's handling of nature which may be considered.

First and obviously he enjoyed intense quasi-mystical experiences which inspired some of his most striking poetry and were to him a constant enrichment of his imagination and "moral being". This enjoyment was not a mere response to the more striking patterns in the natural order. He found that nature and man were interdependent and exquisitely fitted the one for the other. His view of nature may be called organic. He saw her as essentially enjoyable to the mind of man and with something mental in her own structure. His poems abound with this sense of an operant nature not simply obeying the laws of her own development, but capable in various ways of an active and effective relationship with man. Not animistic; nature for him was not so much inhabited by spirits as the dwelling place of Spirit which seems to have needed the contemplation of mankind for its complete fulfilment. Perhaps it would be true to say that for Wordsworth, at any rate in the days when he was writing *The Prelude*, man and nature were both manifestations of the same spiritual life which was differentiated between them and reunited by the act of contemplation.

Secondly, "the return to nature" may well have been a final effort, not so much consciously made by Wordsworth as unconsciously made through him, to find once again a common background of experience which all men could share and in terms of which they could express their common situation. It was an attempt to find a universal mythology in an age whose outlook tended more and more, despite its humanitarian interests, to be mathematical, mechanical and materialistic. It is a pity that the accident of Wordsworth's habitation and life-long preference has made him known as a "Lake-poet". He is an earth-poet. Not the green earth of the pastoral poetry of Pope and Gray and Philips, but the ancient bitter earth from which men wrest a living. The earth of Hesiod and of *Piers Plowman*. It is perhaps unfortunate that he knew more of pasture than of agriculture; coming as he did from high sheep-country, the full hardship entailed by the curse that fell on Adam escaped his knowledge. A little of what Stephen Duck tells us of the back-breaking routine of the cultivator would have been a valuable addition to his own experience of the hardships of shepherds who "amid the heart of many thousand mists" pursued their calling. The country life which Wordsworth knew best was highly specialised, and the freeholders of Cumberland and Westmoreland were not typical of an age of increasingly scientific farming. Subsistence farming was dying out in populous England; of necessity it was becoming an activity not less concerned with profits than the manufacturing of the Lancashire cotton towns. Wordsworth's successors, notably Tennyson, exchanged his vision of man solitary and laborious on the high hills, man the food-producer, the basis of all civilisation, for pastoral idealisations, full of favour and of prettiness. Once again perhaps Wordsworth was too personal in his treatment to get the richest results. Even the Lucy poems plucked from the very heart of his most intimate musings have in them something that speaks of theory as well as of contemplation. Lucy is a shade too Wordsworthian to be the Eve of a new poetic Eden.

But his actual accomplishment was very great. Not even Coleridge realised its full immensity. Without the security of an ancient faith and with no high power of reasoning to aid him, he has given the fullest representation of the human situation since Shakespeare. His lonely figures are types of humanity in a machine-age: herding together in great towns and cut off from a full communal life, people experienced a loneliness never felt before. Like the blind beggar Wordsworth saw in London they are symbols of the new solitude, the solitude felt amidst crowds of strangers. Man, the wanderer, the alien, the dispossessed, has never been presented before with such poignant immediacy. But he is still mankind with the recourses of his "unconquerable mind", forgotten but not diminished. Wordsworth stated the problem and found out the remedy.

His lofty moral code and high sense of endeavour flood scores of his poems. *Resolution and Independence*, *Michael*, *The Happy Warrior*, the *Ode to Duty*, the series of great patriotic sonnets, are indicative in different ways of his wisdom. He is the last of our poets with the old tragic sense of the reality of both freedom and necessity: by accepting the necessity in a voluntary act of will he makes terms with it and finds his freedom.

Coleridge, on whom some further notes will be found in the chapter on the philosophers, was the one Englishman who might have elaborated a genuine Aesthetic. Certainly he is our most stimulating and bewitching critic. His intuitions are brilliant, his judgment somewhat less sure. He founded the school of Shakespearian criticism, of which the late A. C. Bradley was the last representative. He is personal, allusive, and refuses to see blemishes. When Homer nods, he ceases to be Homer; someone else, some dwarfish thief, has assumed the giant's robe. Like Hazlitt, Coleridge is a supreme appreciator and a communicator of his delight. But he has far more knowledge and wisdom. "Logician, metaphysician, bard", his mind is as comprehensive as Shakespeare's, but lacks full philosophic or intuitive unity. He well understood and frequently expounded the weakness which he never overcame. His life and work alike were fragmentary and diffuse.

His collaboration with Wordsworth was the most fruitful in our literature. They were not simply complementary one to another as were Addison and Steele, nor merely partners. Each was an inhabitant of the other's mind. And this not only during their period of friendship and collaboration. Coleridge was Wordsworth's best critic, the man who sympathised most completely with his aim and understood his art the best. Each was most fully himself when in the other's company, actual or recollected. Even when their personal relationship was remote or strained, it was alive in memory.

The most exciting thing that could happen to a young

writer in the last years of the eighteenth century was to meet Coleridge. He inspired enthusiasm and reverence, in his talk

> Worlds on worlds were rolling ever
> From creation to decay.

His work is abundant in high promise and since the day of his death posterity has been trying to cash his I.O.U.'s. Much now reads dully and much is fragmentary, but he has touches of sheer perfection.

The Ancient Mariner is the only finished poem in which he is completely at ease and completely himself. First published in *Lyrical Ballads* of '98, it was reprinted with much sham archaism pruned away in 1800; not until *Sibylline Leaves*, seventeen years later, did it appear accompanied by the running prose Argument that comments so superbly on the verse.

To that convenient fiction, the man-in-the-street, Coleridge is the poet of *The Ancient Mariner* and the romantic movement in poetry is the movement which produced *The Ancient Mariner*. It is perhaps the most perfectly unified and harmonious poem of the time, save only the great odes of Keats. Even the moral that appears towards the end is part of the poem itself and not a lesson to be learnt from it. The mariner by his adventures and sufferings has become the man he is, a man subdued to a kind of elementary simplicity, and the moral is no more and no less a part of the story than the adventures.

> Farewell, farewell! but this I tell
> To thee, thou Wedding-Guest!
> He prayeth well, who loveth well
> Both man and bird and beast.
>
> He prayeth best, who loveth best
> All things both great and small;
> For the dear God who loveth us,
> He made and loveth all.

This is not addressed to the reader as an attempt to improve an occasion, but to the Wedding-Guest as a close to the mariner's tale. It is the Wedding-Guest who must accept it, not we. It is as much a part of the poem as the shooting of the albatross itself.

The poem has for its theme a haunting. The Mariner is haunted by the whole voyage, not simply by something that happened during it, and the only relief he can get is to tell his story. He follows men about like a fiend, not frightful, but long-winded, and whomsoever he overtakes to him his tale he teaches. But narrator and listener are alike inside the poem. It is not Coleridge who is talking, as too often it is Wordsworth who talks and not his characters, but a figure made by Coleridge, a figure that no one else could have made. It is a tale of wonder and terror and sweetness and desolation, but they are all remote and our everyday security is delighted and untroubled. It is one of the great poems of the world.

Christabel was conceived in bits and ran dry on its author. Its music haunted the ears of a generation of poets and the last changes have not yet been rung. *Dejection*, which successive revisions have not improved, should be read in conjunction with Wordsworth's *Intimations*. Both poems mourn the passing of a glory from life; for Wordsworth this passing is one of time's casualties, Coleridge, more modestly, finds the cause in personal failure. Wordsworth ends on a note that is strong but forced. Nature that takes away delight will bring wisdom. Coleridge, downcast still, invokes a blessing as he makes his farewell, but the storm which has arisen during the course of the poem is still raging.

His best poems were written between 1796 and 1802; very occasionally in his later years he was able to revive his former magic.

Southey, once Coleridge's most intimate friend, is now hardly remembered as a poet, though we do not forget what Byron said of him in his *Vision of Judgment*. His excellently written *Life of Nelson* and the more scholarly but less vital *Life of Wesley*, are still read. Time has not been kind to his reputation. Some of his ballads still afford pleasure.

III

Byron's discomfort in English society gave him something of the detachment of a foreigner. This discomfort did not arise, like Shelley's, from a profound alienation of the spirit. His early poverty, his unsatisfactory relations with his mother, his physical deformity, tended to make him dramatise himself. He was unable to assume naturally and as a matter of course the position which he inherited. He was ill at ease with his own title, with his own talents, and in his own company. He seems to have felt that he was an actor in some kind of heroic play, and till the last year of his life he could not find a part to suit him. He arranged his features for public exhibition as others might a cravat.

Old English baron, world-weary cynic, capricious lover, damned soul, democrat, all had possibilities and he did some painful rehearsing for them all. But in vain, for he never knew his lines on the night. His poses were attempts at appropriate behaviour in a world which he knew well enough either to entertain or to satirise, but not well enough to live in. In public—and Byron's sense of publicity sometimes accompanied him into the most intimately private situations—he behaved like a gauche, brutal and wanton schoolboy. He had no instinctive sense of rightness. He was well aware of his deficiencies, but powerless to remedy them. A good tutor might have saved him early or a good wife later. But the former he did not meet with and of possible candidates for the latter role he chose the worst. It was no use trying to reform Byron until his education was completed. Perhaps if Lady Melbourne had been younger she might have taught him delicacy and self-respect and tact, but she was growing old, and though she had a genuine affection for him she seems to have regarded him also with a good deal of detached amusement and curiosity. Her experience might have conferred upon him the freedom he was always seeking and could never find. To her he wrote before his marriage hoping that his wife would "govern" him and declaring that nothing else would do. But governesses make bad governors and his last chance of overcoming his ignorance of how things are done passed. Extremely suggestible, he was powerless to defend himself against any appeal to his vanity, and Whig society made little appeal to anything else. He was never a lover except in the sense that he made love, and this he did half to prove to himself that he was an initiate and knew the game. But he never quite deceived himself.

Byron's excesses whether in life or letters were not the result of strong passions or of any special gift for depravity; they were due partly to his ignorance of what else to do, and partly that the attention of the world flattered him and fed his vanity. So he hardly dared to refuse an affair—something *real* might happen to him at last—and still less did he dare to refrain from publishing with an elaborate apparatus of hints and gestures the stories of his indiscretions. He was terrified lest he should not be found out.

At the end he found a cause which satisfied his sense of drama and made limitless calls on his enormous reserves of courage and generosity. In her sordid way Greece matured him and he found freedom in her service. But he did not survive his own coming-of-age.

It is impossible to talk about Byron's work without mentioning his life and character. It is not easy to talk sensibly about either. His own nervousness is infectious.

Byron's sense of his failure to live as he wished is shown in all his work. He is afraid that the world may not give him credit for being quite grown up and knowing all about wickedness. And *Manfred*, the greatest of his confessional works, shows that his knowledge was pathetically small. *Cain*, his most ambitious attempt at a metaphysic of evil, is, in spite of occasional good things, childish and a thing of postures.

But he was greater as a man than he ever dared to suspect and his poems and letters are the last great record of the speech and life of Whig civilisation.

His tales of adventure in far places, his garrulous confessional habits, his attitude to history and liberty proclaim him a romantic; his admiration for Dryden and Pope and his interest in the social round, his keen eye for the ridiculous and his strong common sense link him with our Augustans. *Don Juan* is a tremendous achievement. It is a fighting retreat from the society in which he was never at home and which had rejected him. He holds up to the world a great distorting mirror in which strange yet familiar countenances appear. Like a true satirist he tells the truth with sufficient shift of emphasis for it to be painful. But, unlike Pope, he had no moral policy, no sense of what *should* be to balance his angry knowledge of what should not. He is a moralist who has neither accepted nor thought out an ethic. But he is a true scourge of villainy; the kettle is not the less black because it is a pot that calls it so.

His highest art is seen in *The Vision of Judgment*, where the perfect raillery of the satire is shot through with touches of pity: *Beppo*, an admirable prologue to *Don Juan* exhibits his gift for story-telling at its best. Like so many good stories it lives as much by its digressions as by its fable. It is the first really free poem that he wrote and in it he found his true manner and his most efficient technique. Byron is the most uneven of poets and the rarer touches are beyond him, but his was one of the coolest intellects of his age and Europe still holds his memory in honour. There have been innumerable lives of Byron, but perhaps the best is still that by his friend Tom Moore, at whose "leadless pistol" he had once mocked, with whom he had once nearly fought a duel. Moore's early Irish patriotism had been watered down by his popularity amongst Whig society, whom he entertained with songs, some of which still keep their charm. His *Diary* is an important and entertaining document.

With him may be mentioned Campbell, whose battle-poems many of us learnt by heart in extreme youth and which some of us can still repeat. His long poems are as dead as those of Southey.

"Strength and Beauty met together" in Shelley, in whom was the knowledge of his own sickness and the sickness of a wider world. His intelligence was vigorous and untiring and his reading very extensive. His greatest weakness was his ignorance of history, in particular the history of institutions. Institutions he saw as so many chains binding the free spirit of man and he failed to understand that these institutions themselves are part of the history of freedom. Of the abuses of authority he was grievously aware, of its necessity he had little understanding. He saw clearly that change is life and acquiescent inertia is death. His faith in human possibilities was immense but he trusted too strongly to the benevolence of human instincts and to the disinterestedness of the human heart. He had something of Blake's strong belief in imagination. "The great instrument of moral good is the imagination." Like Blake he preferred the imagination to the reason as a means of finding out the truth, although he delighted in argument and was himself something of a dialectician. *Prometheus Unbound* shows at once his strength and weakness and that of much of the poetry of his contemporaries. His lofty moral outlook and powerful lyrical impulse have full play. Prometheus, himself purified by suffering, redeems an enslaved world by his endurance. In superb blank verse he expounds his own situation and the actions that are involved in it. But the myth is not firmly conceived. Metaphysically and ethically the poem is right enough, but the translation into the terms of an actual story is a failure. Shelley has a strong sense of the woes of the world, of the evils that men suffer. Equally strong is his joyous imagining of the contrary: of a free and happy world where men love and respect their neighbours and triumph over their dark past. Shelley never thinks of the one without the other. The contradiction between a poet's sense of man's shortcomings and his sense of man's possibilities is present throughout. But the transition from one state to the other is not dramatic, it is lyric. One picture fades out as another lightens. One mood is replaced by another. This is not enough for drama and drama *Prometheus Unbound* purports to be. A vision of Jupiter reigning is succeeded by Jupiter unkinged. The affair is plotless and unplanned. Moreover Shelley is not quite sure what to do about Prometheus and Asia. Tyranny has clearly enough separated Life from Love, but in places Shelley talks as though these great and eloquent sufferers were having an "affair". A touch of vulgarity very rare indeed in Shelley, who is one of the most delicate and sensitive of poets. Meta-physic, myth, and poetry are not perfectly harmonised, and though *Prometheus* is rich in wisdom and aflame with poetry it lacks the unity of a work where means and ends are conceived together.

The figure of Christ haunts Shelley's mind curiously. Anti-clerical as he is, he sees in the spectacle of Christ's crucifixion—the final torture inflicted on Prometheus—a type of fate which man, organised in institutions, inflicts on his prophets and saviours. First death, painful and ignominious, and then the work they tried to perform is undone by the formation of a cult in honour of themselves by means of which the evils against which they fought are perpetuated and strengthened by the authority of their own names.

> Thy name I will not speak,
> It hath become a curse. I see, I see
> The wise, the mild, the lofty, and the just,
> Whom thy slaves hate for being like to thee,
> Some hunted by foul lies from their hearts' home,
> An early-chosen, late-lamented home;
> As hooded ounces cling to the driven hind;
> Some linked to corpses in unwholesome cells:
> Some—Hear I not the multitude laugh loud?—
> Impaled in lingering fire. . . .

Behind the God of the churches and priests Shelley holds—at times—that there is an unknown God whose enemy is the traditional religion which Shelley always associates with intolerance and bigotry. In *Hellas* he sees this unknown power more truly, and accepts the cross as the symbol of its operations on behalf of liberty.

> A power from the unknown God,
>   A Promethean conqueror, came;
> Like a triumphal path he trod
>   The thorns of death and shame.
>   A mortal shape to him
>   Was like the vapour dim

Which the orient planet animates with light;
　　Hell, Sin, and Slavery came,
　　Like bloodhounds mild and tame,
Nor preyed, until their Lord had taken flight;
　　The moon of Mahomet
　　Arose, and it shall set:
While blazoned as on Heaven's immortal noon
　　The cross leads generations on.

The "Prometheans" are doubly doomed, in life contemned and in death invoked by the forces of oppression. Such a one Shelley at times sees himself to be.

A pardlike Spirit beautiful and swift—
A Love in desolation masked;—A Power
Girt round with weakness. . . .

A herd-abandoned deer struck by the hunter's dart

.　.　.　.　.　.　.　.

　　　　　　　　　　sad Urania scanned
The Stranger's mien, and murmured, "Who art thou?"
He answered not, but with a sudden hand
Made bare his branded and ensanguined brow,
Which was like Cain's or Christ's—oh! that it should be so.

To return to *Prometheus Unbound*. No poem includes a clearer vision of the nature of suffering and of the redemptive power of suffering voluntarily accepted: no poem embodies a nobler view of the function of poetry itself.

On a Poet's lips I slept
Dreaming like a love-adept
In the sound his breathing kept;
Nor seeks nor finds he mortal blisses,
But feeds on the aërial kisses
Of shapes that haunt thought's wildernesses.
He will watch from dawn to gloom
The lake-reflected sun illume

100

The yellow bees in the ivy-bloom,
Nor heed nor see, what things they be;
But from these create he can
Forms more real than living man,
Nurslings of immortality!

But no poem is more open to the charges which so many romantic poets incur. It lacks compelling connection: as soon as we cease to read the magnificent Fourth Act we cease to believe in the excellence of its reborn world. It is ill-proportioned—note the long and comparatively futile curse of Prometheus set against the awful terror its very memory is said to bring—and, owing to Shelley's inability to handle, perhaps to discover, a mythology adequate either for his metaphysic or for his poetry, there is an underlying disharmony of impulse.

But these comments are ungracious in connection with a poem which has afforded and will continue to afford so much pleasure.

Hellas is much more firmly conceived; the theme is that of victory and defeat. The Turks are victorious but fear, the Greeks are defeated but triumph. But here, except for two great lyrical outbursts, the level of writing is far below that of *Prometheus*.

At the end we come to where we should perhaps have started; with Shelley's lyrics. No more spontaneous voice than his has ever sung our joys and sorrows and their near neighbourhood.

To quote and comment on the rich variety of his odes and elegies, songs and choruses would take much space and add nothing to the enjoyment of his work which a single reading affords. Shelley's detractors should reread *Adonais*. Once again the slight narrative element suffers from incoherence, an incoherence amply amended by the unity of the inspired mood and the felicity of music and phrase. It ends with the typical Shelleyan collapse back into reality, that fluttering fall from rocket-like ascent which characterises his typical poetic movements.

Shelley treated life frequently enough as a work of fiction—

in real life in the midst of Chapter Six we cannot go back
and rewrite Chapter Two—but in his fiction he has added
a new vision and a new type of prophecy to our heritage.
It is possible that the unfinished *Triumph of Life*, with its
unusually disinterested and self-disregarding point of view,
would have been a masterpiece. But the thing remains a
fragment and what it might have become is a matter for
speculation.

Keats offers us an almost total contrast. His early maturity
is amazing. From his earliest years he seems to have lacked
the capacity either of Wordsworth or of Shelley to be
hurt by human frailty and inconsistency. He expected less
of mankind and in his instinctive way perhaps he had more
knowledge. For him, to be alive was to experience crisis,
and he looked for no all-healing millennium. He is the most
Shakespearian poet of the age. What Shakespeare seems
to have valued in man is the capacity he has for self-know-
ledge. At no time in his life did Keats "but slenderly know
himself". He was as disturbed by his own deficiences and as
acutely aware of them as any hostile critic could have been.
His letters hold a tale of triumphant progress in knowledge
of himself and his art. His own resolutions and his advice
to others have the wisdom of ripe experience. Instinctively
he chose the right books to read and took from his rather
shabby band of friends what they had to give. His early
tendency to over-writing and over-luxuriance he conquered,
and at the end, achieved a style which is a miracle of richness
and chastity.

He has left us few perfect poems; a handful of odes, half
a dozen sonnets, *La Belle Dame Sans Merci*. Noble fragments
like *Hyperion*, fine beginnings like *The Eve of St. Mark*, are
hardly less full of pleasure for us. He never achieved a completely successful narrative poem. In one kind *The Eve of St.
Agnes*, in another *Lamia* come to it nearly.

In *Hyperion* his sympathies are too evenly distributed
between his two sets of figures for the story to gain momentum. Compared with *Prometheus* it has the solidity of history
as against the stirring windiness of a manifesto. For *Hyperion*
is not revolutionary or apocalyptic. It is a dignified and cool

statement of law. Once again the myth failed the poetry. In the re-written version Keats shows a profound under-standing of his own situation, but the total effect is less satisfying.

His early and abused *Endymion* is a much better and more delightful poem than those who have not read it believe. It is clearly experimental. The final objective is by no means always clearly seen, and the style has painful patches, but it is the real thing—an exercise in poetry perhaps, but an exercise by one who is in training for a great event.

In the great odes he is a quiet, almost still poet. He has none of Shelley's bewilderingly rapid movements, he changes his position unobtrusively. These poems are as final in their smaller way as any of Shakespeare's tragedies. In them the romantic, questing impulse for exploration of experience and for full and free expression is controlled by a classic sense of form and dignity.

IV

SOME PROSE WRITERS

Lamb and Hazlitt represent two variants of the same type of criticism. With both, style and taste are more con-spicuous than profound intelligence. Both are highly personal and an element of autobiography runs through their writ-ings. Both abound in reminiscence, and link their aesthetic appreciations with their own developing awareness of the world. Perhaps their greatest common excellence is the power of indicating what is unique in the books and authors in which they delight. Their criteria of value are not trans-ferable. To enjoy their criticism is more a matter of sharing their imaginative responses than of intellectual assent to their judgments. No critics have been better at pointing out how one author differs in essence from another, in showing what one alone could do. Their technique is not unlike that of the wine- or tea-taster. The flavour is the thing and their senses are always alert. Hazlitt had practised painting and dabbled in metaphysics before he became a

great critic. For years he wrote with difficulty and his style
was the result of long effort. At his best he is a model of
vigorous English; words are at his command and he is
never the slave of his own excellence. He can scourge or
praise or ruminate or recollect with equal ease. Characters
real or imaginary, pictures, politics, physical exercise, alike
interest him. He would to-day have been a perfect sports
commentator for the B.B.C. But perhaps his voice or, in
times of stress, his manners would have failed. He married
twice but remained a bachelor all his life in outlook and
habits. He reminds us of some dweller outside the pale
who raids a peaceful empire on whose fringe he lives.
Nervous, gauche and self-conscious, he was quick to take
offence, and when he moved there was the sound of the
stirring of arms. He could teach Gifford of the *Quarterly*
something of the craft of battle. All this in the wars of the
pen. Personally he was less formidable. Lamb's dicta on
him are the justest and wisest. "Hazlitt does bad actions
without being a bad man" "I wish he would not quarrel
with the world at the rate he does. . . . I should belie my
own conscience, if I said less, than that I think W. H. to
be, in his natural and healthy state, one of the wisest and
finest spirits breathing. So far from being ashamed of that
intimacy, which was betwixt us, it is my boast that I was
able for so many years to have preserved it entire; and I
think I shall go to my grave without finding, or expecting
to find, such another companion".[1]

Lamb's personality is the stronger and many of his admirers are apt to treat him as a personal friend. They claim
that to get the best from Lamb one must develop a personal
allegiance to him. Either one knows him intimately or not
at all. He has no acquaintances. This insistence on his
personal character, well known to us from memoirs and
letters, rather than on his authorship has been of doubtful
advantage to his fame. But it is not inexcusable. It is true
that Lamb, when he writes about what he cares for, gives
us rather a way of looking at objects than objects to look

[1] Letter of Elia to Robert Southey, Esq. Printed in *The London Magazine*,
Vol. VIII, p. 400 (October 1923).

at. Hazlitt is more wary. Despite his eagerness to share his pleasures and his admirable power of communicating his enthusiasms, his attitude is often a defiant one, and he appears to enjoy what so many of his fellows enjoy, despite the fact that he is not quite at home with them. Hazlitt initiates his readers; Lamb adopts them into his strange family. You have to utter his passwords, to respect his reserves. Lamb was a fairly persistent minor poet and has two or three fine things to his credit. But it is as "Elia" that he is chiefly read and as "Elia" that he lives. Not that his *Tales from Shakespeare*, which he wrote with his sister Mary, his life-long companion and colleague, are not by far the most effective retelling of this sort that has been done. His notes to his *Specimens of English Dramatic Poets who lived about the time of Shakespeare*—published in 1808, the same year in which Coleridge commenced lecturer—show knowledge and insight, as well as appreciation of a class of literature that he, like Coleridge and Hazlitt, was doing so much to bring back into fashion. But "Elia" is Lamb. His best criticism, his tenderest reminiscences, his rarest appreciation are here, in the two series of essays. He adjusts his memories as an antique dealer does his wares. They are not for all markets; to be given away to his friends; to be sold to the connoisseur; to be withheld from the stranger. We *do* come back to the personal relationship after all. If you do not know Lamb and, perhaps, care for him, his stock is not for you, and you will make a bad bargain. Like so many of his contemporaries, there is an eternal immaturity about him. None of them made this often irritating quality so rich a source of delight. Lamb is always looking back; to his old quaint favourites among authors, Burton, Fuller, Margaret, Duchess of Newcastle, and to his own experiences in extreme youth which he had shared with his sister. He understood childish terrors as none before him and few since, and he can still shudder at their recollection. He never lost the taste of childish enjoyments that long ago caressed his palate and he can persuade us that we too know their elusive flavour. The threatening shadows on the nursery wall and the long-expected, long-deferred treat, the expedition to play or countryside, form some of his best material. He was most at home in his imagination amidst the years when terrors and pleasures alike spring from slight matters and endure long. He reminds us that our childhood was real and is not quite extinguished.

His style is like himself, allusive, whimsical, remote, familiar and almost wanton. As Hazlitt is perhaps as good a model for English prose, after Dryden, as the writers dealt with in this essay afford, so Lamb is perhaps the worst. To repeat his magic is to turn it to folly. His English written by others, who have neither his knowledge nor his limitations, is one of the most irritating languages that ever affronted the sensibilities with obsequious and mannered parade of quaintness.

There was no profound speculation in the eyes of either Scott or Jane Austen. The metaphysical interests of so many of their contemporaries were not for them. Scott writes of wonders but feels none; Jane Austen sheds a silvery satiric light on an everyday world, the everyday nature of which it is her first interest to maintain. Scott is only a great artist in part. The speech and characters of his splendid array of figures drawn from the lower ranks of his own countrymen; action and counteraction, the ebb and flow of men in array of battle, the turns of fortune in the single combat; the hazards of a hard journey; the traditions of war and song of a proud poor race; for these things he can find full expression in language that is virile and flexible. His sense of history is the most powerful of his imaginative gifts. The traditions of the border-country dwelt in him throughout his life, adventure and heroism were his delight. He is simply the most fertile and procreant genius of the age; characters swarm in his novels as in a busy town, rare human types are as "plates dropped from his pocket". His history is not a mere fancy dress parade. The apparel proclaims the man and the man is a product of his time. Scott understood as few writers have done the relation between a people's history and its characters. In his great novels, the novels that deal with Scottish history and Scottish character, he moves easily through past times, and makes those aspects of the past that appealed to him wear an appearance that is both strange and familiar. Familiar in that the quality of life that he reveals is like a boy's dream of history, all tension and bustle and movement; strange because in his best moments his romances combine this boyish zest for action with a sympathy with and insight into human motives. If history did not in fact look to its actors as it did to Scott, they would nevertheless have recognised his account of their ·struggles and perhaps have been content that they should have thus been handed down. For Scott does understand what historical events are about. If we do not get a complete account of the motives and outlook of Cavalier and Covenanter, Whig and Jacobite, we are at least not led seriously astray. If he does not give us their creeds in full he does show us the kind of life that their creeds induced them to live. Man in the light of his environment, ancestors, and beliefs, all these being clearly related, this is Scott's great subject. Without any attempt at a philosophy of history, or any profound ethical interest, he does contrive to write in a way that shows his faith in human worth and human virtues. His usual happy endings are what his public no less than himself desired; his very ordinariness of outlook in many ways is an excellence in his kind of work. Always anxious to share with his readers a full measure of interest and excitement, he placed no obstacle between himself and them. Perhaps indeed he cared more for his stories than his art.

Even if he had never in a happy hour turned to prose fiction, he would still have held a high place. Editor, scholar, lyric and narrative poet, he had one of the fullest and the most bounteous minds of his generation.

Miss Austen's pulses kept time more temperately. Like Keats and Lamb she understood very well the limits of her power. Unlike Scott she cared more for her art than its subject. Superbly workmanlike in her use of material, she unites the comic tradition of Congreve with that of the reticence and good-breeding of an English gentlewoman who never breaks decorum. The union is astoundingly fertile. Her unsleeping humour recognises its proper food and spreads a rare banquet for us all. It even mocks itself. She has something of the slyness of Chaucer and conceals her traps in unsuspected places. While Congreve exploited the excesses of the world of fashion she recognised that respectability and complacency were no less dangerous to the health of society than the more lurid vices. The wearisome formula of wickedness of the Restoration rake is less insidious than. the vulgarity, intolerance, and stupidity of the technically virtuous well-to-do. Jane Austen takes her way through a world of stupidity, leaning on the arm of a favourite character who is no more exempt than a lover in Shakespearian comedy from raillery and reproof. Jane Austen has no panacea for the state of affairs at which she mocks. She would change nothing and is content to enjoy. But she recognises that goodwill and good sense are as rare as heroic virtues, and her loved characters, Elizabeth Bennet, Emma Woodhouse, Fanny Price, are set to learn their lessons in a society singularly free from them.

Her art is exquisite in its economy. Compared with Scott's vast wastefulness and narrative inconsequence it seems to be altogether of another class. He is the born romancer; movement, colour and character justify him abundantly; she has full scope in a narrower world of petty troubles and unmajestic follies. She knows more than her characters do but not so much as to make us feel that their shortcomings are not exhibited rather for our delight than for our edification.

CHAPTER V

BRITISH PHILOSOPHY, 1689–1830

By H. A. HODGES, Professor of Philosophy in the
University of Reading

THE period here in question is the great or classic age
of modern British philosophy, the age in which the
British Isles perfected their distinctive contribution to European thought.

The ruling temper of British philosophy, in mediaeval
and modern times alike, has always been empirical, con-
trasting notably with the speculative tendencies of our Continental neighbours. This is certainly not due to any lack of
speculative interest or capacity in our people. For some
reason, however, what is speculative in the British mind
has always tended to come out in poetry rather than in
philosophy. Instead of a Leibniz to write a *Theodicy* we
have Milton justifying the ways of God to man in epic and
drama. Our Fichte and Schelling and Hegel are Blake and
Wordsworth and Shelley, and the English counterpart of
Nietzsche is William Morris. Accordingly, when the British
mind does give itself up to philosophy, it does so in a more
critical spirit, suspicious of metaphysical systems, but closely
allied with scientific inquiry into nature, as well as with the
study of moral and political questions, in which an obvious
practical interest can be found.

These characteristics show themselves very plainly in the
philosophy of our period. The eighteenth century was an
age of criticism, even in the arts, an age when correctness
was combined with brilliance, when good sense was the
norm of taste, when poetry and painting were given
over to character-study and social satire. On the political
side the country had come through the Revolution of 1688
into a period of tranquil development, and the British

people congratulated themselves on having found out how
to combine freedom with order, tradition with progress.
At the same time, the age was fruitful in scientific research.
The dreams of Bacon in the *New Atlantis* had found realisation through the foundation of the Royal Society, and the
classic achievement of Newton, whose physics and astronomy
dominated the world until the present century, inaugurated
a period of continuous scientific progress. It is not surprising
to find the philosophy of this period characterised by a
blend of scientific with moral and social interests, with a
spirit of criticism ruling over all.

The father of the British School of philosophy is John
Locke (1632–1704) the interpreter and apologist of the
Glorious Revolution, and also of the scientific outlook and
teaching of Newton and his colleagues.

A long friendship with Anthony Ashley, the first Lord
Shaftesbury, made Locke a member of the liberal circle
which stood in opposition to James II before and after his
accession to the throne, and which ultimately engineered
the successful rising against him. Locke's *Two Treatises on
Government* (1690) contain the theoretical justification of
what the men of 1688 had done, and stand to this day as a
classic expression of the principles of British and American
democracy. A passion for freedom and toleration runs
through his writing, and he does all he can to secure the
right of the individual to the pursuit of happiness in whatever way seems best to him, provided only that he concedes
the same right to other individuals as well. The State is
shown as the interpreter and guardian of the rights of men,
the fundamental and indefeasible rights of life, liberty and
property. The State has no authority to act at all except for
the upholding of these rights, and cannot trench upon them,
even, e.g., to the extent of taking a man's property from
him by way of taxation, without the consent of the governed.
The English Parliamentary system is set forth as the best
form of constitution, in that it makes the executive subordinate to the legislature, and the legislature to the people
themselves who elect it. The watchwords of the American
Revolution, the principles of the Declaration of Independ-

ence and the Constitution of the United States, are an echo of these doctrines of Locke.

But this was only one side of Locke's activities. His work in logic and the theory of knowledge summed up in his *Essay concerning Human Understanding* (1690) deserves to be considered at greater length, for it laid the foundations of a most significant movement of thought both here and abroad.

Behind the *Essay* lies the impatience of a scientific mind with the obscurities of philosophy and theology. Locke himself, in his student days at Oxford, had found the traditional philosophy of the place little better than a battle of words—a complaint which Thomas Hobbes had made before him—while he found satisfaction in the pursuit of medical studies. In later years he became a Fellow of the Royal Society, and followed with admiration the progress made by scientific research in the hands of Boyle, Newton, and others of that group. In contrast with the success of mathematics and natural science, the condition of philosophy appeared to him very unsatisfactory. He tells us that the immediate occasion of his beginning the *Essay* was a conversation at which he was present in Oxford, where the principles of morality and religion were under discussion. Impressed by the inconclusiveness of the debate, Locke suddenly threw out the idea that the whole discussion was vitiated by a fault of method, in that the disputants were addressing themselves to the most profound and abstruse problems without having first asked themselves whether the human mind is really capable of doing what they demanded of it. From that moment Locke's mission as a philosopher was settled. It was to undertake a revision and renovation of the fabric of philosophy and of human knowledge in general by making a thorough inquiry into the powers of the human mind, the nature and sources of its knowledge. At first sight this seems a modest task, and it seemed so to Locke himself. He was not trying to contribute anything new to the sum of human knowledge. That task he left to "such masters as the great Huygenius, and the incomparable Mr. Newton", and regarded himself only as an "under-labourer" clearing the rubbish out of the way. Yet in fact, by his artless proposal, Locke was giving a new dimension to philosophic thought, and setting before all future philosophers and scientists the initial problem of explaining and justifying their own activity. The *Essay concerning Human Understanding* is the direct ancestor of Kant's *Critique of Pure Reason*.

Locke's performance was not equal to the greatness of his task. He began by assuming that the way to a just appraisement of the range of human knowledge lies through a study of the workings of the mind, i.e., through psychology. He further supposed that the workings of the mind are clearly visible to introspection, so that his psychology need only follow the "historical plain method" of looking into his mind and writing an account of what he saw there. It is not surprising that the account that he gives, though superficially simple and attractive, is found on examination to bristle with confusions and ambiguities. His conclusion is that all thought and knowledge are derived from sensation. Ideas come into the mind through the senses, and are then made the objects of thought, which by various processes of distinguishing, combining, abstracting, inferring and the like, builds up the system of knowledge. Locke undertakes to show in detail how this is done, a task in which by common consent he fails.

He then advanced his views as to the range of human knowledge. True knowledge, i.e., certitude as distinct from well-grounded opinion, he thinks is possible only in a narrow field. We are certain of the truth of mathematical propositions. We are certain of our own existence, which we know by direct acquaintance, and of God's existence, which we can infer with certainty from our own. But (paradoxically in view of his intellectual background) Locke denies that we have anything that deserves to be called knowledge in the strict sense about the natural world. We have no direct acquaintance with this world, but only with the sensations which we believe it causes us to have. Behind these sensations we conceive a world of objects more or less resembling them, and Locke believes there are convincing reasons for

holding that the objects do not possess the secondary qualities, e.g., colour, taste, hotness, coldness, but do possess the
primary qualities, e.g., size, shape, weight, movement. It
is the relations between these qualities, between magnitudes
and masses and velocities, etc., that we study in science,
and science finds that some of these qualities regularly
co-exist, or succeed one another in a regular way, according
to principles which are the laws of nature. But while we
have good reason to believe in these co-existences and
sequences, we cannot see why they must be as they are.
They remain for us brute facts, which we cannot resolve
into intelligible connections. We cannot see why gold must
be at the same time yellow and malleable; we only see that
in fact it is both. To put the matter in a technical phrase,
although the qualities of things are accessible to us, their
real essence or substance is not. And therefore we cannot
be said to have knowledge of them. Indeed, since the senses
are admittedly open to illusion, there is never absolute certainty even of the existence of any particular thing, nor,
consequently, of the physical world as a whole; though
Locke, like most people, thinks it would be quite absurd
to doubt this.

The absurdity was not obvious to George Berkeley (1685–
1753: Bishop of Cloyne, 1734–52) who made himself
notorious by embracing the possibility which Locke rejected. His philosophy is the direct result of accepting
Locke's principles and pushing them to their conclusion
with more courage and rigour of argument than Locke had
shown.

In spite of Locke's admiration for natural science, his
account of the nature and extent of scientific discovery is
far from complimentary. It denies to science the very possibility of explanation as explanation was then understood,
i.e., of grasping the essential nature of a thing and seeing
how the characteristics of the thing flow from its nature by
an intelligible necessity. What Locke allows to us is something less than this, viz.: a codification of the characteristics
of things as they appear simultaneously or successively
according to a rule. If this is explanation, it is explanation

113   H

in a new and very limited sense. And this is where Berkeley comes in. He urges that the codification of the primary qualities of things according to laws is not explanation at all, because it leaves out the element of necessity. To explain an event is to show that it was causally necessitated, and by necessity Berkeley means a constraining force. What happens happens because something caused it, i.e., forced it to happen; but primary qualities cannot force anything, hence they are not causes, and there can be no explanation in terms of them. Berkeley adds that the only experience we have of force or causal action is in our own minds, where we are able to observe a substance and all its activities from within. Neither substance nor causality can mean anything to us except on the analogy of this, and therefore if natural phenomena are to be explained by reference to substance and cause, this means that they must be explained as manifestations of mind. And what mind can this be, if not the Mind of God? Thus Berkeley is led to the conclusion that our sensations are not the effects produced in us by an independently existing world of material objects with which we have no direct acquaintance, but are themselves the real world, the only world there is, a world of sensible qualities in complex groupings, produced in our consciousness by the action of God upon us, and existing only in being perceived by us. The *esse* of the natural world is *percipi*, and when we say that a natural object exists we mean, or ought to mean, simply that it is perceived by someone, or that in certain assignable circumstances it would be perceived.

If nature is no more than a succession of perceptions produced in us by God, it follows that the laws of nature are simply God's plan of action. For man's convenience, in order that the world may be interpretable and controllable by us, God has elected to produce sensations in us in accordance with rules, and it is these rules that science discovers. Berkeley agrees with Locke that scientific discovery consists in finding out how phenomena accompany or succeed one another according to rules, but he adds that the connections so discovered between phenomena are not cause-effect relations, but merely principles of interpretation whereby from the observation of an event we can infer the past, present, or future occurrence of other events. What we call a cause is really only a sign that what we call the effect will follow, and the so-called effect is a sign that the so-called cause has gone before; but in fact the only causes at work anywhere are the Will of God and the wills of finite agents like ourselves.

Again, if to exist in nature means simply to be perceived or at least perceivable, what are we to say of scientific theories which introduce, as real entities, things which by their very nature could never be perceived? Such theories are plainly illegitimate. The application of this test leads Berkeley into a bold critique upon contemporary mathematics and science, in which he rejects, among other things, the doctrine of absolute space and motion which is the foundation of the Newtonian physics, and embraces a thoroughgoing scientific relativism. His arguments on this and kindred points are open to criticism in detail, but they certainly led to a deeper understanding of the part played in thinking by symbols and imaginary constructions. His attack upon Newton in Newton's own lifetime was an act of great intellectual courage; and some of his arguments against absolute space were adopted and developed, over a century later, by the physicist Ernst Mach.

So far Berkeley is simply the successor of Locke. But there was also another element in his philosophy. A strong religious consciousness drove him on from these logical and epistemological inquiries into speculative metaphysics, where he finally worked out a system in the Platonic, or rather in the Neo-Platonic vein. The natural world is a manifestation of the character of its Creator, and in His Mind subsist the eternal archetypal Ideas, of which the ideas that He imprints upon our senses are a distant reflection. The perceived world is His message to us about Himself, couched in the language of sensible things. Science is the study of the grammar of this language, but it is for speculative metaphysics to read the text of the message. This side of Berkeley's work had no effect upon the main current of British philosophy, but it had a considerable influence upon the speculative poets of a later age, Blake, Coleridge, and Shelley, in all of whom the influence of Berkeley blends with that of Plato and Platonism.

The work of Locke was carried still further by David Hume (1711-76) in whom the logical and epistemological line of inquiry and the moral and political line came together in a common dependence upon psychology. His *Treatise of Human Nature* (1739) begins by urging that every branch of knowledge is logically dependent upon a prior inquiry into the nature of the mind which knows, so that psychology is the foundation of all the sciences. Hume further suggests that the time has come to put the whole of human knowledge on a firm basis by introducing into psychology those experimental methods which have approved themselves in physical science. He sees difficulties, indeed, in transferring methods appropriate to natural science into the very different conditions of psychological investigation, but he waves them aside; and, as the work proceeds, it becomes clear that his methodological conscience is not as rigorous as his opening words would suggest. It was actually more than a century after his time that the first really experimental psychology was established by the work of Fechner. What Hume gives us is still the introspective psychology of Locke, extended and systematised.

The analysis of perception and thought is carried out on Locke's principle, that all thought comes from sensation. There is nothing in the mind except impressions (i.e., sensations) and ideas (i.e., mental images), and all ideas are derived from impressions previously received. Out of these elements the structure of thought is built up, not, as in Locke and Berkeley, by the purposeful activity of the thinking self, but by processes of recall and combination which take place in accordance with the laws of memory and association. Ideas become associated mechanically, by resemblance or by virtue of occurring together in experience. The process is subject to all the contingencies of experience, without any rational activity of selection or control; on the contrary, it is this very process of association which constitutes reason, and thinking is neither more nor less than associating. It is thus that we obtain all the fundamental ideas which give meaning to our world, and in particular the idea of causality. Hume agrees with Berkeley that there is no explanation without causality, and that causality involves activity or the exercise of power. But he urges that our belief in causality as a fact of nature is reached by a process which is logically indefensible. We find certain phenomena tending to recur in the same order. The ideas of these phenomena become associated in our minds, and the idea of one of them brings with it, by a gentle constraint, the idea of the rest. We assume, without logical ground, that the phenomena in question always recur in the same order, according to a law; and, equally without logical ground, we transfer the feeling of constraint, with which the idea of one phenomenon leads us to the idea of another, into the phenomena themselves, and suppose that the one event constrains the other to happen. So we think we have an idea of causal action, though in fact we have only the illusion of such an idea. And this applies not only in respect of the sensible world, but also in respect of our experience of our own minds. There, too, according to Hume, the alleged experience of activity and causal efficacy through our will reduces itself on analysis to an awareness of mental events succeeding one another according to psychological laws. The substantial unity of the self is equally an illusion. On close examination, we find in our minds only a multitude of distinct impressions and ideas arising and associating according to the laws of the mind. The "self" is just this group of psychic events; of any deeper-lying unity there is no trace.

This is the notorious scepticism of Hume; for, if the ideas of substance and causality are without logical basis and, indeed, in the last analysis, without meaning, the whole structure of our beliefs about ourselves and the world falls to pieces, and philosophy, which set out in Locke to establish our beliefs on a firm basis, becomes simply that inquiry which reveals the impotence of human reason. But Hume's own verdict upon this situation is "so much the worse for philosophy". The beliefs which philosophy undermines are

yet indispensable to the conduct of life, and to take philosophy too seriously would be to inhibit life itself. Fortunately,
there are forces in human nature which overcome any
such inhibition. And the moral is that it is to these
forces, rather than to reason, that the conduct of life should
be entrusted. "Reason is and ought to be the slave of the
passions." It is not surprising that the man who could say
this was a friend of Rousseau, the prophet of the romantic
cult of feeling. And the *Treatise of Human Nature* itself, after
having established the sceptical conclusions, goes on at
once to make a study of the passions and the development
of the moral life. By virtue of this part of his work, Hume is
one of the founders of the utilitarian school of moral philosophy, which holds that the only test of the rightness or
wrongness of any action lies in the amount of happiness
which it is likely to bring about. The same interest in human
conduct and the passions which inspire it helps us to understand how Hume, in addition to being a philosopher, could
also be an eminent historian.

The main tradition of British philosophy after Hume
developed along the lines laid down by him. It was known
as the "philosophy of experience". At the root of everything
it placed a psychology governed by the twin principles of
associationism and hedonism: all imagination and thought is
association of ideas, and all action aims at the achievement
of pleasure and the avoidance of pain. The "philosophy of
experience" was disdainful of metaphysics, but took an
interest in logic and the study of scientific method. Its
ruling interest, however, was in moral and social questions.
In Hume's friend, Adam Smith (1723–90), in Jeremy Bentham
(1748–1832), and in James Mill (1773–1836) an associa-
tionist psychology was combined with a moral philosophy
based on the pleasure-principle, a science of economics
based on the assumption that every man seeks, and ought
to seek, his own advantage first and last, and a political
philosophy which demanded that the individual be left
free to seek his own happiness with as little interference as
possible from governments and institutions. This was the
teaching of the "philosophical radicals", the philosophy of

Manchester and the Industrial Revolution, the theoretical background of nineteenth-century reform and free trade. Much might be said about its inadequacy as a philosophy, but its influence for good in the reform of law and social institutions is beyond question.

The inadequacies of the "philosophy of experience", both in its account of perception and thought and in its moral theory, provoked a movement of opposition in the shape of the Scottish School, whose leading representatives are Thomas Reid (1710-96) and Dugald Stewart (1753-1828). In controversy against Locke and Hume the Scottish philosophers were on the whole victorious, demonstrating that the explanation of thought in terms of sense is inadequate, and that there is a distinctively intellective element, as well as a sensuous one, in even the lowliest acts of perception. They were, however, devoid of creative power, and made no first-rate contribution to philosophy. The claim sometimes made, that Reid anticipated some of the work of Kant, is so exaggerated as to be absurd.

More significant is the revolt represented by the romantic movement, which, though belonging primarily to the history of literature, was saturated with philosophic ideas. In Samuel Taylor Coleridge (1772-1834) these ideas took shape as an actual philosophy.

Coleridge had originally been a follower of Hume's disciple, Hartley, but from 1801 onwards, under the influence partly of Neo-Platonism and partly of Berkeley, he came to believe that the "philosophy of experience" was unable to account for the plain facts of experience. Hume in his psychology had pushed analysis so far that he had blinded himself to the unity of the mind, and the group of mental events, which is all that he has left, has hardly more unity than a heap of stones. To begin with, this does not do justice to the poet's experience. Mechanical recall and casual association do not yield a credible account of the process of creative imagination, which Coleridge was able to observe in himself and in his friend Wordsworth. Wider reflection convinced him that even perception cannot be accounted for on the lines of Hume, and that Berkeley was right in finding throughout experience, from perception upward through all the levels of imagination and thought, a free activity of the mind. The reading of Kant and Fichte confirmed Coleridge in these views, and gave him a technical language in which to express them.

On this basis he proceeded to work out a subtle and distinctive philosophy of the imagination. He did not deny the existence of the mechanism of recall and association described by Hume, but he urged that it is overlaid and controlled at all points by the influence both of rational interpretation and of feeling, an influence which rises to its height in the creative imagination of the poet. Carrying further Berkeley's point about symbolism, Coleridge further showed how language is not a mere mechanism of signs, but a product of imagination, endowed with a life and growth of its own, and how thought is so far dependent upon it that no logic can be complete unless it is supplemented by a study of imagination and language, which he calls "poetics" or "philology".

So far Coleridge was working on the same ground as the school of Locke and Hume, though in a different spirit from theirs. But in him, as in Berkeley, the religious consciousness became a force which drove him farther afield into speculative metaphysics. His work here is more closely dependent upon Kant and Schelling, though he always borrows with discretion, and the resulting system is his own. The processes of nature, he holds, are not mechanical, but quasi-organic; nature is a whole composed of wholes, rising from the lowliest units of matter, through organic life, up to rational wholes like a person, a nation, or a language. Above the whole order of nature stands God, the supreme rational Will from which it is derived. The manner in which Coleridge reasons his way to God is closely akin to that of Kant, and the whole of his metaphysic seems to offer a hint of what Kant's own philosophy might have been like if the Platonic elements, which are undoubtedly present in some parts of it, had been allowed free scope to develop.

Coleridge was an isolated figure in his own generation, but his philosophy has had an influence, considerable though not spectacular, upon many British thinkers since his time. He stands as a living witness to a certain idealist strain which, though not usually dominant, has rarely been absent altogether from the philosophy of these islands.

CHAPTER VI

EIGHTEENTH-CENTURY ART

By GEOFFREY WEBB, Slade Professor of Fine Arts in the
University of Cambridge.

THE normal development of European art in the eighteenth century may be summed up as from Baroque
through Rococo to neo-Classic; and England is no exception. The middle or Rococo period has certainly been
somewhat obscured by the influence of Palladio on the
architects, which produces the effect of a precocious neo-
Classicism long before Winckelmann had confirmed that
movement in Italy and Germany, and by the specially
literary romantic aspect that the Rococco took with us. For
the earliest manifestations of the Gothic revival and the
Picturesque movement in landscape gardening and painting
are not only the visual counterparts of a literary romanticism, but the English version of the Rococco. True Rococco
does exist in England, though we do not often mention it,
in the Pagoda at Kew, in the work of some of the plasterer
decorators, and, most famous and respectable of names, in
much of the furniture called Chippendale. Such was the
strength of the romantic quality in English Rococco that
from it derived the true renewal of Gothic as a way of
monumental building, and a profound and often most
fortunate modification of the nature of the revived classic,
and most important of all, one of the greatest schools of
landscape painters Europe has ever known. The full maturity
of these fruits was, however, delayed until the nineteenth
century.

Unquestionably the most important aspect of English

art history of the first quarter of the eighteenth century is the flowering of the native English school of baroque architecture. This is best seen in the churches erected under the Act for the building of fifty new churches in 1709-10, whereby the proceeds of the London Coal Tax, which had financed Wren's city churches and the rebuilding of St. Paul's, were diverted to the building of new churches in the suburbs and to the continuance of the work on Greenwich Hospital. Before this time the most important works in which the baroque had been foreshadowed were the finishing of St. Paul's, the beginning of the work at Greenwich, the finishing of some of the City church towers, e.g., St. Vedast and St. Magnus, and, perhaps most important of all, Vanbrugh's two great palaces, Castle Howard and Blenheim. These two last have occupied the attention of students of the period rather to the exclusion of other works; and as at both of them, and at Greenwich also, Nicolas Hawksmoor served as an assistant to a more famous man, his outstanding abilities have been rather overlooked. Moreover, the position of many of his churches, as Christchurch, Spitalfield, St. Anne's, Limehouse, St. George's in the East, St. Alfrege's, Greenwich, in parts of the town not otherwise distinguished for their amoenity, has tended to increase his obscurity. His works at Oxford, interesting and fine as they are, cannot compare in quality, except for the interior of the Hall at All Souls', with his London churches, though they are by far the best known among his works.

Hawksmoor and Vanbrugh, the earliest outstanding figures of this movement, were both of the entourage of Sir Christopher Wren in his later years, as was also James of Greenwich whose best known work is St. George's, Hanover Square. But there were other men whose connection with the great seventeenth-century master was not so close, or at least is much more uncertain. Thomas Archer, whose earliest documented work is the finishing of the North and West ranges of Chatsworth, appears as the equal of the best men of his time in his churches at Deptford and Birmingham. His Westminster Church, St. John's, creates an unfortunate impression by reason of the stumpiness of its towers, but there is evidence that these are not as the author intended them and in other respects the building is a fine thing. The two London churches of James Gibbs, together with his buildings at Cambridge and his great library at Oxford, serve to place him among the first flight of these English baroque architects, and the magnificent sites of both these churches—St. Mary's-le-Strand and St. Martin-in-the-Fields—have more than made up to Gibbs in posthumous reputation for the fact that Hawksmoor got more commissions under the new Act than he.

It will be seen that the English baroque architects have at least one quality of a flourishing school, a considerable number of artists each with his own individuality and yet sharing certain unifying characteristics. One of these latter is the use of Portland stone, which since the later seventeenth century had become established as the London building stone par excellence; and Portland became such a habit with these men that Gibbs used it for his Cambridge building in preference to the Ketton more usual in that town. A more important unifying factor is that all these architects were building for the Protestant rite of the Church of England, and with this should be taken and considered the precedents developed for them by Sir Christopher Wren in his great church building period of the sixteen-seventies and eighties, and reinforced by his own essay on the requirements of Anglican church building drawn up especially for the advice of the Commissioners under the new Act. This is perhaps the most interesting aspect of the movement. These buildings represent the most considerable body of religious art ever produced for a Protestant community up to that time, for they were designed on a monumental scale and without any restrictions of parsimony. The Coal Tax brought in a very considerable revenue, and sums such as £36,000 for St. Martin-in-the-Fields and £24,000 for St. John's, Westminster, for a building of this size, shows that expense was not spared either for materials or for quality of workmanship in the fittings. They are appropriately the visible monument of that good churchwoman, Queen Anne; and if we have little reason to believe that her architects had the personal piety of the designers of the great Roman churches of the mid-seventeenth century, they are none the less religious architecture. They have that quality of learning and eloquence which distinguished the church of the seventeenth century, and which may certainly be said to have lasted at least till after the time of Atterbury, to whom the engraving of St. Paul's, Deptford, is dedicated, and they have the true baroque emotional quality. Baroque is essentially the architecture of religion, and though the literary expression of English High Churchmanship perhaps belongs to an earlier generation, the opportunity of an architectural embodiment of it did not occur till almost too late, for after this first group of churches the few later ones of the middle of the century are of a less rhetorical and more reasoned architecture. It may indeed seem a paradox to suggest that any form of religious art is an important feature of English life in the eighteenth century. We are too apt to look back at that time from the point of view of the nineteenth century church reformers, who denied to their immediate predecessors any claim to adequate religious expression in the sense that they enjoyed it themselves. But the first twenty-five years of the century were still very largely dominated by the violent religious feeling of the generation that had preceded it. It is the time of Sacheverel, and even if the style of the sermon has been said to have deteriorated under the influence of Tillotson, so that we can hardly read early eighteenth-century sermons with the pleasure to which we turn to those of 100 years before, yet it is certain they played as large a part as ever in the tense religious life of their time, and the churches of Hawksmoor and Gibbs are the visual settings of a ceremony which was dominated not by a dramatic but an oratorical climax. Critics have said that already the sermon had become more a reasoned discourse than an emotional religious appeal, and the writer is not in a position to question such a suggestion; but presumably like all historical criticisms it is made to some degree with the eye on the future, and it may be reasonably supposed that the architects of the early eighteenth century were perfectly conscious of something more than mere reasoned theology in the religious requirements of the churchgoers or the clergy for whom they catered. Hawksmoor's great churches, with their compositional motives often deriving from mediaeval sources, are the embodiment of this early eighteenth-century religion which had not yet forgotten the fervours and glories of the great age of English Churchmanship, which we from our rather convenient distance can see to have gone by before he started to build.

There is little other visual art in England that reflects the religious feeling of these opening years of the century. If such a monument as Bird's for Dr. Busby may perhaps be considered favourably in this light, such a product of the later studio of Gibbons as the Sir Cloudesley Shovel in Westminster Abbey, hardly encourages us to seek it among sculptors, and the single figures of prophets or evangelists which occasionally appear in the sculptural decoration of buildings, good as they often are, can hardly be considered as more than a reflection of the vigorous Catholic art of the low countries. The most important names in painting of the time are Kneller and Thornhill, and some of the former's greatest works belong to this time, for example, the Sir Christopher Wren in the National Portrait Gallery. Kneller is a portrait painter to the exclusion of every other interest. Thornhill, however, might repay study as a religious artist. His work on the dome of St. Paul's has not indeed been greatly appreciated, but on occasion, as at Wimpole House, where he decorated the chapel, his paintings are far from inconsiderable; and his drawings, which exist in considerable quantities, are of a generally high standard. Among them is a considerable quantity of work on religious themes, but even this is little enough as compared with Continental countries, and for the most part Thornhill is remembered as a decorator of the great salons in noblemen's palaces or public buildings, such as the Hall of Greenwich Hospital.

Thornhill, with Kneller, was one of the founders of the first attempt at serious technical education for artists in this country. The Academy that they founded had a somewhat chequered career, but from 1711 onwards there hardly

seems to have been any time when there was not some in-
stitution where young men could learn to draw and have
their drawings criticised. There seems to be no important
native successor of Thornhill unless we are to take Hogarth
as such, but that is hardly justifiable. There is no question
that the type of religious art that is represented by Thornhill's attempts in that direction has not, until recently, been
much appreciated as such, and Thornhill himself, with his
elaborate system of delegated work and highly organised
team of studio assistants, cannot always show even a high
standard of detailed quality; but a study of any considerable
number of his drawings leaves one with a far greater appreciation of his really fine qualities. Other painting on large
scale such as Thornhill's was mainly in the hands of Italians
such as Ricci and Amiconi. William Kent, the architect, in
his early days, did important works in this manner both for
the King at Kensington and Sir Robert Walpole at Houghton. Kent's altarpiece for St. Martin-in-the-Fields brought
on him the ridicule of Hogarth, so that it has been fashionable to deride him as a painter ever since.

These attempts at grandiose figure composition on an
Italian scale are of course relatively unimportant as compared with the art of portrait painting, which has always
in this country been the most successful and the most attractive form of art. In the early eighteenth century Kneller is
still capable of his greatest work. The high quality of
eighteenth-century portraiture might seem a very remarkable phenomenon if we consider the conditions under which
the artists worked. Fashionable painters such as Kneller
and, after him, Hudson and Ramsay and later, indeed, Sir
Joshua Reynolds, had practices of such enormous dimensions
that they could not possibly carry out the painting of the
portraits with their own hands. There was, of course, the long
tried studio system for the painting of large parts of the
picture by assistants and pupils, leaving only the face and
possibly the hands to be done by the master. In this period,
however, another system came into vogue, that of the outside drapery painter. These men made fortunes which were
comparable with, if not as great as, those of the successful

portraitists themselves, and they were treated with the very greatest respect by the most eminent masters. Indeed the popular drapery painter could command respect because if he liked to turn nasty the celebrated portraitist might be left very high and dry. The public were perfectly aware of this system and approved it, and it might be said that if a rich man or a fashionable lady had gone to a painter and discovered that the master painted the picture entirely with his own hands, they would have had the suspicion that they had not chosen as eminent a practitioner as they had hoped. All this commercialisation would seem hardly conducive to the production of the highest forms of painting, but over against this awkward system we must set the fact that the rewards in portrait painting were so great that that branch of art inevitably attracted the greatest talent, and though the system would explain the inequality of works of many of the most important masters, it must not be supposed that because Hudson did not often paint the main area of his canvas he was incompetent to do so.

Among the portraitists of the first part of the century, an interesting figure is Jonathan Richardson. His practice was a large one, but he is perhaps best remembered for his writings on the subject of art. These took the form of a plea for the dignity of the painter's profession, stressing the relations that it bore to scholarship and literary pursuits in a series of books which are in a sense guides or handbooks to a knowledge of the great classic masters of Italy. Richardson is one of the first signs of the movement which was to produce serious art history and criticism in this country, and with him should be mentioned George Vertue the engraver, who formed with Gibbs and Wootton and Humphrey Wanley, librarian to Lord Oxford, a circle which in its early days was also adorned by Matthew Prior. Vertue's great collection of notes of artists practising in this country and of collections in private houses was eventually to form the basis of Horace Walpole's anecdotes on painting, the first serious attempt to write a history of the arts in England. Another member of the group which may perhaps be said to have centred round Lord Oxford was John Michael Rysbrack, the first of a series of remarkable sculptors who worked during the middle years of the century. Rysbrack came over to England from Antwerp about 1720, and very soon made a reputation for himself for portrait busts. Scheemackers, who appears about the same time, left England for Rome for a few years in the late twenties, only to return again and stand out as Rysbrack's most important rival. Better known than these two men, Louis François Roubiliac did not establish himself until the late seventeen-thirties. It is fair to say that the standard of quality of the portraits of these men is as high as anything that was achieved by the painters before the emergence of Reynolds and Gainsborough in the seventeen-sixties. Rysbrack and Scheemackers may be said to bridge the gap in English portraiture between Kneller and Allan Ramsay, and both had large practices and undoubtedly employed pupils. Scheemackers in particular was famous for the quality of instruction to be gained in his studio. The evil practice of making a figure in miniature and having it enlarged by your pupil with a pointing instrument had not yet arisen, and portrait busts of the first half of the eighteenth century have an authenticity in the modern sense which is all too rare among painted portraits. Besides portraits of contemporaries the work of these sculptors included a genre which seems peculiarly English and is surely a reflection of the predominating literary character of our culture, that is, the idealised portrait of the great literary or philosophic figure. Besides such special collections as the busts in the Temple of the Worthies at Stowe, or the similar collection made for Queen Caroline at Richmond, it became the fashion to have busts of the great poets and philosophers to adorn the tops of the shelves in the libraries of the great houses, and all these sculptors produced heads of such figures as Milton, Shakespeare, Locke, Bacon, Inigo Jones, etc., and some of these are certainly to be accounted amongst their finest works. The two versions of Milton produced by Rysbrack, his Bacon, and his Locke, are as fine imaginative works as could be found in any portrait art. The sculptor, who frequently was called upon to produce a bust for a tomb or some other commemorative purpose, had often to work from a painted portrait, even when dealing with men who were his contemporaries, and so the difference in kind of work between the imaginative portrait of, say, Milton, by Rysbrack, or his astonishing bust of the first Lord Shaftesbury at Wimborne St. Giles, or a figure such as Roubiliac's Newton in Trinity College, Cambridge, and their busts of contemporaries is not so very great. It is fair to say that Rysbrack's and Roubiliac's portraits of Newton far surpass any painted representation of the great man that we possess.

Besides these contemporary and imaginative portraits the sculptors' main work lay in the enormous allegorical tombs, of which the finest ensemble is in Westminster Abbey. These show two interesting tendencies in the history of English taste, those chiefly of Scheemackers and Rysbrack having an antique almost neo-classic flavour, while many of Roubiliac's have a dramatic emotional quality which descends to him via the German and French sculptors of his student days, direct from the great Italian masters of the mid seventeenth century, for whom Bernini stands as a symbol. These tombs are perhaps outstanding examples of religious art of the middle of the century, and in face of John Wesley's commendation in this sense of Roubiliac's Nightingale monument at Westminster, it would be presumptuous in our generation to deny them their religious quality.[1] The neo-classic tendency of Rysbrack and Scheemackers which shows itself particularly in the quality of their allegorical figures is no doubt partly due to the sources from which they derive their symbols and allegories, chiefly the great compilation known as Ripa's Iconologia, a work of the sixteenth century, in which types of symbols and allegory had been accumulated from antique sources, often from coins, medals and engraved gems, not to mention an immense display of erudition from the classic poets; but it also represents an aspect of that return to the classic which is the most striking quality of the architecture of the seventeen-twenties and thirties. The movement was led by Richard Boyle, third Earl of Burlington, in his earlier days in association with the Scottish

[1] See *Journal*, March 16, 1764 and March 25, 1771.

architect, Colin Campbell, and later in collaboration with William Kent. It is hard to exaggerate the importance of Burlington's and Kent's position as leaders of taste in the seventeen-thirties and early forties. Burlington himself has been celebrated more than once by Pope, and though Kent and he were unable to achieve their darling ambition, the reconstruction of Whitehall and Westminster on a monumental scale suitable to the centre of government and administration, what they did achieve in the Royal Mews, (on the site of the National Gallery) the Horse Guards and the fragmentary centre part of the Treasury Building and in the partial reconstruction of the Law Courts at Westminster Hall (now destroyed), was sufficient to stamp the character of that most important part of London throughout this period; and enough remains even now, in spite of the accumulation of post-nineteenth-century building, to dominate Whitehall. Their influence on other architects was not only important by example, but furthered by important publications financed by Lord Burlington's great fortune. Burlington and Kent may be said to represent in art, besides a return to a stricter form of antique classicism, the leadership of an aristocracy whose education was completed in Italy. They stood for the tradition of the great masters of figure painting in the grand manner, and it was their example that the sculptors small and great largely followed; it is against them that Hogarth so vigorously revolted. It may be said that Burlington and Kent acted as a corrective to any tendency to the development of a rococo style in this country comparable with that which obtained in, say, Germany and Austria, though this is too sweeping a statement to be made without reservation; for though their insistence on the grand manner in painting brought them into conflict with Hogarth, and the effectiveness of their authority may be considered to have driven that painter away from the elegant decorative painting for which he was particularly gifted in the direction of the type of propagandist art for which he is most famous, Kent himself is among the earliest practitioners of rococo Gothic both at Westminster Hall and Henry Pelham's villa at Esher; while

his work as pioneer of landscape garden design shows that
certain of the most important aspects of rococo and early
romantic art in this country came directly from the inner-
most circle of the Palladianist neo-classics.

The relations of the Burlingtonian group with Alexander
Pope are well known. A more obscure but equally interesting literary contact was that with Bishop Berkeley the
philosopher. Berkeley himself was keenly interested in architecture, and it has been suggested that it was this interest
that brought him into contact with Burlington. It is possible
that the two men met in Rome in 1717–18 and Berkeley's
Alciphron of 1732 contains a remarkable passage which
certainly refers to Burlington. "Crito upon this observed
that he knew an English nobleman who in the prime of life
professeth a liberal art, and is the first man of his profession
in the world; and that he was very sure he had more pleasure
in the exercise of that elegant art than from any sensual
enjoyment within the power of one of the largest fortunes
and most bountiful spirits in Great Britain." Berkeley's own
taste in architecture, as shown by the entries in his Italian
Journeys and various remarks in letters, is of the most enlightened kind; and though he is filled with admiration for
the advanced rococo or late baroque of Lecce, his real
enthusiasm seems to have been reserved for the Greek monu-
ments that he visited in Sicily; and it is extremely unfortunate that we have only references in letters to this enthusiasm as the Sicilian part of his Italian Journey has been
lost. This taste for real Greek architecture is very remarkable
at so early a date, and there is nothing to compare with it
until well after the middle of the century, but it suggests a
leaning to a severe and archaeological type of classicism
which is very much in accordance with the ideas of Lord
Burlington, though we have no evidence that Burlington
himself had any knowledge of Greek architecture. It is
perhaps fair to say that the whole of this "neo-classic re-
action" against the baroque of Hawksmoor and Vanburgh
and the early Gibbs, the period in short of the Fifty New
Churches, represents the final fruit of that rationalist movement whose effects are certainly perceptible much earlier

than this, though in the work of the earlier masters judgment had not gained such an entire mastery over fancy, to make use of a phrase of Hobbes, almost the favourite critical contrast of the baroque masters themselves.

The movement towards Romanticism and the picturesque, which appears just perceptibly in some of the works of Vanbrugh, and more clearly as we have suggested above in Kent, particularly in his work as a landscape gardener, is certainly the most obvious point at which the fine arts and the literature of the eighteenth century came nearest together. Miss Mainwaring and Mr. Hussey have pointed out that the earlier nature poets such as Thomson of *The Seasons*, are looking at the countryside through the eyes of the most admired landscape painters of their day, Claude Lorraine, Salvator Rosa and others of the seventeenth-century classic school. The fashion for Claude and Salvator is presumably a reflection of the strongly Italianate taste of the upper classes due to the completion of their educational system in Italy, and if they took their ideas of architecture from what they saw at Venice and Vicenza, they certainly took their taste in landscape painting from the Claudes in the great Roman collections and, one may say further, their taste in scenery from their excursions in the Campagna. It would be a mistake, however, to suppose that this taste for classic seventeenth-century landscape only arose in the second quarter of the eighteenth century, when indeed it was confirmed and widened by the forces we have mentioned. Earlier landscape painting in England reaching back even to the seventeenth century itself, would seem to have been equally dominated by the classic Roman landscapists and their Dutch followers, though the whole of this aspect of the subject has been little studied largely because the surviving examples of such landscape work are few and of relatively poor quality; but to anyone who has noticed the character of the painted landscape over-doors in the great early eighteenth-century houses, such as Castle Howard, or the painted landscape panels in the Hall at Stoke Edith, the upper part of which was decorated by Thornhill, must realise that this conception of landscape was certainly the predominating one in this country for some considerable period before William Kent attempted to translate it into actual trees and water, or Thomson into words. Landscape gardening itself, besides being the visual embodiment of a whole attitude towards nature, and besides the obvious example of Shenstone's garden at Leasowes, which is well known by reason of Dr. Johnson's comments, produced a considerable literature of its own. In the later eighteenth century Chambers, Mason, Gilpin, Uvedale Price and Payne Knight, and finally "Dr. Syntax in Search of the Picturesque," are all concerned with this subject; and the importance of the movement not only in regard to the growth of the English landscape school, perhaps the most important achievement of this country in any visual art, but also on the architecture both of the latter part of the century and indeed its successor, can hardly be exaggerated.

The other aspect of Romanticism in the visual arts which is best known is the Gothic Revival. Kent's attempts at Gothic have been mentioned, and before him are the Hawksmoor towers of All Souls' and Westminster Abbey, and perhaps even more striking the mediaevalising compositions of Vanbrugh, such as the great fortified wall along the ridge at Castle Howard, the astonishing building at Esher, and last, but not least, his own house which still exists at Maze Hill near Greenwich. These Vanbrugh Gothicisms have a special interest, for they derive from mediaeval military rather than from church architecture; and in what may be called the second phase of the early Gothic revival after the Esher Villa and Strawberry Hill were already well known, it is this romantic castle style which is undoubtedly the most important. How strong the fashion for mediaevalising architecture became in the third quarter of the century can only be appreciated when it is realised that an architect such as Robert Adam, whose name seems to stand for all that we mean by the most elegant Georgian classicism, includes in the catalogue of his drawings, designs for no less than forty different buildings in the Gothic or castellated manner. Some of his earliest works were done in this taste, and in his mature period of the late sixties and seventies, some of his grandest compositions, e.g., Culzean in Ayrshire. It is in the castle manner of Adam that eighteenth-century Gothicism grows up from being merely a matter of drawing-room or garden decoration, such as it appears in the works of Batty Langley, and even at Esher and Strawberry Hill (for the latter was hardly more than an enlarged overgrown garden pavilion), to the full stature of a way of monumental architectural design. The effects of this development are to be seen in the most famous of early romantic Gothic building, Beckford's Fonthill, by Wyatt, and the same architect's Ashridge (though the latter was built in the first years of the nineteenth century). In these Wyatt buildings the Gothic detail of Strawberry Hill and Esher and Batty Langley is married with the type of dramatic picturesque composition which has been developed in the great Adam houses in the castle manner. The cycle of taste had gone full circle, and it is not surprising to find that the critics of the latter part of the century, including Adam, Sir Joshua Reynolds, and, later, John Carter, are concerned to vindicate the reputation of Vanbrugh as against the strictures of the Palladianist Burlingtonian critics. The other architectural fashion of this early romantic period, the neo-Greek, is of much less importance than the Gothic. The neo-Greek movement which is always said to have been initiated by Stuart and Revett, who made drawings of the Athenian buildings in the early seventeen-fifties, had hardly got under way before the end of the century. This seems to have been due to some extent to the personal character of Stuart, who was extremely dilatory in publishing the results of his work in Greece; and indeed, and this is very remarkable in an eighteenth-century architect, made no attempt to publish the buildings executed by himself after his return from the Near East. Though he attained to an extraordinary position of influence and social consideration, this was confined to a relatively small circle, and the manner of Robert Adam with his refined neo-Roman type of decoration, which one of his great contemporaries unkindly described as Mr. Adam's filigree toywork, dictated the fashion both for the major forms of external architecture and the niceties of interior decoration, to the exclusion of the more learned style. The piety of nineteenth-century critics in the midst of the true Greek revival undoubtedly led them to exaggerate the importance of the work of Stuart and Revett, at any rate with regard to its influence on their contemporaries.

Undoubtedly the most commanding figure in English art of the century is Sir Joshua Reynolds, and there is in his learned art a quality of magniloquence which makes him a suitable companion for Dr. Johnson; but Reynolds is not only the most learned and sophisticated of English portrait painters, he is the great advocate of the grand manner in the history of English art criticism. In the great discourses he gave as President of the Royal Academy, which are supposed to have been revised by Dr. Johnson himself, is summed up all that feeling and reverence for the great Italian tradition of the Renaissance for which in a sense in Reynold's youth Burlington may be said to have stood. It is usually said that what Reynolds so splendidly preached he was quite unable to practise, and certainly great imaginative figure compositions, history painting in the grand manner as the eighteenth century would have called it, was not for him; and equally certainly the more intimate, tender, one had almost said sentimental, portraits of Reynolds are often among his very best; but it is a mistake to be led away too far by this paradox. Pictures like the Lord Heathfield or Mrs. Siddons as the Tragic Muse, are evidence of what the grand manner can do or had done for Reynolds; and in such pictures as the Lord Carlisle in the robes of the Thistle it is delightful to find that all the tropes and elaborations of classic eloquence can be used with every degree of virtuosity to serve a slightly ironical intention. Too much has been said about the pompous President: the President very well knew how to be pompous, and what he was about when he was doing it; and in this delightful picture, how to smile discreetly at pomposity on occasion. Just as the paradox of the failure of Reynolds's history painting has proved a tempting simplification of our view of him, so the contrast with Gainsborough has been probably over-emphasised. It is certain that the obvious contrast between

136

Gainsborough, who works always in an extremely personal manner, and Reynolds whose work is constantly reflecting his knowledge and admiration of the great masters of the past, is a sound one, and was recognised by the painters themselves. Gainsborough is in a sense the perfect embodiment of what the rococo movement meant in this country. He is the romantic painter par excellence, with his passion for landscape, the extraordinary refinement and elegance of his handling, the delicacy and subtlety of his colour.

Of the other eminent painters of the time, Romney is the master who should represent the neo-classic tendencies of the Rome of Wincklemann and Mengs, but it would have needed a greater man than Romney to have established neo-classicism here with any real authority comparable to that which it obtained in France. In spite of which it can be said that while Reynolds and Gainsborough's reputations both underwent a severe slump shortly after their deaths, Romney in much of his painting seems to forestall the work of the generation that follows him. Two other figures cannot be omitted from any essay on the art of the eighteenth century in relation to its literature. They are Flaxman and Blake. Flaxman's importance seems rather to belong to the first years of the nineteenth century when the influence of his illustrations to Homer began to make itself felt among the French. As a sculptor he is curiously disappointing, and his attempts at the grand heroic manner are among the most unfortunate of his works. There is no doubt that his particular gift for elegant decorative low relief owed very much to his work for Wedgwood, and it cannot be too strongly insisted that that collaboration was not one of the gifted artist condescending to assist the man of commerce, but of the young and unformed student being drilled, one had almost said licked into shape, by the experience and dominating personality of the greater potter. Blake is altogether too complicated a problem to be treated with any propriety in a concluding paragraph. Besides a real feeling for mediaeval art, he shared with Flaxman a curious deflated classic idiom of drawing derived in Flaxman's case from his study of late Hellenistic and Roman

137

antiques, perhaps more particularly gems, and in Blake's' partly from Flaxman himself, partly from Fuseli, and partly from engravings after Michaelangelo. Fuseli was of the family whose connection with Wincklemann is so close, and he and Flaxman are the most authentic representatives of the true neo-classic as it was known on the Continent; but neo-classicism was not enough; and it needed the exaltations and agonies of Blake to vitalise these feeble shapes and put them together with such Primitive conviction that, as a great critic has said, "When he declared that the Byzantine style had been divinely revealed to him it looks as if he had some justification."

CHAPTER VII

THE ECONOMIC BACKGROUND OF EIGHTEENTH-CENTURY LITERATURE

By F. J. Fisher, M.A.
London School of Economics

TO tell in any detail the economic history of the years between the Glorious Revolution and the Great Reform Act would need a whole volume rather than a single chapter, for they saw, in a very real sense, the birth of modern England. Among their contributions to our civilisation were such diverse and important institutions as the steam engine and the factory system, the scientific breeding of cattle and the smelting of iron with coal, the Bank of England and the income tax, classical economic theory and the beginnings of modern socialist thought. But although the details are complicated, the main theme of the story is simple enough. There was, during those years, a considerable growth both in the population of this country and in its foreign trade. That growth implied an increased demand for the products of English industry and agriculture and, through the medium of a rise in prices, that demand was translated into an increased output. In many cases the desired supplies were obtained without any change in the existing methods of production; the growing population provided ample labour, and a greater number of men working with the old methods were able to keep the market furnished with what it needed. But that solution was not always adequate, and in some of the country's most important economic activities—agriculture, mining, the iron and textile industries, transport—the necessary output of goods and services was obtained only by the adoption of drastic improvements in technology. The eighteenth century was, in fact, the first period in which inventions played a significant part in the economic development of England. To finance those inventions and the commerce which they served, a new banking system had to be created; to permit of their free use economic policy had to be re-modelled; and with them came important changes in the organisation not only of industry and agriculture but also of society itself.

The England of the later Stuarts, although possessed of a considerable empire and a world-wide foreign trade, was still a poor, thinly-peopled, and economically backward country. Its population seems to have amounted to less than six million souls, and its methods of production were generally so crude that one half of those six millions were said normally to earn too little for their maintenance, and to be kept alive only by charity, poor relief or plunder. In agriculture, although enclosure had been progressing slowly for centuries, most of the land was still cultivated under the old open-field system. The average farmer, that is to say, still grew his corn, not in separate fields of his own, but on a number of small unfenced plots scattered around the village among similar plots belonging to his neighbours. He still kept his animals upon the village common and upon the arable lands when they lay fallow or were thrown open for grazing between harvest and seedtime. In some places a considerable degree of efficiency was attained even under such conditions; but generally the system was inadequate to the growing needs of the time. It was extremely wasteful of land, for the arable lands had to be left fallow every third or fourth year in order to conserve their fertility; and large areas were left permanently as rough common for the support of the village livestock. The cattle which it maintained were poor, for not only did the indiscriminate herding of all animals together prevent selective breeding, but the almost complete absence of root crops meant an acute shortage of winter feed. Its output of cereals was normally low, for the usual rotation of crops was too crude and the supply of animal manure too scanty for heavy yields to be possible. In industry, although capitalism and large establishments had been creeping in for at least a century, most manufacturing, even for export, was still carried on in cottages or domestic workshops by wage-earners or small masters using their own simple tools and having at their service no power but that of their own muscles. For transport, although there was a flourishing coast trade, the country was still largely dependent upon the inadequate system of parochial roads which it had inherited from the Middle Ages.

But although the economic system was still crude it was expanding, and men had long been conscious of its shortcomings. The king of Brobdingnag spoke for many of Swift's contemporaries when "He gave it for his opinion that whoever could make two ears of corn or two blades of grass to grow upon a spot of ground where only one grew before would deserve better of mankind and do more essential service to his country than the whole race of politicians put together", and the improvement of the existing means of production was one of the liveliest issues of the day. Agriculture was advanced by the steady progress of enclosure. New methods of finance, manufacture and cultivation were introduced from abroad, particularly from Holland. Inland trade was stimulated by the dredging and embanking of rivers, and by the beginning of a system of turnpike roads maintained not from the parochial rates but from tolls on the traffic which used them. Many an artisan and farmer experimented in an effort to reduce his costs and increase his output. And the members of the newly-founded Royal Society, devoting as they did much of their time to problems suggested by the needs of the business world, were rapidly establishing that alliance of science and technology which lies at the basis of modern life. To exaggerate the immediate effects of the improvements made during the late seventeenth and early eighteenth centuries would be easy. Many of the claims put forward by inventors were absurd and merited the satire which Defoe and Swift poured upon them. Some of the new devices were kept secret by their discoverers; those that were made public seem to have been

adopted but slowly; none of them had at first anything like
a revolutionary impact upon the country's economic system.
Yet they were by no means insignificant. Among them were
two destined to be of the utmost importance; for Abraham
Darby's process for smelting with coke instead of charcoal
made possible the growth of the modern iron industry;
and the steam engine constructed by Newcomen for pump-
ing the Cornish tin mines first harnessed for man's use the
motive power to which he has since owed so much. And,
as a whole, they provided a fund of knowledge upon which
later inventors were to draw with profit.

Experience shows that once technological advance has
begun it tends to be carried forward by its own momentum.
The lower costs made possible by the new methods open
new markets, and in turn those widening markets give a
stimulus to further invention. But on this occasion that
tendency was reinforced by two other factors. The new
science that was beginning to transform industry and agriculture was also being applied in other fields, and in none
did it bear richer fruit than in that of medicine. For the first
time in English history the study of disease was placed upon
a sound empirical basis. The work of the Hunters opened a
new chapter in the development of surgery. The teachings
of White and Smellie so improved the handling of maternity
cases that during the latter half of the eighteenth century
the dangers of childbirth fell rapidly; in the British Lying-in
Hospital, for example, the death rate of mothers declined
from one in 42 to one in 288 and that of babies from one in
15 to one in 77. After 1798 the scourge of smallpox was
partly tamed by Jenner's discovery of vaccination; it accounted for nearly 10 per cent of London deaths in 1785–98
but for only 5 per cent in 1808–14. Some advance was also
made in the treatment of fevers. Nor was this knowledge
restricted to a few leading men and their wealthy patients.
One product of the great humanitarian movement which
swept over England at this time was a system of voluntary
hospitals which, although they were too few to provide
direct treatment for many, were invaluable as schools where
doctors and midwives could learn something of the new

ideas and the new treatments; and the same movement provided a network of charitable dispensaries through which the benefits of the new medicine were passed on to the poor. At the same time as doctors were becoming more proficient in the curing of disease, the causes of disease themselves were being brought under control by contemporary improvements in urban sanitation and by the decline of excessive drinking after the Licensing Act of 1751. Soon the result was seen in a rapid decline of the death rate, which fell from 28.6 per thousand in the decade 1781–90 to 21.1 per thousand in 1811–20. As there had been no corresponding fall in the birth rate there inevitably followed a rapid increase in the population. In 1689 there had been rather less than six million people in England and Wales; by 1750 there were probably not more than six millions and a half; but there were seven millions and a half in 1780, nine millions in 1801 and fourteen millions by 1831. And the same period saw a rapid expansion of foreign trade due partly to the earlier inventions but largely to the increasing demands of a growing population abroad for English goods, and of the growing population at home for imports.

Thus, by the latter half of the eighteenth century, English producers were faced with opportunities such as their predecessors had never enjoyed. Both domestic and overseas markets were expanding and the profits which they offered spurred on the progress of invention. In particular, the new conditions placed an ever-increasing strain upon the country's agriculture, which had to meet the rising demand for food, and upon the textile industries, which not only had to clothe the growing population but also had to provide the bulk of the nation's exports. For a time, therefore, agriculture and the textiles definitely took the centre of the stage in the drama of English economic development and their performances were very similar. Both sought to meet their problems by improving their technique of production; and in both the new methods that were devised brought with them changes in organisation. For two generations after 1760 scientific farming became a fashion led by no less a person than the king himself, who ran a model estate at

Windsor, contributed to agricultural periodicals under various pseudonyms, and earned for all time the nickname of "Farmer George". It was, in fact, the golden age of the gentleman farmer. New rotations of crops were introduced that not only abolished the necessity of frequent fallows but also solved the problem of winter feed for cattle; as more winter feed became available there followed improvements in the breeding of livestock; and the enclosure movement which had been spreading slowly since the fifteenth century now swept over the country in a wave that by 1840 left scarcely an open-field village in existence. In the textile industries there was a gradual improvement of both spinning and weaving machinery; as machinery became heavier and more complicated it was harnessed first to water power and then to the steam engine that Watt had adapted to provide a rotary motion; and as mechanical power supplanted that of human muscles the industry gradually moved from the cottage to the factory. But although agriculture and the textiles held the centre of the stage they did not monopolise it. In many less important trades similar although less important changes were being made, and in the transport and capital goods industries there were developments of quite major significance. The need of the new factories for machinery, and of the armies sent against Napoleon for weapons, led to the rapid development of an engineering industry with new processes and large establishments. The need of that industry for iron produced better means of smelting, refining, rolling, drawing, cutting and working that metal. The need of the new furnaces and steam engines for coal gave rise to improved methods of draining, ventilating and generally operating the mines. Above all, the universal need for better communications inspired a minor revolution in transport. The turnpike system was extended to cover most of the country; the quality of the roads was improved by the technical discoveries of men such as Metcalf, Telford and Macadam; the most important commercial areas were linked together by means of canals; and by 1830 England was on the eve of the railway age.

So great were the technical changes made in the century after 1760 that historians have long called that period the "Industrial Revolution". To-day that label is out of fashion. It ignores the fact that changes occurred in all branches of economic life rather than in industry alone. It hides the fact that those changes were an acceleration rather than a reversal of the trends which had gone before. Yet the term revolution as applied to those years contains within it a serious truth. For all its obvious similarities, the England of 1830 was separated by profound differences from that of 1689. By the early nineteenth century this country had acquired not only a far greater population but also a far richer capital equipment in the form of mines, furnaces, factories, machinery, roads, canals and docks; and in acquiring that equipment it had considerably altered its economic and social structure.

The most obvious manifestation of that alteration was the new balance between agriculture and industry. During the eighteenth century the former had prospered greatly. In 1831 it still directly employed some 28 per cent of the families in the country and, together with the rural crafts dependent upon it, probably supported almost one half of the total population. But the progress of the metal and textile industries, and in particular of cotton, had been even more spectacular. Despite the enclosures and the improvements in technique, agriculture had lost its export trade by the seventeen-eighties, and by 1830 was no longer fully able to meet the home demand for foodstuffs. By contrast, the cotton industry not only strengthened its grip on the English market but after 1780 built up enormous sales overseas. The amount of raw cotton consumed by English manufacturers rose from one million pounds in 1710 to three million in 1760, eighteen million in 1785, fifty-six million in 1800, and two hundred and sixty-nine million in 1830; and although the woollen, coal and iron industries never equalled that pace they also expanded more rapidly than agriculture. By 1830, therefore, industry and commerce were absorbing a far greater proportion of the country's resources than they had been in 1689 and the growth of their relative importance in the national economy had repercussions that were far-reaching.

Geographically that change was reflected in the rise of new manufacturing towns on the northern coalfields, in the drift of population from the countryside to them, and in the weakening of that preponderance which the south had enjoyed since the days of the Romans. Politically, it was reflected in the struggle of the new interests for greater representation in Parliament; a struggle which culminated in the Great Reform Act of 1832 which gave seats to the new towns of the north and enfranchised the middle classes throughout the country. In the realm of economic thought and policy it was reflected in the emergence of those doctrines of *laissez faire* and free trade which were to reign until our own day. Under the later Stuarts the business world had been subjected to an elaborate although chaotic system of governmental interference. Although foreign trade was growing, the vast majority of Englishmen were still producing for the home market and, at their request, that market was preserved for them by a high tariff. As much of the existing foreign trade was devoted to supplying colonial markets and re-exporting colonial goods there were complicated regulations to preserve those fruitful activities for English merchants and shipowners; in particular, the colonists were forbidden to trade directly with Europe or to develop industries that might diminish the demand for English goods. As much English capital was invested in the empire, imperial sugar and other produce was admitted to this country at preferential rates. By the last quarter of the eighteenth century, however, that system was being widely questioned. Adam Smith and his disciples suggested that it was unprofitable; the American rebellion suggested that it was politically unwise; and as industry achieved an efficiency that killed the bogey of successful foreign competition its leaders found that the tariffs and restrictions which had previously sheltered them at home were now serious barriers to the expansion of their sales abroad. During most of the eighteenth century the main problem of industry had been to make production keep pace with the growing demand; by the early nineteenth technical progress had been so great that the difficulty was to find markets for the swelling output; and the result of that change was to marshal the forces of industry and trade behind the banner of free trade. Their struggle was destined to be long, for not only had they to fight the vested interests of agriculture in a Parliament constituted predominantly of landowners, but harassed Chancellors of the Exchequer had to find alternative sources of revenue at a time when the industrialists themselves objected strongly to all new forms of taxation. But by 1820 the war had definitely been started and by 1830 the preliminary skirmishes had been won.

The Industrial Revolution, moreover, altered the balance of English life not only horizontally, as between industry and agriculture, but also vertically, as between capital and labour. One of its major fruits took the form of the emergence, far more clearly than ever before, of a definite proletariat. By the eighteenth century, of course, a class of wage-earners had long been in existence. But the position, at least of the more skilled workers, differed considerably from that of their modern descendants. On the one hand, many of them retained some degree of independence and some measure of ownership over the means of production. In the open-field village the labourers often had a strip or two of arable land and were usually able to keep some poultry and possibly a cow or pig on the common. In industry the craftsman often worked in his own home and with his own tools and, although his hours might be long and his wages low, he was subject to no discipline but could work to suit himself. On the other hand, as production in both agriculture and industry was usually on a small scale there was an economic ladder up which the energetic wage-earner could hope to climb to complete independence. The village labourer, by purchasing or renting additional strips in the open fields as they became available and his savings permitted, could hope eventually to become a small farmer. The enterprising weaver could hope, by gradually employing others, to become a clothier in his own right. In many trades that situation was to obtain until well into the nineteenth century;

but in those in which technical changes were rapid those conditions were swept away. Enclosure meant that the village labourer lost his use of the village common, and as he could seldom produce in defence of his old rights a title which the lawyers would respect he was seldom compensated with an allotment. Scientific farming, moreover, meant large scale farming. "Where," asked Arthur Young, "is the little farmer to be found who will cover his whole farm with marl at the rate of 100 or 150 tons an acre; who will drain all his land at the expense of £2 or £3 an acre; who will pay a heavy price for the manure of towns and convey it thirty miles by land carriage; who will float his meadows at the cost of £5 an acre?" The answer was that he was seldom to be found at all. The small owners seem to have held on fairly successfully until the post-war depression after 1815 swept many of them to ruin, but the eviction of small tenants in favour of large was well under way by 1780. By 1830 the clearly divided trinity of landlord, capitalist tenant farmer, and landless labourer had been firmly established over large parts of the country. And in those industries in which expensive and power driven machinery was being introduced the same story was repeated; the worker was withdrawn from the semi-freedom of his home to the discipline of the factory and saw his dreams of ultimate independence fade away.

To argue that this change normally meant a deterioration in the purely material welfare of the men concerned would be dangerous, for there is abundant evidence that many of them had enjoyed the fruits of their situation not in the shape of an addition to their monetary income but in the form of what their critics called idleness and their sympathisers preferred to call leisure. As so often happens in countries where the standard of living is low they were often content to exist at subsistence level and work no more than was necessary to maintain it. But in whatever way they had exercised their old semi-freedom its loss was bitter. Many a village labourer felt that he had been deprived of what was his by right and summed up the position in the words of the popular jingle :—

The law locks up the man.or woman
Who steals the goose from off the common
But leaves the greater villain loose
Who steals the common from the goose.

Many an artisan refused to enter the new factories in which
discipline was galling, and employment long carried a
social stigma. And among the results of this increasing separa-
tion of the workers as a distinct class were two which greatly
alarmed their social superiors. Among many it led to an
apathy which expressed itself in a drunken improvidence
that matched anything which their old semi-independence
had produced. By contrast, among the tougher spirits it
produced the first real working class movement in English
history. The late eighteenth century was so fertile in trade
unions that the old conspiracy laws had to be furbished up
to keep them in check, and between 1799 and 1825 they
were prohibited altogether. The labour agitation for a
voice in parliament seemed so dangerous to a generation
with the example of the French Revolution before it that
it also had to be suppressed by law. And as working men
found their hopes of independence vanishing they began
to evolve the basic doctrine of modern socialism that the
private ownership of capital was the root of all evil.

From all these changes in technology and organisation,
supported as they were by improvements in banking and
finance, there emerged one major result; the national income was enormously increased. With its greater labour
supply and capital equipment the country was able to
produce an ever-growing stream of wealth. Yet that wealth
did not immediately produce anything like a general advance in the standard of living. Much of it was dissipated in
the long wars with France. The growth in population so
increased the number of mouths to be fed and bodies to
be clothed that, until the end of the 'thirties, there were
men who saw the whole economic progress mainly as a race
between population and production and, at least for a time,
it was not considered absurd to predict that production
would lose. For years Malthus found a general acceptance

for his theory that the human race tended, unless restrained by war, vice or self-control, to breed until its numbers reached the maximum which the economic system could maintain at subsistence level; English experience seemed to prove that to be but too true. For years reformers attacked the problem of poverty from that angle, and while the more respectable preached the virtues of late marriages, the more realistic launched the first birth-control movement in English history. There is, unfortunately, too little evidence to say whether England was in fact over-populated or whether the national income per head actually rose or fell. But it is clear that, as in all times of rapid changes, there were certain groups upon whom the new conditions bore heavily and who gained little or nothing from the new riches.

Agricultural employment seems to have been increased rather than diminished by the spread of enclosures and high farming. But, at least in the south of England, the supply of labour was increasing so rapidly that wages failed to rise enough to compensate the worker for his loss of commons, the decline of by-industries such as spinning, and the larger family which the lower death rate was leaving him to support. Consequently, when in the 'nineties the war-time inflation sent prices soaring upwards, a crisis threatened to explode at the basis of rural society. It was temporarily warded off by the adoption, in county after county, of a system of subsidising agricultural wages out of the poor rate according to the size of the labourer's family and the price of bread. Seldom has a hastily devised remedy proved more expensive than did that. Its immediate result was to force down wages still further until not even single men could live on them, and nearly the whole of the agricultural workers of southern England were pauperised. For the next generation the major social problem of England was the rehabilitation of the country labourer from the state of poverty and degradation into which he had sunk; and the nineteenth century had almost passed before that task was finished. In industry one result of the new methods of production was the appearance of technological unemployment. "Where," asked a pamphleteer in 1833, "is the combing and spinning, cotton-weaving, silk-filling, cruel-filling, hemp-dressing, sack-weaving, paper-making, hand-sewing, hot-pressing, and printing; where the employment general until these last few years? All absorbed in machinery. Where is the distaff and spindle, where the employment in knitting, in the manufacture of hemp and flour? Where the employment for women and children, formerly carrying comfort and independence to the *home* of every cottager? All absorbed by machinery or sacrificed to the cry of the cheap." Outside of the factories there remained a pathetic mass of underemployed and underpaid labour that took a long time to disappear. Nor were the workers in the factories always to be envied. Although their wages were often relatively good their hours were long; before the Factory Act of 1833 began to curb the worst exploitation of child labour they often had to begin their labours at the age of six or seven; dependent as they were upon foreign markets they were periodically thrown out of work when trade fell off; and the towns in which they were forced to live were so devoid of the elementary amenities that are necessary to make urban life tolerable that they became a scandal throughout Europe.

It would be easy to fill page after page with contemporary descriptions of the sufferings of the southern agricultural labourers, of the miners, of the factory children and of the obsolescent handworkers during the early nineteenth century. But to conclude from them that the period under review saw any general decline in the standards of working-class life would be to go beyond the evidence. The lot of the poor had not been happy under the later Stuarts; the spectacular sufferings for which there is so much evidence did not appear much before 1790 and may have been preceded by years of gradual amelioration; those craftsmen whose trades were not affected by sweeping technical changes and those agricultural labourers whose wages were not violently depressed by parish subsidies probably gained from the changes from which their fellows suffered. Were it possible to measure it, one might well find that the life of the ordinary working man in 1830 was more comfortable, as it was certainly longer, than that of his prototype in 1689. But one thing is certain; whatever gains the working classes may have made they were negligible compared with those of their betters. As was only natural at a time when labour was abundant and capital scarce, there were handsome rewards for those who could supply the savings needed by the expanding economic system. For the landlord, for the farmer wealthy enough to finance the new enclosures and adopt the new methods, for the merchant, for the new industrialist, for the investor with funds to spare for turnpike companies, canal companies, insurance companies and government loans, the eighteenth century was a golden age which ushered in the modern economic system appropriately enough by exalting the middle classes to new levels of prosperity.

Thus the literature of the years between 1689 and 1832 was produced against a background of rapid economic and social change and in a society which was rapidly increasing in wealth. What influence did that background exert on literary development? That is a question by no means easy to answer; for although it is almost a canon of modern criticism that art is profoundly influenced by the social environment within which it is produced, the channels through which that influence is exerted are devious and as yet almost unexplored. Yet certain contacts between the economic developments described above and the literature of the time are obvious enough. In the first place, the contemporary preoccupation with material progress produced a spate of descriptive and theoretical writings on economic and social problems; and among those writings were certain pieces, such as Defoe's *Tours*, Cobbett's *Rural Rides* and Hume's *Essays* that have won for themselves a place in the world of letters. In the second place, it was upon this background that writers drew in their search for local colour. But above all, the effect of the growth in population and of the rising standard of living at least in its upper ranks was enormously to increase the reading public. "I suppose," wrote the book-seller Lackington towards the end of the eighteenth century, "that more than four times the number of books are sold now than were sold twenty years since. The poorer sort of farmers, and even the poor country people in general, who before that period spent their winter evenings in relating stories of witches, ghosts, hobgoblins, etc., now shorten the winter nights by hearing their sons and daughters read tales, romances etc., and on entering their houses you may see *Tom Jones*, *Roderick Random*, and other entertaining books stuck up on their bacon racks. . . . A number of book clubs are also formed in every part of England where each member subscribes a certain sum quarterly to purchase books. . . . And the Sunday Schools are spreading very fast in most parts of England which will accelerate the diffusion of knowledge among the lower classes of the community and in very few years exceedingly increase the sale of books." The writer of the eighteenth and early nineteenth centuries was, in fact, in a position similar to that of the business men of those times. He was faced by an expanding market, and like the business man he responded by increasing his output. What was even more important, the expansion of his market brought with it a marked change in his social status and outlook. When the reading public had largely been confined to court circles writers had catered to the taste of those circles and, depending as they often did upon the patronage of some noble for their existence, had learned to look at the world through the eyes of the upper classes. Now that they wrote mainly for the middle classes, and now that their sales gave them the status of professional and business men, they were brought into closer sympathy with those classes. And, as Leslie Stephen pointed out, "the whole character of contemporary literature was moulded by the social conditions of the class for which and by which it was written". It was no mere coincidence that the Industrial Revolution came at the same time as the rise of the novel and as the transition from classicism to romanticism; for the novel and romantic literature generally are essentially bourgeois forms of art.

BIBLIOGRAPHY

LIST OF ABBREVIATIONS

C.H.E.L.—Cambridge History of English Literature
Cl. P.—Clarendon Press
C.U.P.—Cambridge University Press
D.N.B.—Dictionary of National Biography
E.L.—Everyman Library (Dent)
E.M.L.—English Men of Letters series (Macmillan)
E.S.M.E.A.—Essays and Studies by Members of the English
     Association (Cl. P.)
H.U.L.—Home University Library (Thornton Butterworth)
M.L.—Muses Library (Routledge)
M.L.R.—Modern Language Review
O.B.—Oxford Book of Eighteenth Century Verse (Cl. P.)
O.B.R.V.—Oxford Book of Regency Verse (Cl. P.)
O.M.—Oxford Miscellany (O.U.P.)
O.P.—Oxford Poets (O.U.P.)
O.S.A.—Oxford Standard Authors (O.U.P.)
O.U.P.—Oxford University Press
P.M.L.A.—Publications of the Modern Language Association
     of America
P.R.—Percy Reprints (Blackwell)
R.E.S.—Review of English Studies
S.P.C.K.—Society for the Propagation of Christian Knowledge
T.L.S.—Times Literary Supplement
U.P.—University Press
W.C.—World's Classics (O.U.P.)

CONTENTS

GENERAL READING

THE following books are recommended as studies of the period as a whole, and of certain aspects of it which transcend the limitations which division into categories inevitably involves.

The History of England:

> G. N. CLARK, *The Later Stuarts, 1660–1714*, Cl. P., 1934. This is a volume in the Oxford History of England. BASIL WILLIAMS's *The Whig Supremacy, 1714–60*, in the same series, has recently (1939) been published. A volume by G. S. VEITCH will cover the period from 1760–1815. For the last years of the period, see E. L. WOODWARD's *The Age of Reform*, 1938.
>
> Lord MACAULAY, *History*, ed. C. H. Firth, 6 vols., Macmillan, 1913-15.
>
> Lord MAHON, *The History of England from the Peace of Utrecht to the Peace of Aix-la-Chapelle*, second ed., 7 vols., Murray, 1849.
>
> Lord STANHOPE, *The History of England, comprising the Reign of Queen Anne until the Peace of Utrecht*, 2 vols., Murray, 1870.
>
> W. E. H. LECKY, *A History of England in the Eighteenth Century*, Longmans, revised ed. in 7 vols., 1892.
>
> I. S. LEADAM, *The Political History of England*, vol. ix, 1702–60, Longmans, 1909.
>
> E. HALÉVY, *Histoire du peuple anglais au xixe siècle* (Hachette, 1912; translation by E. I. Watkin and D. A. Barker, 2 vols., 1924; in 3 vols. in the 'Pelican' series).

Religious and Ecclesiastical History:

> J. H. OVERTON, *Life in the English Church, 1660–1714*, Longman, 1885.
>
> J. H. OVERTON and F. RELTON, *The English Church from the Accession of George I to the End of the Eighteenth Century* (Macmillan, 1906).

N. SYKES, *Church and State in England in the XVIIIth Century*, C.U.P., 1934.

H. W. CLARK, *History of English Nonconformity*, vol. ii (Chapman and Hall, 1913).

History of Thought:

L. STEPHEN, *History of English Thought in the Eighteenth Century*, 2 vols., Murray, 1876. B. WILLEY, *Eighteenth Century Background*, Chatto and Windus, 1940. See also two papers by A. O. LOVEJOY, *Optimism and Romanticism*, P.M.L.A., vol. 42, 1927, and *The Parallel of Deism and Classicism*, Modern Philology, vol. 29, 1932.

History of Literature:

O. ELTON, *The Augustan Age*, Blackwood, 1899.
    A Survey of English Literature, 1730–80, 2 vols., Arnold, 1928.
    A Survey of English Literature, 1780–1830, Arnold, 1912.

T. SECCOMBE, *The Age of Johnson*, Bell, 1900.

C. H. HERFORD, *The Age of Wordsworth*, Bell, 1897.

Social History:

W. C. SYDNEY, *England and the English in the Eighteenth Century*, Grant, 1891.

J. ASHTON, *Social Life in the Reign of Queen Anne*, rptd., Chatto, 1929.

A. S. TURBERVILLE, *English Men and Manners in the Eighteenth Century*, Cl. P., 1929.

M. D. GEORGE, *London Life in the XVIIIth Century*, Kegan Paul, 1925; *England in Transition*, Routledge, 1931.

Lord ERNLE, *English Farming Past and Present*, ed. Sir A. D. Hall, Longmans, 1936.

A. TOYNBEE, *Lectures on the Industrial Revolution*, Longmans, 1884. See also under Cobbett, Arthur Young, Torrington, Woodforde, Ryder.

BASIL WILLEY, *Background of Eighteenth Century*.

Life and Letters:

A. BELJAME, *Le Public et les Hommes de Lettres en Angleterre au dix-huitième siècle*, Hachette, second ed. 1897.

L. Stephen, *English Literature and Society in the Eighteenth Century*, Duckworth, rpt. of 1927.

Johnson's England, Cl. P., 2 vols., 1933. A collection of essays by various writers on various aspects of eighteenth-century life. Useful bibliographies are appended to each essay.

The Romantic Movement:

M. Praz, *The Romantic Agony*, O.U.P., 1933.

K. Clark, *The Gothic Revival*, Constable, 1928.

A. O. Lovejoy, *On the Discrimination of Romanticisms*, P.M.L.A., vol. 39, 1924.

I. Babbitt, *Rousseau and Romanticism*, Houghton Mifflin, 1919.

W. P. Ker, "On the value of the terms 'Classical' and 'Romantic' as applied to literature," in his *Collected Essays*, vol. 2 (Macmillan, 1925).

I

POETRY

R EADERS of poetry during this period were served by
several collections of which the most famous is that
initiated by Dryden and continued by Tonson the publisher.
The first vol. (*Miscellany Poems*) was published in 1684,
the second (*Sylvæ*) in 1685, the third (*Examen Poeticum*)
in 1693, the fourth (*The Annual Miscellany*) in 1694, the fifth
(*Poetical Miscellanies*) in 1704, and the sixth (*Poetical Miscellanies*), which contains the *Pastorals* of Pope and Ambrose
Philips, in 1709. This collection is sometimes known as
Dryden's, sometimes as *Tonson's Miscellany*. The 6 vols. were
rptd. in 1716 and 1727.

The collection which best represents the poetry of the
middle of the eighteenth century is Dodsley's *Collection of
Poems*, which was published in 3 vols. in 1748. Several additions were made for the second ed. which appeared the
same year, and were rptd. as a fourth vol. in 1749. A 4-vol.
ed. was published in 1755, and a 6-vol. ed. in 1758. The 6-
vol. ed. was rptd. in 1763, 1765, 1766, 1770, 1775, and with
notes by Isaac Reed in 1782. A valuable guide and index to
the contents was made by R. W. Chapman and published
in the *Oxford Bibliographical Society's Proceedings and Papers*,
vol. 3, pt. 3, 1933. See also W. P. Courtney's *Dodsley's Collection of Poetry: its contents & contributors* (1910).

An appendix to Dodsley's *Collection* was published in
twelve monthly parts in 1763 entitled *The Poetical Calendar*.
The editors were Francis Fawkes (1720–77), the translator of
Theocritus (1767), and William Woty.

Eighteenth-century poetry is also well represented in

Anderson's 13-vol. ed. of the *Poets of Great Britain* (1792–5; 14th vol., 1807), and in Chalmers's 21-vol. ed. (1810). Useful selections have been compiled by D. Nichol Smith (*The Oxford Book of Eighteenth Century Verse*, Cl. P., 1926) and K. W. Campbell (*Poems on Several Occasions*, P.R. 1926; *An Anthology of English Poetry: Dryden to Blake*, H.U.L.). A good selection of verse from 1780 till 1830 is H. Milford's *Oxford Book of Regency Verse* (Cl. P., 1928).

POMFRET, John (1667–1702)

Pomfret's poems were published in 1699, but it was not until the next year that he published the poem which made his fame, *The Choice* (rptd. in O.B.). It epitomises much of the philosophy of life, which men of culture were then adopting; and Johnson, who wrote Pomfret's life, declared that "perhaps no composition in our language has been oftener perused".

SETTLE, Elkanah. See p. 296.

PRIOR, Matthew (1664–1721)

Prior's collected poems were published in 1709 and 1718. The best modern ed. is by A. R. Waller (C.U.P., 1905), who prepared a further volume containing *Dialogues of the Dead and other works in prose and verse* in 1907. Selections from the "familiar" shorter poems, by which Prior is chiefly remembered, have been made by Austin Dobson (Kegan Paul, 1889) and by F. Bickley (Abbey Classics, 1923). His life was written by Dr. Johnson; and more recently, by F. Bickley (Pitman, 1914) and L. G. Wickham Legg (C.U.P., 1921), who pays more especial attention to his diplomatic career.

BLACKMORE, Sir Richard (1655?–1729)

If Prior was the best poet writing at the turn of the century, Blackmore was the most prolific. By profession he was a physician, and was knighted (1697) by William III for his professional merits. Poetry, he explained more than once, was his recreation and the entertainment of his idle hours; but the imagination is overtasked in estimating the probable extent of his output, if he could have given his undivided attention to writing verse. The first fruits of his recreation was *Prince Arthur. An Heroick Poem. In Ten Books* (1695), the success of which encouraged him to produce *King Arthur. An Heroick Poem. In Twelve Books* (1697).

But "his head still teemed with heroick poetry, and (1705) he published *Eliza* in ten books" (Johnson). His masterpiece appeared in 1712. This was *Creation. A Philosophical Poem. In Seven Books*, designed to counter the spirit of scepticism by employing the harmony of numbers in demonstrating "the Self-Existence of an Eternal Mind from the created and dependent Existence of the Universe". Addison commended this poem, in a *Spectator* mainly devoted to the exposition of *Paradise Lost*, as "one of the most useful and noble productions in our *English* verse", an opinion which Dr. Johnson was almost inclined to share. The merits of *Creation*, however, are not revealed in a cursory inspection. Its sequel, *Redemption: A Divine Poem, in Six Books*, followed in 1722. Once more "the sweetness and beauties of poetic diction" were engaged to relieve and entertain the reader who wished to see the truth of revealed religion demonstrated. In 1723, Blackmore returned to heroic poetry and published *Alfred. An Epick Poem. In Twelve Books*. To each of these poems he contributed prefaces censuring the lewdness and impiety of modern wits, a subject which he also treated in verse in *A Satyre upon Wit* (1700), the most notorious but not the longest poem in his *Collection of Poems on Various Subjects* (1718). Blackmore's work is characterised by its bathos. The chief pleasure it affords the reader is to watch the poet "sinking from thought to thought, a vast profound!" But as Dryden remarked in the Preface to the *Fables* (1700), we must deal civilly with his poems, "because nothing ill is to be spoken of the dead". The most recent study of Blackmore's work is by Dr. Johnson in *The Lives of the Poets* (see p. 222); but a few pages are devoted to it in H. N. Fairchild's *Religious Trends in English Poetry*, vol. 1 (Columbia and O.U.P., 1939).

WALSH, William (1663-1708)

Dr. Johnson wrote of Walsh, "He is known more by his familiarity with greater men, than by anything done or written by himself." In the opinion of Dryden, who wrote an introduction for his prose *Dialogue concerning Women* (1691), Walsh was "the best critic of the nation", an opinion which Pope endorsed in the *Essay on Criticism*, ll. 729-44. It was Walsh who advised Pope to aim at "correctness" in poetry: their correspondence, first published by Pope, is rptd. in vol. 6 of the Elwin-Courthope ed. of Pope's works. Walsh's own aim in poetry was no more than to be elegantly pastoral and mildly erotic. Most of his poems, with his prose *Letters Amorous and Gallant*, were published in Tonson's *Miscellany*, pt. iv, 1716. A collected ed. was published by Curll in

1736. Walsh collaborated with Congreve and Vanbrugh in an adaptation of Molière called *Monsieur de Pourceaugnac or Squire Trelooby*, 1704 (see p. 298).

GRANVILLE, George, Lord Lansdowne (1666-1735)

Another friend and critic who encouraged Pope's early attempts in poetry was Lord Lansdowne, a poet himself, who modelled his lyrics and complimentary addresses on those of Waller. A collection of these was published in 1712 and reached a fourth ed. in 1726. His most important single poem, however, is *An Essay on Unnatural Flights in Poetry*, first published in Gildon's *New Miscellany* (1701). Lansdowne was also a dramatist. *The She Gallants*, an early example of sentimental comedy, was produced in 1696. It was later revised and renamed *Once a Lover; and Always a Lover*. His best play, commended by Dryden, is a tragedy in blank verse called *Heroick Love* (1698). Granville also produced an adaptation of *The Merchant of Venice* called *The Jew of Venice* (1701), and an opera called *The British Enchanters: or, No Magick Like Love* (1706). A collected ed. of *The Genuine Works in Verse and Prose, Of the Right Honourable George Granville, Lord Lansdowne* was published in two sumptuous quarto vols. in 1732. E. Handasyde's biography, *Granville the Polite*, was published by O.U.P. in 1933.

GARTH, Sir Samuel (1661-1719)

Garth was a fellow of the Royal College of Physicians, a poet, and a friend both of Dryden and of Pope. His *Dispensary* (1699) is a mock-heroic poem in six cantos describing a contest between the physicians and the apothecaries, and bears obvious resemblances to Boileau's *Lutrin* which preceded it, and to Pope's *Rape of the Lock* which was to be written thirteen years later. The poem was corrected and enlarged in subsequent editions, of which a ninth was published in 1726. *A Compleat Key to the Dispensary* was published in 1714. The best ed. of the poem is by W. J. Leicht (Heidelberg, 1905). Garth also wrote *Claremont* (1715) a "local" poem admittedly modelled on Denham's *Cowper's Hill* and Pope's *Windsor Forest*. His poems were first collected for publication in *The Minor Poets*, vol. 1, 1749. They may also be found in such collections as Chalmers's *English Poets*. His life was written by Dr. Johnson.

PHILIPS, John (1676-1709)

Philips gained a large contemporary reputation as the author of three Miltonic imitations, a mock-heroic called *The Splendid Shilling* (1701), an allegorical poem about ale, called *Cerealia* (1707), and a "georgic" on *Cider* (1708). His poems were first collected in 1712, and have recently been edited by G. Lloyd Thomas (P.R., 1927). His life was written by Dr. Johnson.

ADDISON, Joseph. See p. 266.

PHILIPS, Ambrose (1675–1749)
   Ambrose Philips is now remembered as a rival and antagonist of Pope in the writing of pastorals (1709); these are poor, but there is better work in his *Winter Piece*, published in *Tatler*, No. 12 (1709), and rptd. in O.B. He gained considerable notoriety by a series of odes (1718–25), in which "he paid his court to all ages and characters, from Walpole the 'steerer of the realm', to Miss Pulteney in the nursery" (Johnson). They were parodied by HENRY CAREY, author of *Sally in our Alley* (c. 1729; see O.B.), in a poem called *Namby Pamby*, a name which stuck. Both Philips and Carey were also dramatists. Philips's adaptation of Racine's *Andromaque*, entitled *The Distressed Mother*, was produced with great success in 1712. An account of Sir Roger de Coverley's visit to the theatre to see this play was published in *Spectator*, No. 335. Carey had been writing for the stage since 1715. His best plays are *Chrononhotonthologos* (1734), a good parody of heroic tragedy, and *The Dragon of Wantley* (1737), a burlesque of Italian opera. Philips's poems have been edited by M. Segar (P.R., 1937); his life was written by Dr. Johnson. Carey's poems have been edited by F. T. Wood (Scholartis Press, 1930).

WINCHILSEA, Anne Finch, Countess of (1661–1720)
   Lady Winchilsea's best known poem is *The Spleen*, published in Gildon's *Miscellany* (1701). She published a vol. in 1713 entitled *Miscellany Poems by a Lady*. Of these poems the best is *A Nocturnal Reverie* (rptd. with other poems in O.B.), whose "new images of external nature" were noted by Wordsworth as exceptional in the poetry of the time (Essay supplementary to the 1815 preface). Wordsworth enlarged on her merits in a letter to Dyce (May 1830), and transcribed a number of her poems for the benefit of Lady Beaumont (published 1905). The best ed. of her poems is by M. Reynolds (University of Chicago Press, 1903). They are also reprinted with the poems of Parnell, Dyer, Green, and Collins in *Minor Poets of the Eighteenth Century* (E.L.). A selection of them

made by J. Middleton Murry was published by Cape in 1928. There are critical essays by Sir E. Gosse in *Gossip in a Library* (1891), and by E. Dowden in *Essays Modern and Elizabethan* (1910).

PARNELL, Thomas (1679–1718)

Parnell's most famous poem is his *Night Piece on Death*, an effusion of graveyard sentiments, first printed in the collected ed. of his poetry published by his friend, Pope, in 1722 (rptd. in O.B.). A fuller collection was published in 1758. The best modern ed. is by G. A. Aitken (1894), and there is a rpt. (see under Lady Winchilsea) in E.L. Parnell's life was written by Goldsmith as a preface to an ed. of his poems (1770), and again by Dr. Johnson. A short study by A. H. Cruickshank appears in E.S.M.E.A., vol. 7.

GAY, John (1685–1732)

Gay published a collected ed. of his poetry in 1720, which contains *Rural Sports* (1713); *The Shepherd's Week* (1714; ed. H. F. B. Brett-Smith, Blackwell, 1924), a series of grotesque eclogues designed to show the readers of Ambrose Philips's pastorals what country life was really like; and *Trivia* (1716; ed. W. H. Williams, O'Connor, 1922), a realistic description of London life. His *Fables* (first series, 1727; second series, 1738; ed. Austin Dobson, 1882) are some of the best in the language, but it is a form which has made no great appeal to English writers (see Moore, Edward: p. 302). Gay's first play, *The What D'ye Call It*, a tragi-comi-pastoral-farce, was produced in 1715; but his fortune and reputation were not made until he produced *The Beggar's Opera* (1728; ed. F. W. Bateson, Dent, 1934), which is included with its sequel, *Polly* (1729), in G. C. Faber's standard ed. of Gay's poetry (O.S.A.). Gay's life was written by Dr. Johnson. There has been no adequate biography in recent times.

DUCK, Stephen (1705–56)

Duck may be mentioned at this point because of his realistic and gloomy description of the farm labourer's life in a poem called *The Thresher's Labour*. Not even Gay's *Shepherd's Week* is such an appropriate comment on the pastoralism of Ambrose Philips; for Duck anticipates Crabbe in "giving you the petrifaction of a sigh". The poem was shown to Queen Caroline who thereupon became Duck's patron. She raised him from the farm labourer's estate to holy orders and made him her librarian. His poems were first published in 1730 and were handsomely rptd. for subscribers in 1736. In this ed. there is an interesting account of Duck's life by Spence, who describes the progress of the farm labourer's education. Later accounts have been written by Southey in *Lives and Works of the Uneducated Poets* (ed. J S. Childers, Milford, 1925) and R. M. Davis (Univ. of Maine studies, 1927).

HUGHES, John (1677–1720)

Hughes was a friend of Addison, a contributor to the *Spectator*, a writer of political poems with a Whiggish flavour (*The Triumph of Peace*, 1697; *The Court of Neptune*, 1699; *The House of Nassau*, 1702), and an amateur musician, who did what he could to stem the popularity of Italian opera by writing librettos for operas and cantatas. His best work is his tragedy, *The Siege of Damascus* (1720), which was frequently revived during the following hundred years. He also published an interesting ed. of Spenser in 1715. A 2-vol. ed. of Hughes's poems, essays and librettos was published in 1735 with a life by W. Duncombe and an appreciation by Steele, rptd. from *The Theatre*, No. 15. This ed. also contains *The Siege of Damascus*. Hughes's letters were published in a 2-vol. collection called *Letters, by several eminent persons deceased*, 1772. The editor was J. Duncombe, who prepared an enlarged ed. in 3 vols. in 1773.

TICKELL, Thomas (1685–1740)

Tickell's name is remembered because he appears to have been "jockeyed" by Addison into meditating a translation of Homer which should rival Pope's. His translation of *Iliad*, Bk. i, was published in 1715 two days after Pope's translation. No more was published by Tickell and probably no more was written. It is not remarkably well done. Tickell's work is seen to much better advantage in his verses written on the death of Addison, published in his edition of Addison's *Works* (1721), in *An Epistle from a Lady in England to a Gentleman at Avignon* (1717), *Kensington Garden* (1722), *Lucy and Colin* (1725), and *On the Death of the Earl of Cadogan* (1726). His poems were first collected in *The Works of the most celebrated Minor Poets*, vol. 2, 1749, and were rptd. in Chalmers's *English Poets*. Many more were first printed by R. E. Tickell in his *Thomas Tickell and the Eighteenth Century Poets* (Constable, 1931), which besides a bibliography contains many interesting documents from the Tickell family papers. The story of the Homer controversy is told by G. Sherburn in his *Early Career of Alexander Pope* (Cl. P., 1934).

WATTS, Isaac (1674–1748)

Isaac Watts, a dissenting minister, is remembered because he wrote "When I survey the wondrous cross", "O God our help in ages past", and numerous other hymns, which he published in *Hymns and Spiritual Songs* (1707), and *The Psalms of David Imitated* (1719). Perhaps there are still some who read his *Divine Songs* (1715) in their childhood, a book which contains "How doth the little Busy Bee", "'Tis the Voice of the Sluggard", and "Let Dogs delight to Bark and Bite", all rptd. in O.B. These poems have overshadowed the undoubted merits of his *Horæ Lyricæ* (1706). An appreciation of Watts by V. de S. Pinto is published in E.S.M.E.A., vol. 20.

HYMN WRITERS

Many other famous hymns which appear in every collection were written during the eighteenth century. Addison's hymns are mentioned in another section (see p. 266). JOHN BYROM (1692–1763), a teacher of shorthand, was the author of "Christians, Awake", published in his *Miscellaneous Poems* (1773). JOHN and CHARLES WESLEY were both voluminous hymn writers. John, who published 23 collections between 1737 and 1786, was not so successful as Charles, who is said to have written over six thousand. Amongst these are "Come O Thou Traveller unknown", "Lo! He comes with clouds descending", "Hark! the herald Angels sing", "Christ, whose glory fills the skies", "Jesu, Lover of my soul", "Let saints on earth in concert sing", "Love Divine, all loves excelling", and "Gentle Jesus, meek and mild". PHILIP DODDRIDGE (1702–51), a nonconformist divine, wrote several hymns, of which "Hark the glad Sound! The Saviour comes", "O God of Bethel", and "Ye Servants of the Lord" are still sung. "Rock of Ages" (1776) was written by A. M. TOPLADY (1740–78), an acquaintance of Dr. Johnson, and "All hail the power of Jesu's name" (1780) by EDWARD PERRONET, a nonconformist minister. In 1779, JOHN NEWTON and WILLIAM COWPER published their *Olney Hymns*. This famous collection contains Newton's "How sweet the name of Jesus sounds", his "Glorious things of Thee are spoken", and Cowper's "Oh! for a closer walk with God", "God moves in a mysterious way", and "Hark, my soul! it is the Lord". JOHN KEBLE's *Christian Year*, which contains

"When God of old came down from Heaven" and other fine hymns, was published in 1827.

SWIFT, Jonathan. See p. 260.

POPE, Alexander (1688-1744)

Collected Works.

Pope published the first volume of his collected poems in 1717, and the second in 1735. Thereafter not a year passed until his death without some of his earlier writings being collected and republished in volume form. In 1751 his literary executor, William Warburton, later Bishop of Gloucester,(see p. 242) prepared an ed. in 9 vols., purporting to be complete and to contain Pope's final corrections; but every subsequent editor has added some piece to the canon. The standard ed. is in 10 vols. (1871–89), ed. W. Elwin and W. J. Courthope. A more complete ed. of the poetry in 6 vols. is in preparation under the general editorship of J. Butt; the fourth vol., containing the *Imitations of Horace, An Epistle to Dr. Arbuthnot*, and *The Epilogue to the Satires* (ed. J. Butt, Methuen, 1939), is published, and vol. 2, *The Rape of the Lock, Eloisa to Abelard*, (ed. G. Tillotson) is in the press. The best 1-vol. edd. of the poetry are the "Globe", ed. A. W. Ward, and H. W. Boynton's (1903).

Early Poetry.

Pope's first published poems, the *Pastorals*, appeared in the sixth part of Tonson's *Miscellany*, 1709. *An Essay on Criticism* was published in 1711 (ed. J. C. Collins, Macmillan, 1896) and in 1712 *The Messiah* appeared in *The Spectator* (No. 378), and the first form of *The Rape of the Lock*, with other poems by Pope, in Lintott's *Miscellany*. *Windsor Forest* was published in 1713, the enlarged form of *The Rape of the Lock* in 1714 (ed. G. Holden, Cl. P., 1909), and *The Temple of Fame* in 1715. These poems were rptd. in the collected works (1717) with *Verses to the Memory of an Unfortunate Lady* and *Eloisa to Abelard*.

Translation of Homer.

The first four books of *The Iliad of Homer, Translated by Mr. Pope*, were published with a preface, an essay on Homer, and observations on each book in 1715. Further vols. were published in 1716,

1717, 1718, and the translation was completed in 6 vols. in 1720. In translating *The Odyssey*, Pope was assisted by Fenton (see p. 178), who translated Books I, IV, XIX, XX, and by Broome (see p. 178), who translated Books II, VI, VIII, XI, XII, XVI, XVIII, XXIII, and prepared all the notes. The first fourteen books were published in 3 vols. in 1725, the remainder in two more vols. in 1726. The most convenient modern rpt. of Pope's Homer is in W.C. (2 vols.).

Editorial Work.

In the meanwhile, Pope had prepared for the press the poems of his friend Thomas Parnell (see p. 170). The ed. was published with a prefatory epistle in verse to the Earl of Oxford—one of the best of Pope's shorter poems—in 1721. In 1723 he performed the same work for another friend, John Sheffield, Duke of Buckingham, and applied the same principles to Shakespeare, his ed. of the plays in 6 vols. being published in 1725. Pope was Shakespeare's second editor. Although the ed. is bad when judged by modern standards, it provides interesting evidence of Pope's taste (see J. Butt, *Pope's Taste in Shakespeare*, O.U.P., 1936).

Later Poetry.

Pope's *Shakespeare* was adversely criticised by Lewis Theobald in *Shakespeare Restored* (1726). Pope resented the criticism and punished Theobald by making him King of the Dunces in his new poem, *The Dunciad. An Heroic Poem. In Three Books*, published anonymously in 1728. *The Dunciad* was issued in an enlarged form in 1729 with the title *The Dunciad Variorum. With the Prolegomena of Scriblerus.* The apparatus of scholarship burlesqued in prefaces, footnotes, appendices, and index, was used not only to continue the attacks upon Pope's numerous victims but also to sharpen the satire on pedantry.

In 1731 Pope published the first of the poems later incorporated into his unfinished plan of a book of *Ethic Epistles;* this was the Epistle to the Earl of Burlington (*Moral Essay*, IV). Three more of the same group were published in 1733, *Of the Use of Riches, An Epistle to . . . Lord Bathurst* (*Moral Essay*, III) and the first three parts of *An Essay on Man*, published anonymously, and completed with a fourth part in 1734 (ed. M. Pattison, Cl. P., 1866).

At the same time Pope found it necessary to defend himself from attacks made on the publication of the Epistle to Burlington.

This he did in *The First Satire of the Second Book of Horace, Imitated* (1733), a poem which provoked further attacks. Pope answered these and others in *An Epistle to Dr. Arbuthnot* (1735), his 'Apologia pro Vita Sua'. The application of Horace's words to modern times proved so congenial to Pope that he started a series of *Imitations of Horace*, nine being published between 1734 and 1739 (ed. M. Pattison Cl. P., 1872 with *An Epistle to Dr. Arbuthnot*, and the *Epilogue to the Satires*, and ed. J. Butt, Methuen, 1939). The best of this brilliant series is *The First Epistle of the Second Book of Horace, Imitated* (the Epistle to Augustus), 1737. The *Imitations of Horace* were rounded off with *The Epilogue to the Satires* (1738), two dialogues upon which Pope is said to have spent more care in correcting than on any other of his poems.

The *Imitations of Horace* did not entirely distract Pope's attention from the *Ethic Epistles*. *An Epistle To . . . Viscount Cobham. Of the Knowledge and Characters of Men* (*Moral Essay*, I) was published in 1734 and *Of the Characters of Women* (*Moral Essay*, II) in 1735. Some material towards a verse essay on education was incorporated in the fourth book of *The Dunciad* (1742). In 1743 *The Dunciad* was issued in a completely revised form, Theobald dethroned, and Colley Cibber (see p. 301) crowned in his stead.

Space forbids an account of Pope's lesser poems, but mention must be made of the recent additions to the canon published by N. Ault in *Pope's Own Miscellany* (Nonesuch Press, 1935). Though critics are not agreed in accepting all Mr. Ault's attributions, he has discovered a considerable number of poems undoubtedly by Pope.

Prose.

There is some justification for suspecting that when Pope wrote letters he usually wrote with an eye to future publication. The letter, for him as for Voiture, was the least formal style of writing consistent with elegance. His letters to Cromwell had been printed without his consent in 1726, and a further batch of letters to Wycherley was published in 1729. Pope would have liked more to be published, but he thought it unsuitable to appear responsible for the publication; so acting under a pseudonym, he managed to persuade Curll the publisher to buy the letters in printed sheets and offer them for sale. Curll did so and published them in 1735. Pope was thus able to object that the publication was surreptitious and that he was forced to put out an authorised ed., which eventually appeared in 1737 (see C. W. Dilke, *Papers of a Critic* (1875), i. 287 ff.). The letters occupy four and a half vols. in the Elwin-Courthope ed. This is the best ed., but it is far from complete, the text is impure, and the dating inaccurate. A new ed. is in preparation by G. Sherburn.

Pope's other prose works have been collected by N. Ault (vol. 1, Blackwell, 1936; vol. 2 not yet published). They consist of satires upon pedantry and bad poetry, periodical essays contributed to *The Spectator* and *The Guardian*, prefaces, and replies to his enemies' attacks. The best of them are *The Art of Sinking in Poetry* (1728) and *A Letter to a Noble Lord* (written 1733; published, 1751).

Biography.

Material for a life of Pope was collected from Pope himself and from his friends by Joseph Spence, who first met Pope about 1728. The life was never written, but Spence's collections were made use of by Dr. Johnson, who wrote the best of the eighteenth-century biographies of Pope in *The Lives of the Poets*. The collections themselves were edited by S. W. Singer and published in 1820 with the title, *Anecdotes . . . of Books and Men*. This is still the best ed. Two nineteenth-century biographies deserve mention, those of R. Carruthers (1853, revised ed. 1857) and of W. J. Courthope (1889, vol. 5 of the Elwin-Courthope ed.); but it should be borne in mind that knowledge, as opposed to understanding, of Pope was increasing throughout the century—partly as a result of the researches of C. W. Dilke, collected in *Papers of a Critic* (1875)—and that therefore early biographies are necessarily defective in point of fact. Much the best is G. Sherburn's *The Early Career of Alexander Pope* (Cl. P., 1934), which unfortunately goes no further than 1727. Edith Sitwell's brightly coloured biography (Faber, 1930) is sympathetic in approach, but adds nothing to our knowledge of Pope.

Criticism.

The earliest full-length study of Pope's poetry is Joseph Warton's *Essay on the Genius and Writings of Pope* (first vol. 1756, second vol. 1782). Though not so unsympathetic as historians tell us, it is garrulous and digressive, interesting chiefly as a document in contemporary taste. See studies by E. Morley in E.S.M.E.A., vol. 9 (1923) and W. D. MacClintock (O.U.P., 1933). No other had been written until the Cl. P. published a valuable study by G. Tillotson, entitled *On the Poetry of Pope*. Another, by R. K. Root, entitled *The Poetical Career of Alexander Pope*, has recently (1938) been published by O.U.P.

Amongst the shorter studies, Hazlitt's lecture in *Lectures on the English Poets* (1818; ed. F. W. Baxter, 1929) must be given pride of place. W. P. Ker's lecture in *The Art of Poetry* (Cl. P., 1923), two *Leslie Stephen* lectures by Lytton Strachey (1925) and J. W. Mackail (1919; rptd. in *Studies of English Poets*, Longmans, 1926), and a lecture by D. Nichol Smith in *Some Observations on Eighteenth-Century Poetry* (O.U.P., 1937) are all admirable; so are two recent 'leaders' in T.L.S. (August 10, 1933, on *The Essay on Man*, and October 25, 1934). Of the more specialised studies, the most important is R. H. Griffith's invaluable *Alexander Pope: A Bibliography* (first vol. 1922; second vol. 1927; a third vol. of Popeana is promised.) Mention must also be made of A. Warren's *Alexander Pope as Critic and Humanist* (O.U.P., 1929) and E. Audra's *L'Influence française dans l'œuvre de Pope* (Champion, 1931).

"The School of Pope".

The School of Pope is a phrase sometimes used by critics of Wordsworth in contemptuous but unspecified dismissal of eighteenth-century poetry. As a matter of fact, few of the major poets of the century can be said to have imitated Pope. Amongst the minor poets, several attained a decent level of sharp and witty satire in Pope's manner. Of these may be mentioned JAMES BRAMSTON (1694-1744), who published *The Art of Politicks* in 1729, and *The Man of Taste* in 1733; JAMES MILLER (1706-44), whose *Harlequin-Horace* (1731) may have helped Pope in the composition of the *Epistle to Dr. Arbuthnot*; and PAUL WHITEHEAD (1710-74) who, as a warning to Pope, was summoned before the House of Lords in 1739 to answer for a satire called *Manners*, which had been deemed libellous. An earlier satire of his, *The State Dunces*, inscribed to Pope, had been published in 1733. Miller also produced two successful adaptations of Molière, *The Mother-in-Law* (1734) and *The Man of Taste* (1735). He collaborated with Henry Baker in a translation of Molière (10 vols., 1739), of which a two-vol. selection is rptd. in E.L.

Another admirer of Pope's works was SIR CHARLES HANBURY WILLIAMS (1708-59), who sometimes wrote satires in Pope's manner and sometimes allowed himself greater metrical variety. He was perhaps the most clever of the satirists whose sympathies lay with Walpole's government. An ed. of his poems in 3 vols., with notes by Horace Walpole, was published in 1822. Two lyrics written in the manner of Prior are rptd. in O.B. His life by Lord Ilchester and Mrs. Langford-Brooke was published by Butterworth (1928).

There are two more satellites of Pope who deserve a brief notice: ELIJAH FENTON (1683–1730) and WILLIAM BROOME (1689–1745). The assistance which they gave to Pope in translating the *Odyssey* has already been mentioned (see p. 174). In addition, each published his vol. of poems, Fenton in 1707, Broome in 1727. Fenton's greatest success was his tragedy, *Mariamne* (1723), and his best piece of work was his ed. of Waller's poems (1729). Broome on the other hand was uniformly mediocre. The life of each was written by Dr. Johnson.

JOHNSON, Samuel. See p. 221.

THOMSON, James (1700–48)

Thomson's first published poem was *Winter* (1726). *Summer* followed in 1727, and *Spring* in 1728. A collected ed. of *The Seasons*, which contained the first printing of *Autumn* and the *Hymn*, was issued in 1730. Thomson revised the text several times, gradually eradicating all traces of Deism. His revisions can be most conveniently studied in O. Zippel's ed. (Berlin, 1908). *The Castle of Indolence*, in which Thomson used Spenser's stanza with great success, was published in 1748. *Rule Britannia* is to be found in the second act of his *Alfred: A Masque* (1740). Thomson also wrote five tragedies, which were well received: *Sophonisba* (1730), *Agamemnon* (1738), *Edward and Eleonora* (1739), which was banned by the censor, *Tancred and Sigismunda* (1745), generally regarded as his best play, and *Coriolanus* (1749). His collected works were published with a memoir by his friend Murdoch in 1762. The best modern ed. (of the poems only) is by J. L. Robertson (O.S.A.) 1908.

Thomson's life was written by Dr. Johnson. L. Morel's *James Thomson, Sa Vie et Ses Œuvres* (Hachette, 1895) is the most detailed study of the poet. G. C. Macaulay's volume in E.M.L. is excellent; so is J. W. Mackail's lecture in his *Studies of English Poets* (Longmans, 1926), and D. Nichol Smith's in his *Some Observations on Eighteenth-Century Poetry* (O.U.P., 1937).

MALLET, David; originally MALLOCH (1705–65)

Mallet had been a fellow-student with Thomson in Edinburgh, and was closely associated with him at the time when *The Seasons* was being written. It is therefore not surprising that Mallet's work in *The Excursion* (1728), should resemble Thomson's in subject and style. Five years later he was writing in moderately successful imitation of Pope, to whom he addressed a satire on

Bentley and Theobald, called *Of Verbal Criticism* (1733). His most famous poem is *William and Margaret*, a ballad written about the year 1723 (rptd. in O.B.). Mallet also wrote for the stage—his *Eurydice* was produced in 1731, and his *Mustapha* in 1739—and published lives of Bacon (1740) and of Bolingbroke (1752). A collection of his works in one vol. was published in 1743, and an ed. in 3 vols. was published in 1759.

DYER, John (1700–58)

It is a pity that Dyer is usually remembered by one poem, and that not his best, *Grongar Hill* (1726), a pretty imitation of Milton's *L'Allegro*. There is better work in *The Ruins of Rome* (1740), and in *The Fleece* (1757), another "georgic" in the tradition which John Philips (see p. 168) had resuscitated with his *Cider*. The most famous tribute paid to Dyer is Wordsworth's sonnet, "Bard of the Fleece". An ed. of his poems with a preface by Edward Thomas was published in 1903, and they are rptd. with the poems of Lady Winchilsea and others in E.L. (see under Lady Winchilsea, p. 169), but the best ed. is still that of R. A. Wilmott (with Akenside's poems in one vol., 1855).

SOMERVILLE, William (1675–1742)

ARMSTRONG, John (1709–79)

Other "georgic" imitators were Somerville, whose racy poem *The Chase* (1735) is said to contain good advice on the management of hounds, and certainly conveys the exhilarating effect of a day's hunting; and Armstrong, a Scottish physician, who published *The Art of Preserving Health*, a blank verse poem in four books, in 1744. A bibliography and appreciation of Armstrong's writings is included in I. A. Williams's *Seven XVIIIth-Century Bibliographies* (Dulau, 1924).

GREEN, Matthew (1696–1737)

Green's witty poem, *The Spleen* (1737), provides instruction in the use of retired leisure. It has been edited by W. H. Williams (Methuen, 1936). An ed. of Green's poems was made by R. K. Wood (Cayme Press, 1925), and they have been rptd. with the poems of Lady Winchilsea, Dyer, and others in E.L. (see under Lady Winchilsea, p. 169).

SHENSTONE, William (1714–63)

Shenstone included *The School-Mistress*, an intentionally

ludicrous imitation of Spenser's style, in *Poems upon Various Occasions* (1737). The poem was enlarged from 12 to 28 stanzas, and published in a separate octavo in 1742. Further additions were made when it was printed in Dodsley's *Collection of Poems*, (1748). The first two versions are rptd. in C. E. de Haas's *Nature and the Country in English Poetry of the first Half of the Eighteenth Century* (Amsterdam, 1928). Shenstone's works were collected in 2 vols. in 1764; a third containing some of his letters was added in 1769. There is no modern ed. of his poetry, but his best poems, *Pastoral Ballad*, and *Written at an Inn at Henley*, are rptd. in O.B. A selection from his prose entitled *Men and Manners* was edited by Havelock Ellis for the Golden Cockerel Press in 1927. M. Williams, who wrote a life of Shenstone in 1935 (Cornish), has recently prepared an ed. of his letters (Blackwell, 1939); another by D. Mallam has been published by Minnesota and O.U.P. (1939). There is a life of Shenstone by Dr. Johnson, an essay on him by W. H. Hutton in *Burford Papers* (1905), a literary 'portrait' by A. R. Humphreys (C.U.P., 1937), and a bibliography by I. A. Williams in *Seven XVIIIth-Century Bibliographies* (Dulau, 1924).

GLOVER, Richard (1712–85)

Glover's contemporary fame rested on a blank verse epic entitled *Leonidas* (1737), which was well received by those who opposed Walpole's government because they detected in it a reflection of their own "patriotic" ardour. A revised ed. was published in 1770, and enlarged from nine to twelve books. More readable is a ballad called *Admiral Hosier's Ghost* (1739) which was rptd. in Percy's *Reliques*. No one has yet undertaken to edit the works of Glover or to write his life.

YOUNG, Edward (1683–1765)

The best of the early poems of Young is a series of satires entitled *The Universal Passion* (1725) and written in a manner which Pope was scarcely to improve when he wrote his *Moral Essays*. But Young's most famous work, *Night Thoughts* (1742–5), a blank verse poem in nine books, appealed to a newer taste for meditations upon mortality. Its popularity both at home and abroad—it was translated into most of the European languages—was second only to Shakespeare's, and though its fame has long since ebbed, it has left its mark with several proverbs of which the best known is "Procrastination is the Thief of Time". There has been no ed. of Young's poetry in recent years. Probably the

Aldine ed., first published in 1830–6 with a life by J. Mitford, is the most easily obtained.

Young also wrote for the stage. Two tragedies, *Busiris* (1719) and *The Revenge* (1721), were popular in his own day and for long after.

In his *Conjectures on Original Composition* (1759) Young showed that he had renounced his allegiance to the Augustan principles of his youth. The essay has been edited by E. J. Morley (Manchester U.P., 1918) and is rptd. in the first W.C. volume of *English Critical Essays*. The standard biography is by H. C. Shelley (Pitman, 1914). A lecture on Young by J. W. Mackail is included in his *Studies of English Poets* (Longmans, 1926).

GRAY, Thomas (1716–71)

The first attempt to collect the writings of Gray was made by his friend William Mason (see p. 182) in 1775. This ed. was far from complete, and subsequent editors (T. J. Mathias, 2 vols., 1814; J. Mitford, 5 vols., 1836–43) each made considerable additions. At present the standard ed. is that of Sir Edmund Gosse (Macmillan, 4 vols., 1884; revised 1902–6), but it is not entirely trustworthy.

The *Ode on a Distant Prospect of Eton College*, written in 1742, was the first of Gray's English poems to be printed (1747). It was rptd. in the following year in Dodsley's *Collection of Poems*, together with the *Ode on Spring* and the *Ode on the Death of a Favourite Cat*. The *Elegy* was published in 1751, *The Bard* and *The Progress of Poesy* in 1757. The best ed. of the English Poems is by D. C. Tovey (C.U.P., 1898; revised, 1904). There is also a good ed., with Collins's poetry in the same volume, by A. L. Poole (O.S.A.); M.L. includes Gray's poems with those of Johnson, Collins, and Goldsmith in one vol.; and E.L. and the Cl. P. publish selections of Gray's letters with his poems. An elaborate ed. of the *Elegy* has been prepared by F. G. Stokes (Cl. P. 1929).

The standard ed. of Gray's letters is by P. Toynbee and L. Whibley (Cl. P., 3 vols., 1935). A selection is published in W.C.

Gray's life was written by his friend, Mason (1775), and later by Dr. Johnson. Gosse's biography in E.M.L. is inaccurate. The only trustworthy account is Roger Martin's *Chronologie de la Vie et de l'Œuvre de Thomas Gray* (O.U.P., 1931). Martin has also published an *Essai sur Thomas Gray* (O.U.P., 1934). The title of A. L. Reed's *Background of Gray's Elegy* (O.U.P., 1924) sufficiently indicates its theme. A brilliant study of the *Elegy* was

published in T.L.S. (July 27, 1933). A bibliography was compiled by C. S. Northup (O.U.P., 1917).

BLAIR, Robert (1699–1746)

The Grave (1743), a sombre poem in blank verse, by Robert
Blair, a Scottish minister, was frequently printed with Gray's
Elegy. There has been no ed. in recent times.

MASON, William (1725–97)

Mason is now remembered only as the friend and biographer
of Gray, but his reputation as a poet seemed sufficiently well
founded to most of his contemporaries. *Elfrida* (1752), a dramatic
poem, "written on the model of the ancient Greek tragedy",
was not intended for the stage, but was a considerable success
when produced in 1772. Its companion, *Caractacus* (1759), was
patriotic rather than pathetic, and was intended to show the
mingling of "Attic art with Shakespeare's fire". Mason's recent
biographer, J. W. Draper, tells us that these two dramatic poems
were regarded as classics for half a century. *Elfrida* contained
some odes, the success of which prompted Mason to publish
a vol. of Pindarics (1756). A vol. of *Elegies* was published in
1763, and a collected ed. of his poems in 1764. Mason's longest
poem, *the English Garden*, began to appear in 1772, subsequent
instalments being published in 1777, 1779 and 1781. It is
one of the many "didactic" poems written during the century
(see pp. 168, 179, 190). Mason also wrote several satires, of which
the most famous was *An Heroic Epistle to Sir William Chambers* (1773).
This poem was published with notes by Horace Walpole. An ed.
by P. Toynbee is published by Cl. P. (1926). A 4-vol. ed. of
Mason's works appeared in 1811.

There is an elaborately minute study of Mason's work by
J. W. Draper called *William Mason. A Study in Eighteenth-Century
Culture* (New York U.P., 1924).

COLLINS, William (1721–59)

Collins published his first vol. of poems, *Persian Eclogues*,
in 1742 and his *Odes* in 1746 (1747 on title page). His longest
poem, and one of the most remarkable, *An Ode on the Popular
Superstitions of the Highlands of Scotland*, was first printed in the
transactions of the Royal Society of Edinburgh in 1788. The
best editions of Collins's poems are those of W. C. Bronson
(Ginn, 1898) and Edmund Blunden (Haslewood Books, 1929).
There are cheaper editions obtainable in O.M. (ed. C. Stone,

1907), in the O.S.A. series (with Gray's poems in one vol.), in M.L. (with the poems of Johnson, Gray, and Goldsmith), and in E.L. (with the poems of Lady Winchilsea, Parnell, Dyer, and Green).

Collins's life was written by his friend, Dr. Johnson. The best modern biographies are Blunden's 'study' prefixed to his ed. of the poems, and E. G. Ainsworth's *Poor Collins* (O.U.P., 1937). *Collins, and the English Lyric in the Eighteenth Century* is the subject of one of J. W. Mackail's lectures (*Studies of English Poets*, Longmans, 1926), and a Warton lecture by H. W. Garrod on Collins's poetry (1928) was expanded into a book (Cl. P., 1928). An essay by A.S.P. Woodhouse on *Collins and the Creative Imagination* is printed in *Studies in English by Members of University College, Toronto* (O.U.P., 1931). I. A. Williams includes a bibliography of Collins in his *Seven XVIIIth-Century Bibliographies* (Dulau, 1924).

WARTON, Joseph (1722–1800)
WARTON, Thomas (1728–90)

Closely associated with Collins were Joseph and Thomas Warton, sons of Thomas Warton (1688–1745), professor of poetry at Oxford, whose poems they published in 1747 (a facsimile of this book was published by the Facsimile Text Society, New York, in 1931). Joseph Warton, later headmaster of Winchester, published a poem called *The Enthusiast* in 1744, whose title rightly suggests that its author was flying a flag of romantic defiance. He and Collins had planned a joint volume of Odes, almost a *Lyrical Ballads* of experiment and reform; but eventually each published his odes separately in 1746. Warton's critical work on Pope has already been mentioned (see p. 176); he also edited Sidney's *Apology for Poetry* (1787) and commenced an ed. of Dryden, his notes being incorporated in the 1811 ed. A vol. of biographical memoirs with selections from his poems and letters was prepared by J. Wooll (1806).

Thomas Warton, professor of poetry and of ancient history at Oxford, published his *Pleasures of Melancholy* in 1747 and collected his poems in 1777. These contain the sonnets which Hazlitt thought some of the finest in the language; three are rptd. in O.B. with his *Verses on Sir Joshua Reynolds's Painted Window at New College, Oxford* (1782). Much of his poetry was inspired by his antiquarian pursuits. His *Observations on the Faerie Queene* (1754) is the first adequate criticism of Spenser, and his ed. of Milton's minor poems (1785) is an excellent piece of work; but his *magnum opus* is the *History of English Poetry* (3 vols., 1774–81; ed. W. C.

Hazlitt, 4 vols., 1871), a task handed on to him from Pope and Gray, which he completed as far as the end of the Elizabethan age. His poems were edited with a memoir and notes by R. Mant (2 vols., 1802), and his life has been written by C. Rinaker (University of Illinois, 1916). His memory is honoured in the British Academy Warton Lectures on English Poetry, of which four have been devoted to the study of his work: W. P. Ker's *Thomas Warton* (1910), rptd. in his *Collected Essays* (Macmillan, 1925), Sir E. Gosse's *Two Pioneers of Romanticism* (1915), D. Nichol Smith's *Warton's History of English Poetry* (1929), and L. C. Martin's *Thomas Warton and the Early Poems of Milton* (1934). E. Partridge's *The Three Wartons* (Scholartis Press, 1927) contains a selection from their poems, an essay and a bibliography.

AKENSIDE, Mark (1721–70)

With the Wartons may be mentioned Mark Akenside. His *Pleasures of Imagination*, a blank verse poem in three books, was published in 1744, and his *Odes* in the following year. The first collected ed. (1772) contains a fourth book of the *Pleasures of Imagination* and additional odes. There has been no ed. of the poems in recent times. Probably one of the Aldine editions, first published in 1835 with a good biography by A. Dyce, is the most readily obtainable (see also under Dyer, p. 179). A bibliography and appreciation of Akenside's writings is contained in I. A. Williams's *Seven XVIIIth-Century Bibliographies* (Dulau, 1924).

SMART, Christopher (1722–71)

More sublimely imaginative is *A Song to David* by Christopher Smart, published in 1763. It has been rptd. with a selection from Smart's other poems, and with a biographical and critical preface, by Edmund Blunden (Cobden-Sanderson, 1924). It is also to be found in O.B. Some recently discovered writings entitled *Rejoice in the Lamb*, have been published by Cape, ed. W. F. Stead, 1939. An edition of Smart's poems by R. E. Brittain is in preparation. *The Case of Christopher Smart* is the title of an English Association Pamphlet (no. 90, 1934) by Laurence Binyon.

LYTTELTON, George, Lord (1709–73)

Lyttelton's best poem—commended by Gray—is his *Monody*, written on his wife's death in 1747. He was also the author of *Blenheim* (1728), a poem on the Duke of Marlborough's seat; *An Epistle to Mr. Pope from a young gentleman at Rome* (1730);

184

The Progress of Love (1732); and *Advice to a Lady* (1733). Lyttelton's prose writings were perhaps more widely read. His *Letters from a Persian in England to his Friend at Ispahan* (1735), which were modelled on Montesquieu's *Lettres Persanes*, reached a fifth ed. in 1744; *Observations on the Conversion of St. Paul* (1747), 'a treatise to which infidelity has never been able to fabricate a specious answer' (Johnson), reached a ninth ed. in 1799; and *Dialogues of the Dead* (1760), suggested by the writings of Lucian, Fenelon, and Fontenelle, reached a fifth ed. in 1768. His most ambitious work was *The History of the Life of Henry II* (1767). The collected writings, ed. G. E. Ayscough, were published in 1774.

Lyttelton's life has been written by Dr. Johnson, Sir R. J. Phillimore (1845), and A. V. Rao (*A Minor Augustan*, Calcutta Book Co., 1934). There is a good essay on Lyttelton in S. C. Roberts's *An Eighteenth-Century Gentleman* (C.U.P., 1930).

CHURCHILL, Charles (1731–64)

The most effective satirist between the times of Pope and Byron was Churchill. He made his reputation with *The Rosciad* (1761), and followed it up with a spate of satires, of which his admirers prefer *The Ghost* (1762–3), in which Dr. Johnson is lampooned as "Pomposo" (ii. 653 ff.), *The Prophecy of Famine* (1763), *Gotham* and *The Candidate* (1764). A collected ed. of his poems was published by W. Tooke in 1804. Tooke's notes are incorporated into the various Aldine editions, one of which is still the easiest collection of his poems to find in the second-hand bookshops. The best ed. is by James Laver (Eyre and Spottiswoode, 2 vols., 1933). A bibliography of Churchill's poems is included in I. A. Williams's *Seven XVIIIth-Century Bibliographies* (Dulau, 1924).

GIFFORD, William (1756–1826)

At least one more satirist before the time of Byron is worth reading. Gifford was a sour man of considerable ability. He translated Juvenal, edited the plays of Ben Jonson, Massinger, and Ford, and conducted *The Anti-Jacobin* and *The Quarterly*. His *Baviad* (1791), an imitation of the first satire of Persius, and *Maeviad* (1795), an imitation of the tenth satire of the first book of Horace, "squabashed—in Sir Walter Scott's phrase—at one blow a set of coxcombs, who might have humbugged the world long enough". These were ROBERT MERRY and his "Della Cruscan" friends, who cultivated the exchange of amorous poetical inanities.

WOLCOT, John (1738–1819)

Another sufferer from Gifford's satirical attentions was John Wolcot, who wrote under the name of Peter Pindar. In 1785 he had commenced an heroi-comic poem on George III's private life called *The Lousiad* (5th canto published 1795), whose success incited him to produce further satires of the same kind, such as *Ode upon Ode, or A Peep at Saint James's* (1787). Gifford's loyal counter-attack was entitled *An Epistle to Peter Pindar* (1800). Wolcot had practised for many years both as priest and physician before he set up as a satirist. His earliest successes were a series of *Lyric Odes to the Royal Academicians* (1782–6). He also satirised Boswell—"the pilot of our literary whale"—in *A Poetical and Congratulatory Epistle to James Boswell, Esq., on his Journal of a Tour to the Hebrides* (1786) and in *Bozzy and Piozzi, or the British Biographers* (1786), Sir Joseph Banks (see p. 284), James Bruce (see p. 284), Hannah More (see p. 305), and several other contemporary figures. A 4-vol. ed. of his works was published in 1794–6, and one in 5 vols. in 1812.

FALCONER, William (1732–69)

Falconer's *The Shipwreck* (1762) is an odd phenomenon. It is a poem in three cantos, the work of a sailor who had determined to record his experiences in the heroic measures of Pope's *Odyssey.* The poem was well received by the reviewers and reached a third (enlarged) ed. in 1769, but Falconer expressed his disappointment "that the gentlemen of the sea, for whose entertainment it was chiefly calculated, have hardly made one-tenth of the purchasers." *The Shipwreck* is rptd. in the Aldine Poets (see any barrow of second-hand books) with a life by J. Mitford.

GOLDSMITH, Oliver (1728–74)

The *Miscellaneous Works* of Goldsmith were first collected in 1775. The contents have been enlarged in subsequent editions, but none is complete. The best are those of Peter Cunningham (4 vols., 1854) and J. W. M. Gibbs (Bohn Library, 5 vols., 1884-6). A new ed. is being prepared by R. S. Crane and A. Friedman.

Goldsmith's best poems are *The Traveller* (1764, dated 1765), *The Deserted Village* (1769; 1770 on the title page), and *Retaliation* (1774). They are collected with other poems in Austin Dobson's excellent ed. (O.S.A.), in the same editor's W.C. and E.L. editions (the E.L. vol. also contains the plays and certain essays), in a vol.

of M.L. with the poems of Johnson, Gray, and Collins, and in a vol. of the Globe Library (ed. D. Masson) with the essays, the plays, and *The Vicar of Wakefield*—this is the most convenient one-vol. selection.

Goldsmith's comedies, *The Good Natur'd Man* (1768), and *She Stoops to Conquer* (1773), are printed with *The Vicar of Wakefield* (1766), in one vol. of O.S.A., ed. C. E. Doble and G. Ostler, as well as in the E.L. and Globe editions of the poems. The best amongst recent editions of *The Vicar* is O. Doughty's (Scholartis Press, 1928). It is also rptd. in W.C., E.L., and The Globe Library (mentioned above).

His two periodical essays, *The Bee* (Oct. 6 to Nov. 24, 1759), and *The Citizen of the World* (1762), are printed with his *Life of Richard Nash, of Bath, Esq.* (1762), in one vol. of O.S.A., as well as in the Globe Library. Eighteen new essays were discovered and published by R. S. Crane in 1927 (University of Chicago Press). Goldsmith also wrote (besides many lesser works) *An Enquiry into the Present State of Polite Learning in Europe* (1759), *An History of England, in a series of letters from a nobleman to his son* (1764), and *An History of the Earth, and Animated Nature* (1774). His *Collected Letters* have been edited by K. C. Balderston (C.U.P., 1928).

Dr. Johnson had once intended to write Goldsmith's life, but he never fulfilled his purpose (see A. Tillotson's *Dr. Johnson and the "Life of Goldsmith"*, M.L.R., Oct., 1933). The best biographies are those of Prior (1837), Forster (1848), and Dobson ("Great Writers" series, 1888). A bibliography of Goldsmith's writings is included in I. A. Williams's *Seven XVIIIth-Century Bibliographies* (Dulau, 1924).

MACPHERSON, James (1736–96)

No one any longer disputes that Macpherson mixed about six parts of his own imaginative work with one part of genuine Gaelic ballads to produce his *Ossian*. He published fifteen *Fragments of Ancient Poetry, collected in the Highlands of Scotland* in 1760, with a preface by Hugh Blair, an Edinburgh professor, who wrote a *Critical Dissertation on the Poems of Ossian* in 1763. *Fingal* followed in 1762, *Temora* in 1763, and the collected *Works of Ossian* in 1765. They were ed. W. Sharp in 1896. The fullest biographical study of Macpherson is T. B. Saunders's *Life and Letters of J.M.* (1894). J. S. Smart's critical study was published by Nutt in 1905, and there is an excellent chapter on his work in E. D. Snyder's *The Celtic Revival* (O.U.P., 1923).

PERCY, Thomas (1729–1811)

The most remarkable literary event of the "sixty" decade was the publication of a large 3-vol. collection of old ballads by Thomas Percy in 1765 with the title, *Reliques of Ancient English Poetry*. It is recorded here partly because of its immense influence on subsequent romantic poetry, partly because it contains some of Percy's own poetry in imitation of the ballad style. The *Reliques* reached a fourth ed., revised by Percy's nephew, in 1794, and has since been ed. in 3 vols. by H. B. Wheatley (1891); it is also included in 2 vols. of E.L. An ed. of the Folio Manuscript from which Percy derived most of his ballads was published by J. W. Hales and F. J. Furnivall in 4 vols. in 1867–8, and re-issued in the King's Classics series, ed. I. Gollancz, 4 vols., 1905–10. An ed. of Percy's correspondence with Farmer (see p. 220) and Malone (see p. 221) is being prepared for the University of Louisiana Press under the general editorship of D. Nichol Smith.

CHATTERTON, Thomas (1752–70)

Another publication which shows the increasing interest in medieval literature was the archaic "Rowley Poems" of Thomas Chatterton, ed. T. Tyrwhitt, the Chaucerian Scholar, in 1777. Tyrwhitt's third ed. (1778) includes an appendix which states that these "fakes" were wholly Chatterton's work, but there were still some who believed in the authenticity of an original Rowley until W. W. Skeat showed in the preface to his ed. of Chatterton's complete works (modernised text, 2 vols., 1871) that "the poems exhibit a phraseology such as no human ingenuity can translate into fifteenth-century English without completely recasting them." Another ed. of the complete words (also in modernised text) by H. D. Roberts is published in 2 vols. of M.L. (1906). The Rowley poems alone have been edited for the Cl. P. by M.E. Hare (1911). The best biographies of Chatterton are those of Sir Daniel Wilson (1869) and E. H. W. Meyerstein (Ingpen and Grant, 1930). A bibliography compiled from the excellent collection in the Bristol Free Libraries is included in E. R. Norris Mathew's *Bristol Bibliography* (1916).

BEATTIE, James (1735–1803)

James Beattie, professor of moral philosophy at Marischal College, Aberdeen, published his most famous poem, *The Minstrel*, in 1771 (Book 2, 1774). The poem is written in the Spenserian stanza and served to show Byron that that measure would suit his purpose in *Childe Harold's Pilgrimage*. It describes the education of an elder brother of Wordsworth's Lucy, and is a highly interesting example of contemporary taste. Gray's detailed criticism of the poem is found in a letter to Beattie, dated March 8, 1771. Sir William Forbes's uncritical life of Beattie (2 vols. 1806) cannot be recommended with any enthusiasm, though it is not wholly devoid of interest.

COWPER, William (1731–1800)

Cowper's *Olney Hymns* (1779) have already been mentioned (p. 172). He published a vol. of satires in 1782, and another vol., containing *The Task* and *The History of John Gilpin*, in 1785. *On the Receipt of my Mother's Picture* and *The Dog and the Water Lily* were issued together in 1798. The most complete ed. of Cowper's writings (including his translation of Homer, 1791) is Southey's in 15 vols. (1835–7). The best edd. of his poems are those of J. C. Bailey (Methuen, 1905) and H. S. Milford (O.S.A., revised ed. 1934).

Cowper is one of the best "familiar" letter-writers of the time. No entirely satisfactory ed. exists. The most complete is that of T. Wright (4 vols., Hodder and Stoughton, 1904), who ed. a further volume of unpublished letters in 1925 (Farncombe). A new edition is being prepared by N. Campbell. There are 1-vol. selections in W.C. and E.L.

Wright has also written a documented life of Cowper (Farncombe; second ed., 1921). The best biographical study is Lord David Cecil's *The Stricken Deer* (Constable, 1929).

HAYLEY, William (1745–1820)

Hayley, the friend and first biographer of Cowper, was himself a poet, but his verses were more numerous than meritorious. By 1788 he had already written enough to fill six octavo volumes of *Poems and Plays*. The most popular of his poems was *The Triumphs of Temper* (1781) "intended to promote the cultivation of good-humour". It is a weak imitation of Pope's *Rape of the Lock. An Essay on Epic Poetry; in five epistles to the Revd. Mr. Mason* (1782) has the adventitious interest of containing a translation by Hayley of the first three cantos of Dante's *Inferno* into terza rima. This was the first printed translation into English of any considerable portion of the *Divina Commedia*. Hayley was aware of the originality of his attempt; he writes in introduction to it, "The Author has since been solicited to execute an entire translation of Dante: but the extreme inequality of this Poet would render such a work a very laborious undertaking, and it appears very doubtful how far such a version would interest our country."

In the same year (1782) CHARLES ROGERS (1711–84) published anonymously a complete translation of the *Inferno*. The first translation of the entire work was published by HENRY BOYD (d. 1832) in 1802. At that time H. F. CARY (1772–1844) had already been at work on his famous translation for five years. It was published in 1814, and is rptd. in E.L. See Paget Toynbee's *Britain's Tribute to Dante in Literature and Art* (British Academy; O.U.P., 1921), and R. W. King's biography of Cary, *The Translator of Dante* (Secker, 1925).

Besides several other poems and some plays, Hayley wrote lives of Milton (1794), Cowper (1803), and Romney (1809), and compiled two volumes of *Memoirs*, which were edited by John Johnson, and published in 1823. There is a short biographical sketch of Hayley in *The Stricken Deer*, ch. 5 (see p. 189).

DARWIN, Erasmus (1731–1802)

Darwin was a naturalist—and the grandfather of a greater naturalist—who attempted to recommend his studies in verse. He published in 1789 *The Botanic Garden, Part II Containing The Loves of the Plants, A Poem. With Philosophical Notes*. Part I was *The Economy of Vegetation*, which was not published till 1791. The work became popular and reached a seventh edition (sixth ed. of Part I) in 1825. Horace Walpole was one of its warmest admirers. It was "the most delicious poem upon earth", he told the Misses Berry, "I defy you to discover three bad verses in the whole stack" (April 28, 1789). Coleridge could have found them (see *Biographia Literaria*, ch. 1); and so could Wordsworth, for though his *Evening Walk* and *Descriptive Sketches* are smudged with Darwinian diction, it seems probable that he was referring chiefly to *The Botanic Garden* when he censured the gaudiness and inane phraseology of many modern writers in the Advertisement to *Lyrical Ballads*. A parody called *The Loves of Triangles*, the work of Canning, Frere and Ellis, appeared in *The Anti-Jacobin* (see p. 212) in 1798. Darwin's *The Temple of Nature; or the Origin of Society: A Poem, with philosophical notes* was published in 1803.

Anna Seward's *Memoirs of the Life of Dr. Darwin* appeared in 1804. H. Pearson drew upon family papers hitherto unused for his *Dr. Darwin* (Dent, 1930). A study by J. V. Logan, *The Poetry and Aesthetics of E.D.*, was published by the Princeton U.P. in 1936. There is also an essay on Darwin in F. Hitchman's *Eighteenth Century Studies* (1881).

BLAKE, William (1757–1827)

No complete ed. of Blake's writings has yet been published, for all his letters have not yet been traced; but with this exception G. Keynes's ed. (Nonesuch Press, 3 vols., 1925) may be regarded as definitive. A cheaper 1-vol. ed. was published by the same press in 1927. These editions have superseded the 3-vol. ed. of E. J. Ellis and W. B. Yeats (Quaritch, 1893).

Blake's poetical writings consist of *Poetical Sketches* (1783), *Songs of Innocence* (1789), *Songs of Experience* (1794), poems from the prophetic books and from his letters; and poems from a sketch book and commonplace book used by Blake between 1793 and 1818, and now known as the Rossetti MS. The best ed. is by J. Sampson (Cl. P., 1905); there is also a good ed. (including the prophetic books) in E.L., by M. Plowman, and selections in W.C. and the O.M. The Prophetic Writings have been edited by D. J. Sloss and J. P. R. Wallis (2 vols., Cl. P., 1926). The same press publishes Blake's letters to Thomas Butts, ed. G. Keynes (1926).

The first, and still the most important, biography of Blake was written by A. Gilchrist in 1863 (2nd ed., 1880), who embodied reminiscences by persons still alive who had once known Blake. The book also contains a selection from Blake's poems, ed. D. G. Rossetti. In addition to its intrinsic value it had the merit of stimulating Swinburne to write his *William Blake, A Critical Essay* (Chatto and Windus, 1868). A more recent biographical essay is that of Mona Wilson (Davies, 1932).

The following books may be recommended for further study: M. Plowman, *An Introduction to the study of Blake* (Dent, 1927), P. Berger, *W.B., Poet and Mystic* (translated D. H. Conner; Chapman and Hall, 1914), S. Foster Damon, *W.B.: His Philosophy and Symbols* (Constable, 1924), D. Saurat, *Blake and Modern Thought* (Constable, 1929). The Grolier Club of New York published a bibliography of Blake by G. Keynes in 1921.

CRABBE, George (1754–1832)

George Crabbe published *The Village*, a severely realistic antidote to Goldsmith's *Deserted Village*, in 1783. The less successful *The Newspaper* followed in 1785, and then for twenty years Crabbe kept silence in a country parsonage. At last, in 1807, he began to publish again, apparently quite unaffected by the enormous developments of the intervening years. *The Parish Register* appeared that year, and its favourable reception encouraged him to produce some more of this rapid and pungent narrative verse.

The Borough followed in 1810, and 21 *Tales* in 1812. His last considerable book was *Tales of the Hall* (2 vols., 1819).

Collected editions of Crabbe's poems were published in 1807, 1823 (5 vols.), and 1834 (8 vols.). The best ed. is A. W. Ward's (C.U.P., 3 vols., 1905–7). The O.S.A. series contains a 1-vol. ed. by A. J. and R. M. Carlyle. Methuen publish a good selection from his poems (ed. A. C. Deane; 2nd ed. 1932).

A life of Crabbe, incorporating his letters and a journal of his early poverty-stricken years in London, was well written by his son, George, as a prefatory volume for the ed. of 1834. It was rptd. in W.C. with an attractive preface by E. M. Forster in 1932. The best modern biography is R. Huchon's *George Crabbe and his Times* (Murray, 1907).

BOWLES, William Lisle (1762–1850)
RUSSELL, Thomas (1762–88)

The Sonnet, which had been successfully revived by Thomas Warton (*Poems*, 1777), became a favourite verse form in the last two decades of the century. Two of the best sonneteers were W. L. Bowles and Thomas Russell. Bowles's first vol., entitled *Fourteen Sonnets written chiefly on Picturesque Spots during a Journey*, was published in 1789, and created a profound effect upon at least one of its readers—Coleridge, who was then a school-boy at Christ's Hospital (see *Biographia Literaria*, ch. 1). The number of sonnets was increased to thirty by the time the 8th ed. appeared in 1802.

In 1806 Bowles's prepared an edition of Pope's poems, in which he bestowed certain strictures upon Pope's moral and poetical character, and was severely rebuked by Byron (or Hobhouse) in *English Bards and Scotch Reviewers* (1809). Pope's cause was again championed by Thomas Campbell (see p. 194) in his *Specimens of the British Poets* (1819), to which Bowles replied with a pamphlet entitled *The Invariable Principles of Poetry*. These were the first shots in a long pamphleteering war, the history of which has been surveyed by J. J. Van Rennes in his *Bowles, Byron, and the Pope Controversy* (H. J. Paris, Amsterdam, 1927).

A collection of Bowles's letters, ed. G. Greever, was published by Constable in 1926 with the title *A Wiltshire Parson and his Friends*.

Russell's only volume, *Sonnets and Miscellaneous Poems*, was also published in 1789. It has been rptd. with the poems of CUTHBERT SHAW by Eric Partridge (Dulau, 1925).

The pensive melancholy of CHARLOTTE SMITH's *Elegiac Sonnets* is also worth tasting. She published a modest collection of 16 in 1784, diffidently appealing for readers "among the few, who to sensibility of heart, join simplicity of taste". Encouraged by their reception from a dazzling list of aristocratic and ecclesiastical patrons, she filled successive editions with more and more sonnets, the 10th (2 vols., 1811) containing 92. Her life (1749–1806) was written by Sir Walter Scott (*Lives of the Novelists*, E.L.).

These three poets are all represented in O.B.

BLOOMFIELD, Robert (1766–1823)

Bloomfield was a young farm labourer who came to London and was apprenticed to a shoemaker. He had published a few verses in the *Gentleman's Magazine* before he made his reputation with *The Farmer's Boy; A Rural Poem, in Four Books* (1800). The poem reached a fifteenth edition in 1827, and was translated into Italian and Latin. Bloomfield also published *Rural Tales* (1801) and *The Banks of Wye* (1811). A collection of his *Remains* in 2 vols. appeared in 1824, with a prefatory memoir by Joseph Weston; and a complete edition of his poems was published by Routledge in 1883. Hazlitt spoke favourably of *The Farmer's Boy* in *Lectures on the English Poets*, No. 5 (see p. 270).

ROGERS, Samuel (1763–1855)
CAMPBELL, Thomas (1777–1844)
MOORE, Thomas (1779–1852)

Students of the great poets writing at the beginning of the nineteenth century can scarcely avoid the names of Rogers, Campbell and Moore, and should not altogether avoid their works; though what they wrote has more interest for the study of taste than intrinsic merit.

Rogers may be described as Goldsmith-and-water. He wrote soft, carefully elegant poetry, without resilience or incisiveness. One line of his characterises his whole work:

"With sighs so sweet, with transports so refined."

The Pleasures of Memory had an encouraging reception on its publication in 1792. *Jacqueline* was printed with Byron's *Lara* in 1814. *Human Life* appeared in 1819, and *Italy* in 1822. An ed. of his poems, elegantly adorned with engravings by Turner and Stothard, was published in 1834.

A reader of these poems might be surprised to learn that Rogers was brilliant in conversation; but *Recollections of the Table Talk of Samuel Rogers* (ed. A. Dyce. 1856) is one of the best "ana" in the language. A companion vol., *Recollections by Samuel Rogers*, was edited by W. Sharpe in 1859. The two were conflated by G. H. Powell and printed in one vol. in 1903. Rogers's life has been written with lavish detail by P. W. Clayden (*The Early Life of Samuel Rogers*, 1887; *Rogers and his Contemporaries*, 2 vols., 1889). A shorter work, derived mainly from these sources, is R. E. Roberts's *Samuel Rogers and his Circle* (Methuen, 1910).

Campbell at his best gives adequate expression to the Trafalgar spirit; at his worst, as in *The Pleasures of Hope* (1799), he provides a lamentable example of the traditions of Thomson and Goldsmith worn threadbare. *Ye Mariners of England* was published in 1801. A collected vol. of his poems appeared in 1803 containing *Hohenlinden*, and another in 1809 containing *Gertrude of Wyoming*, *Lord Ullin's Daughter*, and *Battle of the Baltic*. That *Gertrude of Wyoming* once had readers is proved by the survival of one line in proverbial quotation:—"'Tis distance lends enchantment to the view." Popular taste accepted Campbell's poetry throughout the nineteenth century, and it is still available in O.S.A. Campbell published *Specimens of the British Poets* in 7 vols. in 1819 (ed. P. Cunningham, 1 vol., 1841)—the critical summaries prefaced to the specimens are still of considerable interest—and on Feb. 9, 1825, he wrote a letter to *The Times* projecting the University of London.

The Life and Letters of Thomas Campbell, ed. W. Beattie, was published in 3 vols. in 1849. Campbell has not been made the subject of any critical study, but students may be recommended to W. M. Dixon's *Thomas Campbell. An Oration* (Jackson, Wylie, 1928) and to G. M. Hopkins's remarks in his *Correspondence* (ed. C. C. Abbott, O.U.P., 2 vols., 1935).

Moore is still remembered by such songs as "The Minstrel Boy" and "The Harp that once through Tara's Halls". These are two of his *Irish Melodies* which were issued, words and music together, in ten folio numbers between 1808 and 1834. Of equal success at the time was his *Lalla Rookh* (1817), an oriental romance which appealed to the readers of Byron's eastern tales. The first collected ed. of Moore's poems was published in 6 vols. in 1819, and the definitive ed. in 10 vols. in 1841-2. There is an ed. by A. D. Godley in O.S.A.

Moore was a friend of Byron. After Byron's death Moore was commissioned to edit his letters and journals and to write his life. This book was published in two vols. in 1830, and is still a work of importance in the study of Byron. Moore's own *Memoirs, Journals, and Correspondence* were edited by Lord John Russell and published in 8 vols., 1853–6. A selection, ed. J. B. Priestley, is published by C.U.P., 1925. Thom & Co. of Dublin have issued a bibliographical handlist of Moore's first editions compiled by M. J. MacManus (1934). There is a life by S. Gwynn in E.M.L., and a more recent study by L. A. G. Strong, entitled *The Minstrel Boy* (Hodder and Stoughton, 1937).

Hazlitt's characters of Campbell and Moore are to be found in *The Spirit of the Age*, and his estimate of the poetry of all three in the eighth of his *Lectures on the English Poets* (see p. 270).

WORDSWORTH, William (1770–1850)

Collected Works.

Wordsworth published the first collected ed. of his poetry in 2 vols. in 1815, grouping his poems under various headings, such as *Poems referring to the Period of Childhood* (e.g., *Alice Fell*), *Poems founded on the Affections* (e.g., *Michael*), *Poems of the Fancy* (e.g., *The Green Linnet*), *Poems of the Imagination* (e.g., *Lines composed a few miles above Tintern Abbey*), *Poems referring to the Period of Old Age* (e.g., *The Old Cumberland Beggar*). In his preface, Wordsworth explained that these groups should be taken as roughly "corresponding with the course of human life", thus "composing an entire work within themselves". This arrangement has been much criticised; but since Wordsworth preserved it in all subsequent editions and disapproved of a chronological arrangement, it has been kept by most of his editors, of whom the best are Dowden (Aldine ed., 7 vols., 1893), and Nowell Smith (3 vols., Methuen, 1908). In Knight's 8-vol. ed. (1882–6; re-issued by Macmillan, 1896) the poems are arranged in chronological order; this is the most elaborate ed., but it is not entirely trustworthy. Of the 1-vol. editions, the O.S.A. (ed. T. Hutchinson) preserves Wordsworth's order, giving the date of each poem, wherever possible; the Globe (ed. J. Morley), which is the only 1-vol. ed. to print *The Recluse* and the notes which Wordsworth dictated to Miss Fenwick, keeps Knight's chronological order.

Separate Publications.

Wordsworth's first published poems were *An Evening Walk* and *Descriptive Sketches*, 1793.

Lyrical Ballads, which contains *The Ancient Mariner* and three other poems by Coleridge, was published anonymously in

September 1798. Such poems as *Goody Blake and Harry Gill, We are Seven, The Thorn, The Idiot Boy*, and *Lines composed a few miles above Tintern Abbey* were first printed in this book. A second ed., to which a second vol. was added, containing *Hart-Leap Well, A Slumber did my Spirit seal*, and *Michael*, was published with an enlarged preface of great importance in 1800. The definitive ed. appeared in 1802, and a rpt. in 1805. Type-facsimiles of the 1798 vol. have been published by Noel Douglas (1926) and in O.M. The best edition is by T. Hutchinson (Duckworth, 1898) A rpt. of the 1805 vol., ed. G. Sampson, was published by Methuen in 1903.

In 1807 Wordsworth published two vols. containing such poems as *She was a phantom of delight, Alice Fell, Resolution and Independence, The Happy Warrior, Yarrow Unvisited, The Solitary Reaper, Ode on the Intimations of Immortality*, and such sonnets as "Westminster Bridge" and "Toussaint l'Ouverture". A type-facsimile of these vols. is published in O.M., and another, with editorial matter by H. Darbishire, by the Cl. P.

Since 1798 or earlier, Wordsworth had been meditating a great philosophical poem to be entitled *The Recluse, or, Views on Man, Nature, and Society*. In preparation for this he started, in March 1798, a poem on the growth of his own mind. He regarded this at first as an integral part of *The Recluse*, but as it grew upon his hands he realised that it had inevitably encroached on his first design. The poem was finished in May 1805, but it was not published; in fact, Wordsworth had told De Quincey in the previous year that the poem would not be published "these many years, and never during my lifetime, till I have finished a larger and more important work to which it is tributary". The poem was corrected in subsequent years and published posthumously in 1850 with the title, *The Prelude, or Growth of a Poet's Mind*. The best ed. is by E. de Selincourt (Cl. P., 1926), who for the first time printed the 1805 and other MS. versions on pages facing the 1850 text. The 1805 text was rptd. in O.S.A. in 1933 with a revised and abbreviated version of de Selincourt's preface and notes.

The Excursion, a poem in nine books, appeared in 1814. Wordsworth explained in the preface that this was intended for the second part of *The Recluse*. Of the first part, only Book 1 survives, and was perhaps all that was written of it. It was first published in 1888 by Macmillan, and is included in the Globe ed., but not in O.S.A. Of the third part nothing survives. To the completed work in three parts, *The Prelude* was designed, in the poet's words, to stand in the same relationship as the antechapel and the body of a gothic church. Continuing this metaphor, he added that his minor poems when properly arranged would have "such connexion with the main Work as may give them claim to be likened to the little cells, oratories, and sepulchral recesses, ordinarily included in those edifices". From the 1815 preface it is clear that Wordsworth did not intend this metaphorical description of his minor poems to conflict with the view that they composed "an entire work in themselves".

Amongst Wordsworth's later poetical publications must be mentioned *The White Doe of Rylstone* (1815); *Peter Bell* (1819), originally intended for publication in *Lyrical Ballads*, and later grouped under *Poems of the Imagination;* and *The Waggoner* (1819).

Prose.

Wordsworth's prose works were first collected by A. B. Grosart (3 vols., 1876); the "standard" ed. is by W. Knight (2 vols.; Macmillan, 1896), whose notions of accuracy were not those of modern scholarship. The most important of these writings are the critical works, a vol. of which, ed. Nowell Smith, is published in O.M. This series also includes his tract on the Convention of Cintra, 1809 (ed. A. V. Dicey), and his admirable *Guide to the Lakes*, 1810 (ed. E. de Selincourt).

Letters.

Wordsworth's letters were first collected by W. Knight in 3 vols., entitled *Letters of the Wordsworth Family* (Macmillan, 1907). A complete ed. with a more accurate text, has been prepared by E. de Selincourt for the Cl. P. (*The Early Letters of William and Dorothy Wordsworth, 1787–1805*, 1935; *The Letters of W. and D. W., 1806–1820*, 2 vols., 1937; *Later Letters, 1821–1850*, 3 vols., 1938). The *Journals of Dorothy Wordsworth*, indispensable for the study of her brother's poetry, were ed. by W. Knight (Macmillan; 2 vols., 1897; one vol., 1924). It is regrettable that Knight's text is both incomplete and inaccurate. Some corrections of it will be found in E. de Selincourt's biography, *Dorothy Wordsworth* (Cl. P., 1933). See also C. M. Maclean's *Dorothy Wordsworth: The Early Years* (Chatto, 1932).

Biography and Criticism.

Christopher Wordsworth, the poet's nephew, published 2 vols of *Memoirs of William Wordsworth* in 1851. E. Legouis's *The Early Life of William Wordsworth, 1770–1798; a study of "The Prelude"*, first appeared in 1896; a translation by J. W. Matthews was published by Dent in 1897 and rptd. in 1921. Of more recent biographies the most important are G. M. Harper's *W.W., his life, works and influence* (1916; revised and abridged, 1919) and E. C. Batho's *The Later Wordsworth* (C.U.P., 1933).

Chs. 4, 17–20, 22 of Coleridge's *Biographia Literaria* (for editions, see under COLERIDGE) are of the first importance in the study of Wordsworth. Many good critical studies have been written in recent years, the most important of which are H. W. Garrod's *Wordsworth* (Cl. P., revised ed., 1927), C. H. Herford's *Wordsworth* (Routledge, 1930), and H. J. C. Grierson's *Milton and Wordsworth* (C.U.P., 1937). There are serviceable bibliographies in the first vol. of Knight's ed. of the poems, and in the Globe ed. (by J. R. Tutin). The most famous selection from the poems is Matthew Arnold's (1879), still rptd. with Arnold's preface in the *Golden Treasury* series (Macmillan).

COLERIDGE, Samuel Taylor (1772–1834)

Poetry and Drama.

More than half of Coleridge's verse was written between the years 1794 and 1799. In 1796 he published his first vol., entitled *Poems on Various Subjects*, and in 1797 a second vol. in which he omitted a third of the poems in the former vol. and added almost an equal number. In 1798 he collaborated with Wordsworth in the production of *Lyrical Ballads*, to which he contributed *The Ancient Mariner*, *The Nightingale*, and two fragments from *Remorse*; and in the same year he published in one vol. *Fears in Solitude; France, an Ode*; and *Frost at Midnight*. His two translations from Schiller, *The Piccolomini*, and *The Death of Wallenstein* appeared in 1800. A collected ed. of his poems was published in 1803, which contained the poems previously published in 1796 and 1797, with the omission of four from 1796 and two from 1797. Ten years later Coleridge began publishing what yet remained unprinted. *Remorse*, a tragedy written in 1797, appeared in 1813; *Christabel*, *Kubla Khan*, and *The Pains of Sleep* in 1816; and in 1817, another collection of his poetical works, entitled *Sibylline Leaves*. Further collected editions, revised by Coleridge, appeared in 1828, 1829, and 1834.

The best modern editions of Coleridge's poems are the Globe ed. (by J. Dykes Campbell; Macmillan, 1893 and frequently rptd.) and the Oxford ed. (by E. H. Coleridge, 2 vols., 1912; a rpt. of this text, omitting the dramas, is available in O.S.A.). The

Oxford ed. is more complete than the Globe, presents a slightly better text, and a full record of the changes which Coleridge made between one edition and another. On the other hand, the Globe provides a valuable commentary and an excellent biographical introduction.

Philosophical Writings.

The chief documents for the study of Coleridge's philosophy are *The Friend*, described by Coleridge as a "Literary, Moral, and Political Weekly Paper", conducted by him during the years 1809 and 1810; *Biographia Literaria* (see below under *Literary Criticism*); *A Preliminary Treatise on Method*, designed as an introd. to the *Encyclopaedia Metropolitana*, and issued separately in 1818; *Aids to Reflection* (1825); and *Confessions of an Inquiring Spirit*, first published by H. N. Coleridge in 1840. Numerous philosophical manuscripts by Coleridge are still unpublished. A survey of them with extracts was made by A. D. Snyder in a vol. entitled *Coleridge on Logic and Learning* (Yale and O.U.P., 1929).

The Friend was issued in vol. form in 1812, and was much revised in 1818. It is rptd. in Bell's Bohn Library. The *Treatise on Method* has been edited by A. D. Snyder (Constable, 1934). *Aids to Reflection* and *Confessions of an Inquiring Spirit* are available in one vol. of the Bohn Library.

Literary Criticism.

Biographia Literaria; or Biographical Sketches of my Literary Life and Opinions was published in 2 vols. in 1817. This is Coleridge's only work of critical importance published during his life. Notes and reports of the lectures which he gave between the years 1805 and 1818 were preserved and many of them published by his nephew, H. N. Coleridge, in *The Literary Remains of S.T.C.* (1836–9). Another group of critical observations which H.N.C. published in *The Literary Remains* were some of the numerous notes left by Coleridge on the margins and blank spaces of books and pamphlets. A third group of critical observations is the record which H.N.C. kept of his uncle's conversation and published under the title *Specimens of the Table Talk of S.T.C.* in 1835. In this group should be included the "hitherto unpublished aphorisms, reflections, confessions and soliloquies, which for the want of a better name I have entitled *Anima Poetæ*", selected from Coleridge's notebooks and pocket books by his grandson, E. H. Coleridge, and published by Heinemann in 1895. *Biographia Literaria* is available in one vol. of E.L. but the best ed.

is J. Shawcross's (2 vols., Cl. P., 1907). *Coleridge's Shakespearean Criticism*, ed. T. M. Raysor, was published by Constable in 2 vols. in 1930, and in 1936 the same firm published a vol. of Coleridge's *Miscellaneous Criticism*, also ed. T. M. Raysor. The *Table Talk* has been rptd. in O.S.A. A vol. of lectures and notes on Shakespeare and other dramatists is published in W.C., and a selection of Coleridge's criticism, ed. J. W. Mackail, in O.M.

Letters.

A few specimens of Coleridge's letters were published during his life and many more in the years immediately succeeding his death, but no complete collection has yet appeared. There are three important and complementary collections: *Letters of S.T.C.*, ed. E.H.C. (2 vols., Heinemann, 1895), described by the editor as a selection from some of the more important letters, intended rather to illustrate the story of the writer's life than to embody his critical opinions or to record the development of his philosophical and theological speculations; *Biographia Epistolaris*, ed. A. Turnbull (2 vols., Bell, 1911), which is an attempt to complete H.N.C.'s unfinished plan of a Biographical Supplement of letters appended to the 1847 ed. of *Biographia Literaria*; *Unpublished Letters of S.T.C.*, ed. E. L. Griggs (2 vols., Constable, 1932), most of which are of a more personal and intimate nature than those published by E.H.C.

Selections.

An admirable selection from Coleridge's poetry and prose, ed. S. Potter, was published by the Nonesuch Press in 1933.

Biography and Criticism.

E.H.C.'s life of his grandfather was unfortunately never completed, but chs. 1, 5 (the year 1796), and 9 (1800) are printed in a vol. of studies on the hundredth anniversary of Coleridge's death, ed. E. Blunden and E. L. Griggs (Constable, 1934). The material which E.H.C. collected has been used by L. Hanson, whose first instalment *The Life of S. T. C.: The Early Years* is published by Allen and Unwin (1938). Another "biographical study" has been written by E. K. Chambers (Cl. P., 1938). Of the earlier biographies, the best is J. Dykes Campbell's *S. T. C.: A Narrative of the Events of his Life* (Macmillan, 1894), a revised and expanded version of his introd. to the Globe ed. of Coleridge's poems.

The best studies of Coleridge's work are J. L. Lowes's *The Road to Xanadu* (Constable, 1927), J. H. Muirhead's *Coleridge as Philosopher* (Allen and Unwin, 1930), I. A. Richards's *Coleridge on the Imagination* (Kegan Paul, 1934), and S. Potter's *Coleridge and S.T.C.* (Cape, 1935). In E.S.M.E.A., vol. 22, E. de Selincourt has published the original version of *Dejection, An Ode*, with an account of its origin. Vol. 21 of the same series contains a valuable essay by J. Isaacs on *Coleridge's Critical Terminology*. J. S. Mill's essay, rptd. in his *Dissertations and Discussions*, vol. 1, is well worth reading.

T. J. Wise's *Bibliography of the Writings in Prose and Verse of S.T.C.* was published by the Bibliographical Society in 1913. This is a standard work for specialists. The General Reader may find V. W. Kennedy's *S. T. C. A selected bibliography* (Enoch Pratt Free Library, Baltimore, 1935) more serviceable.

COLERIDGE, Hartley (1796–1849)

S. T. C.'s son published a vol. of poems in 1833. These and others were rptd. in 2 vols. by his brother, Derwent, in 1851. The standard ed. is by R. Colles (M.L.). Hartley Coleridge also wrote a number of critical essays, which were collected in 2 vols. by his brother in 1851. His letters have been ed. by G. E. and E. L. Griggs (O.U.P., 1936). Derwent Coleridge prefixed a memoir of his brother to his ed. of the poems. Two studies have appeared in recent years: *H. C., His Life and Work*, by E. L. Griggs (University of London Press, 1929), and H. Hartman's *H.C.* (O.U.P., 1931).

SOUTHEY, Robert (1774–1843).

No attempt has ever been made to collect all Southey's numerous writings. Nor would such an attempt be valuable. There is not even a complete ed. of his poems, for he himself rejected a number from his 10-vol. ed. published in 1837–8 (rptd. 1853), and this is still the most complete. A selection, ed. M. H. Fitzgerald, is published in O.S.A., which contains *Thalaba* (1801), *Madoc* (1805), *The Curse of Kehama* (1810), *Roderick* (1814), and some of his minor poems, but omits such poems as the *Botany Bay Eclogues*, *Wat Tyler*, and *A Vision of Judgement*, which Byron has made famous by reference and parody. The *Vision* has been published in a cheap rpt. with Byron's *Vision* (see p. 203).

Southey's prose is usually preferred to his verse. The famous *Life of Nelson* appeared in 1813, and is available in O.S.A. and

E.L. The *Life of Wesley* was published in 1820. It is rptd. with Coleridge's notes, ed. M. H. Fitzgerald, in 2 vols. of O.S.A. A "Shandyan" work entitled *The Doctor* was commenced in 1812 and published in 5 vols. between 1834 and 1838. There is a complete ed. by J. W. Warter (1848) and a convenient abridgement, ed. M. H. Fitzgerald, was published by Bell in 1930. It contains the famous nursery tale of the Three Bears. *The Journal of a Tour in Scotland in 1819* was first published by Murray in 1929 with editorial matter by C. H. Herford.

Southey's *Life and Correspondence* was published by his son in 6 vols. in 1849. A selection from his letters, ed. M. H. Fitzgerald, is available in W.C. There is an excellent biography by E. Dowden in E.M.L. No study of Southey would be complete which did not consider the impressions recorded by Byron in *The Vision of Judgement* and *Don Juan*, by Hazlitt in *The Spirit of the Age*, and by De Quincey in *Recollection of the Lakes and of the Lake Poets* (see pp. 270–1).

BYRON, George Gordon, Lord (1788–1824)

Collected Works.

A uniform ed. of the poems and letters was published by Murray. The poems were edited by E. H. Coleridge in 7 vols. (1898–1904), and the letters and journals by R. E. Prothero in 6 vols. (1898–1901).

Poems.

Byron's first vol. of poems was entitled *Hours of Idleness* (1807). It was reviewed so severely in the *Edinburgh Review* that Byron was prompted to write his *English Bards and Scotch Reviewers* (1809), in which he first showed his satiric powers. The first two cantos of *Childe Harold's Pilgrimage* appeared in 1812; a third followed in 1816, and a fourth in 1818. In the meanwhile he had started a series of tales in verse, all quite readable but of no conspicuous merit; these are *The Giaour*, and *The Bride of Abydos* (1813); *The Corsair* and *Lara* (1814); *The Siege of Corinth*, *Parisina*, and *The Prisoner of Chillon* (1816); *Mazeppa* (1819). Two at least of his dramas are more pleasing, *Manfred* (1817), and *Cain* (1822). His three mature satires are *Beppo* (1818); *Don Juan*—undoubtedly his greatest poem—in 16 cantos (1819–24); and *The Vision of Judgment* (1822), provoked by Southey's poem with the same title, written in his laureate capacity on George III's death.

One-vol. collections are published by Murray (containing the whole of E. H. Coleridge's text and a selection of his notes) and in O.S.A. (which does not contain the new matter in Coleridge's edition.) A copious selection with an introd. by H. J. C. Grierson was published by Chatto and Windus in 1923, and a selection of the satires, containing *English Bards*, *The Vision* and extracts from *Childe Harold* and *Don Juan* was edited by Joan Bennett for C.U.P. in 1937. *Don Juan* is edited by F. H. Ristine (Macmillan, New York, 1927) and *The Vision of Judgment*, with Southey's *Vision*, by E. M. Earl (O.U.P., 1929).

Letters.

Selections from Byron's letters are published by Murray (ed. J. Murray, 1922), the Cl. P. (ed. V. H. Collins, 1928), and Dent (E.L.).

Biography and Criticism.

Several memoirs of Byron were written after his death, including Thomas Moore's biography (see p. 194), T. Medwin's *Journal of the Conversations of Lord Byron* (1824) and E. J. Tre- lawny's *Recollections of Shelley and Byron* (1858), which is issued in O.M., ed. E. Dowden. The number of modern studies shows that his personality has lost little of its fascination. Of these the most notable are R. Edgcumbe's *Byron, The Last Phase* (Murray, 1909), E. C. Mayne's detailed biography (revised ed., Methuen, 1924), H. Nicolson's *Byron, The Last Journey* (cheap reissue, Constable, 1934), and P. Quennell's *Byron, The Years of Fame* (Faber, 1935). J. Nichol's vol. in E.M.L., though by no means up-to-date, is a good short account.

By comparison, little has been written about Byron's poetry. The famous estimates of Arnold and Swinburne are well reviewed in H. J. C. Grierson's Warton Lecture (British Academy, O.U.P., 1920).

SHELLEY, Percy Bysshe, (1792–1822)

Collected Editions.

There are two collected editions of Shelley's writings—one, ed. H. Buxton Forman in 8 vols. in 1880, the other, ed. R. Ingpen and W. E. Peck in 10 vols. (Benn, 1927–9). The first collected ed. of Shelley's poems was prepared by his widow and published in 4 vols. in 1839. Notable editions have since been published by W. M. Rossetti (3 vols., 1878), and C. D. Locock (2 vols., Methuen, 1911). The best ed. in one vol. is by T. Hutchinson (Cl. P., 1904; also available in O.S.A.).

Poems.

Shelley's most important publications in verse were *Queen Mab* (1813); *Alastor; or, The Spirit of Solitude* (1816); *The Revolt of Islam* (1818); *The Cenci* (1819); *Prometheus Unbound* (1820)—a vol. which contains, amongst other poems, the *Ode to the West Wind*, *The Sensitive Plant*, and *To a Skylark; Oedipus Tyrannus; or, Swellfoot the Tyrant* (1820); *Epipsychidion* (1821); *Adonais. An Elegy on the Death of John Keats* (1821). In 1824 Mrs. Shelley published a vol. of *Posthumous Poems*, which contains, amongst others, *Julian and Maddalo; The Witch of Atlas; The Triumph of Life;* and *Stanzas Written in Dejection, Near Naples*. A further vol. of posthumous poems was published by R. Garnett in 1862 with the title, *Relics of Shelley*. A rpt. of the *Prometheus* vol. is published in O.M., and an ed. of it by A. M. D. Hughes is published by the Cl.P. Facsimiles of *Alastor*, *The Cenci*, *Epipsychidion*, *Adonais*, and other works were published by the Shelley Society between 1886 and 1892. A facsimile of *Adonais* was also published by Noel Douglas in 1927.

Prose Works.

Shelley's prose has been edited by H. Buxton Forman in 4 vols. (1880), and by R. H. Shepherd in 2 vols. (Chatto, 1888). A *Defence of Poetry*, written in reply to Peacock's *The Four Ages of Poetry*, was first published by Mrs. Shelley in *Essays, Letters from Abroad, Translations,* and *Fragments*, in 1840. It was rptd. with Peacock's *Four Ages* and Browning's essay on Shelley in P.R., ed. H. F. B. Brett-Smith (1921). A vol. of his literary and philosophical criticism, ed. J. Shawcross, is published in the O.M. Shelley's letters have been ed. by R. Ingpen (2 vols., 1909; rptd. in Bohn Library, 1915).

Biography and Criticism.

Memoirs of Shelley were written by three of his contemporaries, Thomas Jefferson Hogg, Thomas Love Peacock, and Edward John Trelawny. These have been collected in 2 vols. (Dent, 1933). Separate editions of Peacock's *Memoirs* (ed. H. F. B. Brett-Smith) and Trelawny's *Recollections* (ed. E. Dowden) are available in O.M. The standard life of Shelley is E. Dowden's (2 vols.,

Kegan Paul, 1886). Another by W. E. Peck was published in 2 vols. by Benn in 1927. The merits of Shelley's poetry have recently been contested by T. S. Eliot in *The Use of Poetry and the Use of Criticism* (Faber, 1933) and Herbert Read in *In Defence of Shelley* (Heinemann, 1936). A new study is being prepared by A. M. D. Hughes. A useful introduction to his work is H. N. Brailsford's *Shelley, Godwin, and their Circle* (H.U.L.). N. I. White reprints "practically every obtainable known contemporary review or article dealing with Shelley" in *The Unextinguished Hearth* (Duke U.P., 1938), as a basis for studying Shelley's reputation. He comes to the conclusion that "Shelley's contemporary critics were not blind to his genius, but merely afraid of it."

HUNT, James Henry Leigh (1784–1859)

Leigh Hunt's prose is treated in the following vol. His poems, which are sometimes said to have had a malign effect upon Keats's early work, were viciously attacked in *Blackwood's Magazine* in a series of articles on "The Cockney School of Poetry" (1817–18). His chief poetical works are *The Feast of the Poets* (1814), *The Story of Rimini* (1816), *Hero and Leander* and *Bacchus and Ariadne*, both published in a 3-vol. collection of his poems in 1819, which also contains one of the most famous of his shorter pieces, *On a Lock of Milton's Hair. Abou Ben Adhem*, a favourite anthology piece, first appeared in S. C. Hall's *Book of Gems* in 1838. Collected editions of Hunt's poetry were published in 1832 and 1860, but neither is complete. The fullest collection is edited by H. S. Milford in O.P.

KEATS, John (1795–1821)

The complete editions are those prepared by H. Buxton Forman (4 vols., 1883; revised, 1889; 5 vols., 1900–1). The best editions of the poems are those by E. de Selincourt (Methuen, 1905; rev. ed., 1926), and H. Buxton Forman (O.S.A.). The Cl. P. has recently published a new ed. by H. W. Garrod (1939). An ed. in M.L., ed. G. Thorn Drury, has an introd. by Robert Bridges. J. Middleton Murry's ed. is published by Eyre and Spottiswoode (2 vols., 1930).

Three vols. of his poems appeared during Keats's life: *Poems* (1817); *Endymion* (1818); *Lamia, Isabella, The Eve of St. Agnes, and other poems* (1820), a vol. which also contains *Hyperion, Ode to a Nightingale, Ode on a Grecian Urn, Ode to Psyche, Fancy,* "Bards of Passion", *Lines on the Mermaid Tavern, Robin Hood, To Autumn,* and *Ode on Melancholy.* A type-facsimile was published by Noel Douglas in 1927. There is another in O.M., and the Cl. P. also publishes an ed. by M. Robertson. Noel Douglas published a facsimile of the 1817 vol. in 1927, and O.U.P. a facsimile of *Endymion* (ed. H. C. Notcutt) in the same year. Most of Keats's other poems were published by R. Monckton Milnes, later Lord Houghton, in his *Life, Letters, and Literary Remains of John Keats*, 2 vols., 1848. *The Fall of Hyperion*, an attempt made in 1819 to reconstruct *Hyperion*, was first published by Milnes in the Philobiblon Society's *Bibliographical and Historical Miscellanies* (1856–7).

The first collection of Keats's letters was made by Milnes (see above). The standard ed. is by M. Buxton Forman (2 vols. O.U.P., 1931).

The earliest life of Keats was written by Milnes (see above), rpts. of which are available in W.C. and E.L. Since then the most notable of many lives has been S. Colvin's (E.M.L.). The following critical studies may be recommended: J. Middleton Murry's *Keats and Shakespeare* (O.U.P., 1925) and his *Studies in Keats* (O.U.P., 1930). H. W. Garrod's *Keats* (Cl. P., 1926), and M. R. Ridley's *Keats's Craftsmanship* (Cl. P., 1933).

CLARE, John (1793–1864)

Clare published 4 vols. of poetry: *Poems Descriptive of Rural Life and Scenery* (1820), which reached a fourth ed. in the next year; *The Village Minstrel and other Poems*, 2 vols. (1821); *The Shepherd's Calendar, with Village Stories, and other poems* (1827); and *The Rural Muse* (1835). He wrote many more which have only recently been published. In 1920 Cobden-Sanderson issued a vol. of *Poems, Chiefly from Manuscript*, ed. E. Blunden and A. Porter; and in 1924 E. Blunden edited a vol. entitled *Madrigals and Chronicles* (Beaumont Press), derived entirely from manuscript sources. A collected ed. by J. W. Tibble, was published in 2 vols. by Dent in 1935. There are selections in O.M. (ed. A. Symons) and in O.B.R.V. *Sketches in the Life of John Clare. By Himself* was edited by E. Blunden in 1931 for Cobden-Sanderson, who has also published (1932) a biography by J. W. and A. Tibble.

DARLEY, George (1795–1846)

Darley published 5 vols. of verse: *The Errors of Ecstasie: A Dramatic Poem. With Other Pieces* (1822); *Sylvia* (1827); *Nepenthe* (1835); and two "dramatic chronicles", *Thomas à Becket* (1840) and *Ethelstan* (1841). These and other poems were

collected in the M.L.ed. Much of Darley's prose is concerned
with systems of algebra, geometry, etc., but he also wrote
a vol. of imaginative prose tales with incidental poems
entitled *The Labours of Idleness* (1826). C. C. Abbott's *Life and
Letters of G.D.* (O.U.P., 1928) is a valuable biographical and
critical study, in which for the first time Darley's letters are
collected and the importance of his art criticism emphasised.
An article by Robert Bridges on *Nepenthe*, Darley's most remarkable poem, appeared in *The Academy* on August 4, 1906, and
was rptd. in his *Collected Essays*, vol. 5 (Cl. P., 1931).

LANDOR, Walter Savage (1775–1864)
Landor's first vol. of poems of which he said he was soon
ashamed, was published in 1795. *Gebir*, the first of his heroic
poems, appeared in 1798, and was revised in 1803; and two others,
Crysaor and fragments of *The Phocæans*, were printed in 1800 and
published in *Poetry by the Author of Gebir* (1802). Another collection,
Simonidea (1806), contains *Gunlaug and Helga*. Still more heroic
and narrative poems appear in *Hellenics* (1847), a revised and
enlarged ed. of which was published in 1859. Later vols. of
poems are *Last Fruit off an Old Tree* (1853), *Dry Sticks, Fagoted*
(1858), and *Heroic Idyls, with additional poems* (1863).
   Count Julian: A Tragedy, Landor's first poetic drama, was
published in 1812. The first and third parts of *Ines de Castro*
were published in 1831, the second part following in 1846.
A trilogy, *Andrea of Hungary, Giovanna of Naples*, and *Fra Rupert*,
was published in 1839–40. There are three more plays to be
mentioned, *The Siege of Ancona* (1846), *Beatrice Cenci* (1851),
and *Antony and Octavius* (1856).
   In the meanwhile Landor had been publishing his *Imaginary
Conversations*, the first collection of which appeared in 1824.
But these are fully treated in vol. 4, pp. 222–3.
   A collected ed. of Landor's poems was published in 1831
with the title, *Gebir, Count Julian, and Other Poems*. The first
collected ed. of his works appeared in 2 vols. in 1846. Another,
ed. J. Forster, was published in 7 vols. (one volume is devoted to
a life of Landor by Forster) by Chapman and Hall in 1876.
Subsequent editions, progressively more complete, are those of
G. C. Crump (10 vols., Dent, 1891–3) and of T. E. Welby and
S. Wheeler (16 vols., Chapman and Hall, 1927–36). Wheeler's
ed. of the poems has been re-issued in 3 vols. by the Cl. P. (1937).
A selection from Landor's poems is published in the Golden
Treasury series (Macmillan); and the 1798 text of *Gebir* and

the 1847 text of the *Hellenics* are rptd. in Dent's Temple Classics.

The best biographies of Landor are those of J. Forster (2 vols., 1869; the biography in his ed. of the *Works*, 1876, is a revised and compressed version) and S. Colvin (E.M.L.). A valuable *Bibliography of the Writings in Prose and Verse of W. S. L.* was compiled by T. J. Wise and S. Wheeler (Bibliographical Society, 1919).

SCOTTISH POETRY

RAMSAY, Allan (1685?–1758)

Allan Ramsay, an Edinburgh wig-maker who abandoned the trade for bookselling, published a vol. of poems in 1720 and a pastoral comedy, entitled *The Gentle Shepherd*, in 1725. Although this was a great success, Ramsay is more interesting as an editor than as a poet. In 1724 he issued two vols. entitled *The Ever Green, Being a Collection of Scots Poems, Wrote by the Ingenious before 1600*, and in the same year he started to publish *The Tea-Table Miscellany*, adding a second vol. in 1726, a third in 1727, and a fourth in 1737. This is a collection of Scottish songs, modified or rewritten by Ramsay and "some ingenious young gentlemen" and set to their old tunes. It was the beginning of an important movement which was to culminate in Burns, a movement also responsible for Hamilton of Bangour's *Braes of Yarrow*, Jean Elliot's and Mrs. Cockburn's versions of *The Flowers of the Forest*, and Mickle's *There's Nae Luck about the House*, all rptd. in O.B. Ramsay's poems were collected in two vols., ed. G. Chalmers (1800), an ed. frequently rptd. in the nineteenth century. His life has been written by B. Martin (Harvard U.P., 1931), who has also compiled a bibliography (Jackson, Wylie, 1931).

FERGUSSON, Robert (1750–74)

The non-lyrical, *Ever Green*, tradition is represented by Robert Fergusson, to whom Burns gave most generous praise. In fact he anticipates much of Burns's non-lyrical work with fainter success. Only one vol. of poems appeared during his life— in 1773—to which a second part was added in 1779. His poems have been rptd. several times, but there is no adequate ed. Nor is there an adequate life. A bibliography compiled by J. A. Fairley was published by Maclehose in 1915.

BURNS, Robert (1759–96)

Collected Works.

Only a selection is possible. J. Currie's 4-vol. ed. of 1800 was reissued in 1820 with additional matter by Gilbert Burns. The Life and Works, ed. W. and R. Chambers, was published in 4 vols. in 1851. The fullest nineteenth-century ed. is W. Scott Douglas's "variorum" in 6 vols., 1877–9. The Waverley Book Co. published a 10-vol. ed. in 1927, comprising six vols. of poems, ed. T. F. Henderson (see below), and 4 vols. of letters, ed. F. H. Allen.

Poems.

Burns, who unites the *Ever Green* and *Tea-Table Miscellany* traditions, published his first vol. at Kilmarnock in 1786— *Poems chiefly in the Scottish Dialect*—in order to defray the expense of his (unfulfilled) journey to Jamaica. A facsimile of this book is published in O.M., and a facsimile with notes by M. S. Cleghorn has been published by the Cl. P., 1913. A second ed., to which *Tam O'Shanter* was added, was published in Edinburgh in 1787, and a 2-vol. ed. in 1793. James Johnson began issuing *The Scots Musical Museum* in 1787 and enlisted Burns's help, who contributed 184 songs which he had either written or collected. This work reached a sixth vol. in 1803. Burns also contributed about 70 songs to *A Select Collection of Original Scottish Airs for the Voice* (6 vols., 1793–1805). The best ed. of the poetry is by W. E. Henley and T. F. Henderson (4 vols., Jack, 1896–7). There are one-vol. collections in E.L. and W.C.

Letters.

The standard ed. is by J. De L. Ferguson (Cl. P., 2 vols., 1931).

Biography and Criticism.

The earliest biography of Burns was written by R. Heron in 1797 (rptd. by Hecht, see below). Other early lives which still retain their interest are Josiah Walker's prefixed to *Poems* (1811), and A. Cunningham's (1834). The most reliable biographies are those of A. Angellier (Hachette, 1893), C. Carswell (Chatto and Windus, 1930), F. B. Snyder (Macmillan, 1932), and Hans Hecht (Hodge, 1936).

Carlyle's essay on Burns first appeared as a review of Lockhart's inaccurate *Life* (1828) in the *Edinburgh Review*. It is rptd.

in the first vol. of his essays in E.L. Henley's estimate is prefixed to his ed. of the poems and to the 1927 complete ed. The second vol. of Angellier's life is critical. There are interesting studies by W. P. Ker in his *Collected Essays*, vol. 1 (Macmillan, 1925), by W. Raleigh in *Some Authors* (Cl. P., 1923), and by F. B. Snyder (*R. B., His Personality, His Reputation and His Art*, O.U.P., 1936). A character-study by J. De L. Ferguson, with the title *Pride and Passion*, has recently been published by O.U.P. (1939).

SCOTT, Sir Walter. See p. 234.

HOGG, James (1770–1835)
James Hogg, "The Ettrick Shepherd", was an uneducated peasant who, as Scott said, had "just talent sufficient to spoil him for his own trade, without having enough to support him by literature". He assisted Scott in collecting materials for the *Minstrelsy of the Scottish Border* (1802–3), and published a collection of ballad-imitations entitled *The Mountain Bard* in 1807. His best work, which is in the ballad-tradition rather than in the traditions of *The Ever Green* or *The Tea-Table Miscellany*, is to be found in *The Queen's Wake* (1813), a narrative poem which contains the famous *Kilmeny* (rptd. in O.B.R.V.) and *The Witch of Fife*. A vol. of parodies and imitations of his contemporaries was published with the title, *The Poetical Mirror*, in 1816; it was rptd. in 1929 with an introd. by T. Earle Welby (Scholartis Press). A 4-vol. selection from his numerous poems appeared in 1822.

Hogg also wrote a large number of prose tales, of which the best are *The Brownie of Bodsbeck* (1818) and *The Private Memoirs and Confessions of a Justified Sinner* (1824; rptd. by Philpot with an introd. by T. Earle Welby in 1924), and collected some Jacobite songs, which he entitled *The Jacobite Relics of Scotland* (2 vols., 1819, 1821). His *Domestic Manners and Private Life of Sir Walter Scott*, which angered Lockhart, appeared in 1834. His death in 1835 was commemorated by the best of Wordsworth's later poems, *Extempore Effusion upon the death of James Hogg*.

The best ed. of his works is T. Thompson's (2 vols., Blackie, 1865). E. C. Batho's interesting study, *The Ettrick Shepherd* (C.U.P., 1927), contains a bibliography.

II

IMITATION AND PARODY

IT is not surprising that parody and imitation should abound at a time when poets derived so much inspiration from books. Most of the poetry written during this period before 1800 is imitative in one manner or another. The purpose of this section is to indicate the chief types and sources of imitation. For bibliographical details the reader will need to refer back to the previous section.

An "imitation", specifically so called, is a loose translation, in which an attempt is made to adapt the words of a Latin or Greek writer to modern conditions. It had been practised in the seventeenth century by Oldham and Rochester, and it is not altogether absent from Dryden's translations of Ovid and Juvenal; but the most successful examples of this way of writing are Pope's *Imitations of Horace*, Johnson's *London* and *The Vanity of Human Wishes*, and Gifford's *Baviad* and *Maeviad*.

This period cannot provide so fine an example as Milton's *Samson Agonistes* of the adaptation of a classical "form". The best it can offer are Gray's Pindaric Odes. These are imitations with a serious intention. But the masterpieces of this period in the adaptation of classical form were written with a comic intention. Such are Pope's *Rape of the Lock* and his *Dunciad*; and unless the reader knows something about the classical epic he will not enjoy them as much as he might. Another ancient verse-form which captured the imagination of later poets was the ballad, reintroduced to modern readers by Percy's *Reliques*. The best imitations are Coleridge's *Ancient Mariner* and Keats's *La Belle Dame sans Merci*. The sonnet is not so old a form as the pindaric ode or the ballad, but it had fallen into general disrepute, except in Milton's eyes, in the mid seventeenth century. Its revival in the seventeen-seventies by T. Warton, and its subsequent use by Bowles, Russell, Coleridge, Wordsworth and others, provides one more example of the adaptation of an obsolete form.

The strongly-marked characteristics of poets' styles gave ample opportunity for that flippant imitation we call parody. John Philips parodied Milton in *The Splendid Shilling* and Shenstone parodied Spenser in *The Schoolmistress*. But both were to discover reasons for more reverential imitation. They came to smile, but they stopped to admire; and later imitators smiled less and less and admired more and more. It would take too long to record all the imitators of Spenser and Milton. Readers of Dyer and of Thomson's *Seasons* cannot fail to observe the results of studying Milton's style; and Spenser's style and stanza are equally manifest in Thomson's *Castle of Indolence*, W. J. Mickle's *Concubine*, and even in Byron's *Childe Harold*. But parody did not always lead to such serious results. Parody is an end in itself in Isaac Hawkins Browne's *A Pipe of Tobacco*, 1735 (imitations of Pope and Young, rptd. in O.B.), in some of the poetry of the *Anti-Jacobin* (see below) in Hogg's *Poetical Mirror*, and in Horace and James Smith's *Rejected Addresses* (see below).

THE ANTI-JACOBIN was a paper conducted in the interests of Pitt's Tory Government by Gifford (see p. 185) during the years 1797 and 1798. Besides recording and commenting on the important events of the week, it published poems mainly the work of GEORGE CANNING (1770–1827), later Prime Minister, and JOHN HOOKHAM FRERE (1769–1846), whose metrical translations of Aristophanes are rptd. in W.C. The best of these poems are the parodies of Southey's sapphics, *The Soldier's Wife*, and *The Friend of Humanity and the Knife-Grinder*, and *The Loves of the Triangles*, a parody of Erasmus Darwin's *The Loves of the Plants*, 1789 (see p. 190). *Poetry of the Anti-Jacobin* was first collected in 1799. The best editions are those of C. Edmonds (1852) and L. Rice-Oxley (P.R., 1924). Methuen publishes a vol. of *Selections from the Anti-Jacobin*, ed. Lloyd Sanders.

SMITH, James (1775–1839) and HORACE (1779–1849)

The occasion of *Rejected Addresses* was a competition initiated by the committee of Drury Lane Theatre for an address to be spoken at the reopening of the theatre in 1812. The Smiths collaborated in a series of parodies of the entries which might have been sent by Wordsworth, Crabbe, Byron, Scott, Coleridge, Cobbett and others, the first four mentioned being generally reckoned the best. There is a useful modern ed. by A. Boyle (Constable, 1929), there are selections in O.B.R.V., and there is an appreciation by E. Blunden in *Votive Tablets* (Cobden-Sanderson, 1931).

III

CRITICISM

Eighteenth-century criticism is surveyed in A. Bosker's *Literary Criticism in the Age of Johnson* (Groningen, 1930).

THE greatest critic writing at the beginning of this period was JOHN DRYDEN, whose work has been treated in vol. 2 (see pp. 368–70). The most interesting of the critical prefaces which he wrote after 1689 are *A Discourse concerning the Original and Progress of Satire* (1693) and the preface to the *Fables* (1700).

RYMER, Thomas (1641–1713)

In marked contrast to Dryden's work is the work of Rymer, who published a translation of Rapin's *Reflections on Aristotle*, with a preface, in 1674. His other critical writings are *The Tragedies of the last age consider'd and examin'd by the practice of the ancients and by common sense*, 1678 (which is largely concerned with Fletcher's *Rollo, A King and no King*, and *The Maid's Tragedy*), and *A Short View of Tragedy* (1693), in which Rymer examined *Othello*. Dryden's criticism is the criticism of a fellow-craftsman, sympathetic, liberal, permitting any reasonable extenuation of the "rules" of art. Rymer's criticism is learned, vigorous, even sprightly; but it is unsympathetic and illiberal. Rymer is never tired of showing "how unhappy the greatest English poets have been through their ignorance or negligence of these fundamental rules and laws of Aristotle". Consequently Rymer mauls Shakespeare as cruelly as William Archer mauled the minor Elizabethan dramatists in *The Old Drama and the New* (1923) with similar methods and similar results. Selections from his work are published by J. E. Spingarn in *Seventeenth-Century Critical Essays*, vol. 2 (Cl. P., 1908–9). Dryden's comments on Rymer were printed by Dr. Johnson at the end of his *Life of Dryden*.

214

Rymer did more useful and lasting work as an antiquary, by collecting and printing the public conventions of England with other powers under the title of *Foedera* (20 vols., 1704–35). See D. C. Douglas's *English Scholars* (Cape, 1939), ch. XI.

TEMPLE, Sir William (1628–99)
Temple's approach was less professional than either Dryden's or Rymer's. He wrote his critical essays with a dilettante's ease. These were *An Essay upon the Ancient and Modern Learning* and *Of Poetry*, both published in the second part of his *Miscellanea* (1692). An ed. by J. E. Spingarn is published by the Cl. P. (1909). For Temple's other writings, see vol. 2, p. 304.

ANCIENTS AND MODERNS

The controversy between the defenders of the Ancients and the defenders of the Moderns was fought out in France with a clearer understanding of the issues than that which prevailed between the antagonists in England. The subject had been debated by Sprat in his *History of the Royal Society* (1667) and by Dryden in his *Essay of Dramatic Poesy* (1668) both of whose sympathies lay with the Moderns. New life was given to the controversy by Sir William Temple's championship of the Ancients in his *Essay upon the Ancient and Modern Learning* (1692) to which he had been stimulated by reading Fontenelle's *Pluralité des Mondes*. Temple was elaborately answered by William Wotton in *Reflections upon Ancient and Modern Learning* (1694); and there the matter might perhaps have been allowed to rest if it had not been for some passing praise casually bestowed by Temple on the *Letters of Phalaris*, which he supposed to be one of the oldest books we have. This passage in Temple's essay was noticed by Richard Bentley, the great classical scholar, who promised to contribute an appendix to Wotton's second ed. proving the *Letters* to be spurious, and also by Henry Aldrich, Dean of Christ Church, who engaged a young pupil of his, Charles Boyle, to prepare a fresh ed. of the *Letters*. This ed. was published in 1695, with some prefatory irony upon the "singular humanity" of Bentley, who had allowed insufficient time for collation of a manuscript of *Phalaris* in his charge. In 1697 Bentley wrote his promised appendix to Wotton's second ed., and took the occasion of answering Boyle's charge and reviewing his book. From this point the controversy is no longer between the champions of the Ancients and of the Moderns, but between Bentley and Boyle, Bentley maintaining the spuriousness of *Phalaris*, Boyle maintaining that Bentley had not proved his case. Boyle's reply, which was largely written by Atterbury, was published in 1698 with the title *Dr. Bentley's Dissertations on the Epistles of Phalaris, and the Fables of Æsop, Examin'd*; Bentley's masterly rejoinder, which far transcends the occasion, was *A Dissertation Upon the Epistles of Phalaris* (1699). There was really no more to be said, except by Swift who wrote the *Battle of the Books* while working at Sir William Temple's about this time, but did not publish it till 1704.

Thus the original issue—between those who chafed at ancient and classical precedent and those who appealed to it from contemporary barbarisim—was obscured by the Phalaris controversy. The larger issue is discussed by J. B. Bury in *The Idea of Progress* (Macmillan, 1920) and by R. F. Jones in *Ancients and Moderns* (Washington University Studies, 1936); the story of Bentley *versus* Boyle is well told by R. C. Jebb in ch. 4 of his *Bentley* (E.M.L.), and by H. W. Garrod in an essay called "Phalaris and Phalarism" contributed to *Seventeenth-Century Studies presented to Sir Herbert Grierson* (Cl. P., 1938).

BYSSHE, Edward

Temple thought that so much paper had been blotted on the subject of the Rules of Poetry, "that 'tis all grown tedious or repetition". Nevertheless Bysshe's *Art of English Poetry* (1702) was so popular that it reached a ninth and enlarged ed. in 1762. It is divided into three parts: I. Rules for making Verses, II. A Dictionary of Rhymes, III. A collection of the most Natural, Agreeable, and Noble Thoughts . . . that are to be found in the best English Poets. This third part is the first of a series of anthologies, of which the best known is ELIZABETH COOPER'S *Muses Library* (1737).

DENNIS, John (1657–1734)

Dennis was well known to his contemporaries as a poet, a dramatist, and a critic, but it is only as a critic that his fame survives. His first essay in criticism was a reply to Rymer, called *The Impartial Critick* (1693). In 1698 he entered the controversy, provoked by Jeremy Collier's *Short View of the Immorality . . . of the English Stage* (see p. 299), with *The Usefulness of the Stage*. His best works belong to the first years of the next century: *The Advancement and Reformation of Modern Poetry* (1701); *A Large*

Account of the Taste in Poetry, prefixed to *The Comical Gallant* (1702), Dennis's version of *The Merry Wives of Windsor*; and *The Grounds of Criticism in Poetry* (1704). *An Essay on the Genius and Writings of Shakespeare* was published in 1712, and *Original Letters, Familiar, Moral, and Critical* in 1721. Dennis is all too well remembered as the unrelenting critic of Pope and Addison. *Reflections upon a late Rhapsody called An Essay upon Criticism* was published in 1711, and was followed by a series of *Remarks—upon Cato* (1713); *upon Mr. Pope's Translation of Homer; with Two Letters concerning Windsor Forest, and the Temple of Fame* (1717); *on Mr. Pope's Rape of the Lock* (1728); and *upon . . . . the Dunciad* (1729).

Dennis's solitary theatrical success was a tragedy, *Liberty Asserted* (1704); he also wrote two other tragedies *Appius and Virginia* (1709) and *The Invader of his Country*, a version of *Coriolanus* (1720).

Selections from Dennis's writings were published in 1718 (*Select Works*) and in 1727 (*Miscellaneous Tracts*). The first vol. of an ed. by E. N. Hooker has recently (1939) been published by the Johns Hopkins Press and O.U.P. J. E. Spingarn's *Seventeenth-Century Critical Essays*, vol. 3 (Cl. P., 1909) contains *The Impartial Critick*; W. H. Durham's *Critical Essays of the Eighteenth Century, 1700–25* (O.U.P., 1915) contains *A Large Account, The Grounds of Criticism in Poetry*, and *Reflections upon . . . An Essay upon Criticism*; and *An Essay on . . . Shakespeare* is rptd. in D. Nichol Smith's *Eighteenth-Century Essays on Shakespeare* (1903). The best study of Dennis is H. G. Paul's *J.D., His Life and Criticism* (Columbia U.P., 1911).

ADDISON, Joseph (1672–1719)

Addison's writings are treated at large on pp. 266–8, to which the reader is referred for details of editions. But in view of the importance of his critical work, it is necessary to draw attention here to certain papers in *The Spectator*. Nos. 411–21, on the Pleasures of the Imagination, are an attempt to apply Locke's doctrines to the subject of aesthetics, and are in fact the first sustained effort to build up an aesthetic theory. In papers 58–63 Addison carried on the discussion of the nature of Wit, which had already occupied Cowley, Dryden, and Locke. In a series of Saturday papers (nos. 267–369), he showed that it was quite correct to enjoy *Paradise Lost*, and in papers 70 and 74 he went even further to show that an admirer of the *Æneid* might also admire *Chevy Chase*. Other interesting critical papers are those on Tragedy (39–44) and the review of Pope's *Essay on Criticism* (253).

217

After Addison and Shaftesbury (p. 239), many writers obliged the reading public with essays on beauty, and in particular on the boundaries of the beautiful and the sublime, a subject examined in great detail by S. H. Monk in *The Sublime: A Study of Critical Theories in XVIIIth-Century England* (Modern Language Association of America, 1935). The most important contributions to these discussions were FRANCES HUTCHESON's *Inquiry into the Original of our Ideas of Beauty and Virtue*, 1725 (see p. 241), JOHN BAILLIE's *Essay on the Sublime* (1747), WILLIAM HOGARTH's *Analysis of Beauty* (1753), EDMUND BURKE's *Philosophical Enquiry into the Origin of our Ideas of the Sublime and Beautiful*, 1757 (see p. 247). The standard bibliographical guide to this subject is J. W. Draper's *Eighteenth-Century English Æsthetics* (Heidelberg, Winter, 1931).

The virtue of Burke's *Enquiry* from the point of view of his contemporaries was that it nicely distinguished the Sublime from the Beautiful, and neatly classified ideas which could bear the Sublime label, such as obscurity, terror, overwhelming power, vastness, and vacuity. Its popularity continued until the end of the century. The next writer on aesthetics, ALEXANDER GERARD (*An Essay on Taste*, 1759), may not have read it, for he looks back to the theories of Shaftesbury, Hutcheson, and Baillie, but it had certainly influenced LORD KAMES, who published his *Elements of Criticism* in 1762, and HUGH BLAIR, who began lecturing at Edinburgh in 1759 or 1760 on Taste, Beauty, the Sublime, etc., and published his lectures in 1783.

"The most purely aesthetic document of the eighteenth century" is ARCHIBALD ALISON's *Essays on the Nature and Principles of Taste*, 1790 (enlarged ed., 1810), in which Alison propounded that it is the association of ideas set up by an object, not the object itself, which produces the sublime or beautiful effect. Alison's views were developed further in RICHARD PAYNE KNIGHT's *Analytical Enquiry into the Principles of Taste* (1795), DUGALD STEWART's *Philosophical Essays* (1810), and FRANCIS JEFFREY's *Essay on Beauty*, contributed to the *Encyclopædia Britannica* (1810).

Knight was vigorous in impugning not only Burke but also his friend, UVEDALE PRICE, who had read William Gilpin's *Essay on Picturesque Beauty*, 1792 (see p. 286), and adopted the word "picturesque" to denominate a third category of effects which were neither beautiful on the one hand nor sublime on the other. His views are expounded in his *Essay on the Picturesque, as Compared with the Sublime and Beautiful* (1794). See Christopher Hussey's *The Picturesque* (Putnam, 1927).

YOUNG, Edward. See p. 180.

WARTON, Joseph and Thomas. See p. 183.

CRITICISM OF SHAKESPEARE

Much work was done during this period in establishing and interpreting the text of Shakespeare. The first ed. (1709) was the work of Nicholas Rowe, the dramatist (see p. 301), who made a somewhat haphazard revision of the text, regularised the stage directions and the scenic divisions, and supplied a biographical introduction. The next editor was Pope (1725), who worked hard at collating texts, but preferred to trust the standard of his own taste (see p. 174). Theobald's ed. (1733) was superior to both of his predecessors' in text and in critical notes. He was the first to print such brilliant emendations as "a' babbled of green fields" (*Henry V*, II. iii. 16) and "lackeying the varying tide" (*Ant.*, I. iv. 46). Of the subsequent editions, the most important are those of Dr. Johnson (1765), whose notes are still of great value whenever scholarship and historical knowledge fail, and Capell (1768), a most thorough collater but unreliable in his choice of readings. Johnson's ed. served as the basis for subsequent editions, those of Steevens, Reed and Malone, the culmination of this work being the great Boswell-Malone variorum ed. of 1821 (see p. 221).

The tone of the criticism of Shakespeare was set by Dryden's "epitome of excellence" in his *Essay of Dramatic Poesy* (1668; see vol. 2, p. 368), of which the critical introductions of Rowe, Pope, and Johnson are amplifications and elaborations. Shakespeare was admitted to have faults; he was a "wild" genius; but there was a degree of beauty and truth to Nature in his irregularity to which the more polished writer could not attain.

The prefaces were general surveys sparing in particulars. But Pope systematically marked Shakespeare's "shining" passages (see p. 174), and Johnson added to his notes an estimate of each play and an examination of a few of the principal characters. The method of character-study was further pursued by THOMAS WHATELY in his *Remarks on some of the Characters of Shakespeare*, (written before 1770, not published till 1785), by WILLIAM RICHARDSON in *A Philosophical Analysis and Illustration of some of Shakespeare's Remarkable Characters* (first series, 1774; ii, 1784; iii, 1789), by MAURICE MORGANN in *An Essay on the Dramatic*

Character of Sir John Falstaff, 1777 (rptd. in O.M.), by Coleridge in his lectures, and by Hazlitt in his *Characters of Shakespeare's Plays* (1817).

Only a few of the other activities of Shakespeare's critics can be mentioned. GERARD LANGBAINE had started to explore Shakespeare's sources in his *Account of the English Dramatic Poets* (1691). A 2-vol. collection was made by CHARLOTTE LENNOX in 1753–4, entitled *Shakespeare Illustrated: or the Novels and Histories, on which the Plays of Shakespeare are founded* (see K. Young's monograph in Univ. of Wisconsin *Studies in Language and Literature*, 1923, and A. T. Hazen's *Johnson's Prefaces and Dedications*, O.U.P., 1937, pp. 104–6). The most important contribution to this study was RICHARD FARMER's *Essay on the Learning of Shakespeare* (1767). A remarkable anticipation of the study of Shakespeare's imagery was made by WILLIAM WHITER in a work called *A Specimen of a Commentary on Shakespeare . . . on a new principle of criticism derived from Mr. Locke's Doctrine of the Association of Ideas* (1794). More widely known are Lamb's essay *On the tragedies of Shakspeare, considered with reference to their fitness for Stage Representation* (1811), and De Quincey's *On the knocking at the Gate in "Macbeth"* (1823).

For later editions of the critical work of Johnson, Coleridge and Hazlitt, see pp. 221, 200, 270. D. Nichol Smith's *Eighteenth Century Essays on Shakespeare* (1903) is a valuable collection of prefaces and essays with an introductory survey, and the same editor's *Shakespeare Criticism* (W.C.) provides a useful selection. The methods of the early editors have been examined by T. R. Lounsbury in *The Text of Shakespeare* (1906), by D. Nichol Smith in *Shakespeare in the Eighteenth Century* (Cl. P., 1928), and by R. B. McKerrow in *The Treatment of Shakespeare's Text by his Earlier Editors, 1709–1768* (Br. Academy Lecture, O.U.P., 1933).

JOHNSON, Samuel (1709–84)

Collected Works.

Johnson's writings were collected in 11 vols. and published with a life by Sir John Hawkins in 1787. Two supplementary vols. containing Johnson's reports of Debates in Parliament (1740–3) were issued the same year. A new ed. in 12 vols. with a life by Arthur Murphy (see p. 303) was issued in 1792 and was frequently rptd. The works were rptd. in 11 vols. in 1825, and again in 2 vols. ("Bohn") in 1850.

Poems.

Johnson's poems were first collected in one vol. in 1785, and were rptd. with additional poems in 1789 and 1820. The most convenient modern rpt. is in M.L. together with the poems of Gray, Goldsmith, and Collins. A new ed. is expected from D. Nichol Smith and E. L. McAdam.

London: A Poem, In Imitation of the Third Satire of Juvenal appeared anonymously in 1738, and its companion piece, *The Vanity of Human Wishes. The Tenth Satire of Juvenal, Imitated* in 1749. They were edited by I. P. Fleming in 1876, by F. Ryland in 1901, and rptd. with an introd. by T. S. Eliot in 1930. Johnson's only play *Irene: A Tragedy* (in blank verse), was acted in 1749 and printed the same year. Of Johnson's other poems it is only necessary to call attention to his verses on *A young Heir's coming of age*, first printed in Mrs. Piozzi's *British Symphony* (1794), and to his lines *On the Death of Mr. Robert Levet*, published in the *Gentleman's Magazine*, August 1783, both rptd. in O.B.

Learned Works.

The *Plan of a Dictionary of the English Language* was published in 1747, the *Dictionary* itself being completed in 1755. Johnson issued an abridged ed. in octavo in 1756, and corrected the folio vols. for a fourth ed. in 1773. The *Dictionary* was revised by H. J. Todd in 1818, and in subsequent years revisions were made by other editors. The last dictionary professing to be based on Johnson's was published in 1883. Johnson's preface is one of his most admired writings.

Johnson's intention of editing Shakespeare was first announced in 1745 when he published *Miscellaneous Observations on the Tragedy of Macbeth*. Fresh proposals were issued in 1756 but the ed. was delayed until 1765. Like the *Dictionary*, the *Shakespeare* became the basis upon which later editors worked. George Steevens assisted Johnson in revising an ed. published in 1773; Isaac Reed's revisions appeared in 1785; the revisions of Edmund Malone and James Boswell, the younger, appeared in the deservedly respected "third variorum" of 1821. Johnson's preface, so frequently praised from his day to our own, is rptd. with the proposals and a selection from Johnson's notes in Sir Walter Raleigh's *Johnson on Shakespeare* (O.M.).

Johnson's first biography, a life of Father Paul Sarpi, was published in 1738. He wrote many more between this and *The Lives of the Poets*, of which the most noteworthy are *The Life of*

Savage (1744), later incorporated in *The Lives of the Poets*, a life of Sir Thomas Browne, prefixed to an ed. of the *Christian Morals* (1756), rptd. by S. C. Roberts with the *C.M.* (C.U.P., 1927) and a life of Ascham, contributed to Bennet's edition (1761). *The Lives of the Poets* was undertaken in 1777 at the request of the London booksellers who intended to put out "an elegant and accurate edition of all the English Poets of reputation, from Chaucer to the present time—with a concise account of the life of each author". The booksellers afterwards limited their project by excluding the poets before Cowley, and Johnson enlarged his. The first four vols., containing 22 lives, were issued in 1779, and the remaining six vols. in 1781. The standard ed. is by G. Birkbeck Hill (3 vols., Cl. P., 1905); there are cheap rpts. in E.L. and W.C.

Other Writings in Prose.

The remainder of Johnson's writings are journalistic, with the exception of *Rasselas* (1759) and *A Journey to the Western Islands of Scotland* (1775). R. W. Chapman is the editor of the best ed. of *Rasselas* (Cl. P., 1927), and of the *Journey* (with Boswell's *Tour* in the same vol., O.S.A., 1930). *Rasselas* is also rptd. in E.L. (*Shorter Novels*, vol. 3) with Beckford's *Vathek* and Walpole's *Castle of Otranto*.

The Rambler is a series of 208 periodical essays, of which Johnson wrote all except Nos. 10, 30, 44, 97, and 100. They were published twice weekly between 1750 and 1752, and were rptd. in revised form in 1753. There is a convenient selection in O.M. Between 1758 and 1760, Johnson contributed a weekly essay entitled *The Idler* to the *Universal Chronicle*. The essays, of which he had written all but 12, were collected in 1761. A selection is published by C.U.P. Johnson also wrote several essays for Hawkesworth's *Adventurer* (1753–4). Two other journalistic enterprises with which Johnson was connected belong to this decade, *The Universal Visiter* (1756), to which he contributed *Further Thoughts on Agriculture*, and *The Literary Magazine* (1756), for which he provided the preliminary address and wrote his famous review of Soame Jenyns's *Free Inquiry into the Nature and Origin of Evil*.

In 1770 Johnson published anonymously the first of a series of pamphlets in support of the government. This was *The False Alarm*, supporting the exclusion from parliament of John Wilkes, the member for Middlesex. *Thoughts on the Late Transactions respecting Falkland's Islands* followed in 1771, *The Patriot* in 1774, and *Taxation no Tyranny; an Answer to the Resolutions and Address of the American Congress* in 1775. They were rptd. in one vol. in 1776.

Coleridge liked these pamphlets better than any other parts of Johnson's work, and pleaded for the merits of *Taxation no Tyranny* in particular. But readers are more likely to agree with Johnson in preferring the "subtlety of disquisition" in *The False Alarm*, or with Boswell in preferring the "fire" of the *Falkland's Islands*.

Johnson's *Prefaces and Dedications*, which show how good a level of workmanship he always maintained, have been collected by A. T. Hazen (Yale and O.U.P., 1937). A valuable review of this vol. by R. W. Chapman was printed in R.E.S., July 1938.

At present the standard ed. of Johnson's letters is by G. Birkbeck Hill (2 vols., Cl. P., 1892). Another ed. is in preparation by R. W. Chapman, who has published a selection in W.C.

Biography.

Boswell's was the sixth life of Johnson (see p. 275). Of the earlier biographers, Sir John Hawkins (1787) wrote with the authority of being Johnson's oldest surviving acquaintance, but did not make the most of his opportunity; Mrs. Piozzi (lately Mrs. Thrale) was the only person who could describe Johnson in his domestic circle, for so he came to look upon her house at Streatham. Her lively *Anecdotes of the late Samuel Johnson* appeared in 1786. It is rptd. in the Cambridge Miscellany, ed. S. C. Roberts (C.U.P., 1932). An elaborately annotated ed. was published by G. Birkbeck Hill in *Johnsonian Miscellanies* (Cl. P., 2 vols., 1897), which also contains extracts from Hawkins and numerous sketches and anecdotes of Johnson by his contemporaries, as well as Johnson's *Prayers and Meditations*. Mrs. Thrale's journal of her visit to France with Dr. Johnson is published with Johnson's journal by the Manchester U.P. (ed. M. Tyson and H. Guppy, 1932). It is not surprising that there have been few subsequent biographers—Leslie Stephen's life in E.M.L. is perhaps the most satisfactory—but any future writer of a Life of Johnson will find that he is deeply indebted to the painstaking biographical collections of A. L. Reade, who has published 9 vols. of *Johnsonian Gleanings* (privately printed, 1909–39).

Criticism.

The best general studies of Johnson are Sir Walter Raleigh's *Six Essays on Johnson* (Cl. P., 1910), D. Nichol Smith's article in C.H.E.L., and J. Bailey's *Dr. Johnson and his Circle* (H.U.L.). There is a lecture on Johnson's poetry in D. Nichol Smith's *Some Observations on Eighteenth Century Poetry* (O.U.P., 1937). Sir James A. H. Murray's Romanes Lecture (1900) on the *Evolution of English Lexicography* is essential to the study of the *Dictionary*, and the relevant pages of W. P. Courtney's *Bibliography of Samuel Johnson* (Cl. P., 1915) should also be consulted. Students of Johnson's Shakespearian criticism should read D. Nichol Smith's *Eighteenth-Century Essays on Shakespeare* (1903) and the same writer's *Shakespeare in the Eighteenth Century* (Cl. P., 1928), Raleigh's introd. to *Johnson on Shakespeare,* op.cit., and K. Young's *Samuel Johnson on Shakespeare* (University of Wisconsin studies, 1923). W. B. C. Watkins's *Johnson and English Poetry before 1660* (Princeton and O.U.P., 1936) is an admirable piece of work. E.S.M.E.A. contain a paper by R. W. Chapman on the problems of re-editing Johnson's letters (vol. 12), and one by D. Nichol Smith on *Irene* (vol. 14). The greatest collection of Johnsoniana in the world is owned by R. B. Adam of Buffalo, N.Y., who has provided an elaborate catalogue in 3 vols. (revised ed., 1929). The first vol. reproduces 250 of Johnson's letters with facsimiles of some of his manuscripts; the second deals with Johnson's books and with more of his manuscripts; the third consists of 266 pages describing and reproducing letters from every person of note mentioned in Birkbeck Hill's editions. A supplement to Courtney's *Bibliography*, op. cit., by R. W. Chapman and A. T. Hazen is published by the Oxford Bibliographical Society, vol. 5, pt. 3, 1939.

HURD, Richard (1720–1808)

Bishop Hurd's most famous critical work is a justification of "Gothic" poetry which, he maintained, must be judged by its own, and not by classical, standards. He named it *Letters on Chivalry and Romance*, and published it in 1762. A rpt., ed. E. J. Morley, is included in O.M. But "the critical spirit of Hurd", which Gibbon commends in his autobiography, had already been displayed in *A Discourse concerning Poetical Imitation* which accompanied his commentary on Horace's Epistle to Augustus (1751), and in *A Letter to Mr. Mason on the marks of Imitation* (1757). His correspondence with Mason has been ed. E. H. Pearce and L. Whibley (C.U.P., 1932). An ed. of his works in 8 vols. was published in 1811. There is an interesting study of Hurd in Bishop Pearce's *Hartlebury Castle* (S.P.C.K., 1926), ch. 12.

REYNOLDS, Sir Joshua (1723–92)

Reynold's literary works, which he regarded with considerable pride, were collected in 2 vols. by Edmund Malone in 1797 (rptd. in Bell's Bohn Library). They consist of three papers supplied to Dr. Johnson for *The Idler* in 1759 (Nos. 76, 79, 82), fifteen

Discourses delivered at the Royal Academy during the years 1769 to 1790, and annotations of Mason's translation of Du Fresnoy's *De Arte Graphica* (1783). The best editions of the discourses are those of J. Burnet (1842), E. Gosse (Kegan Paul, 1884; with Blake's annotations, also published in G. L. Keynes's edition of Blake), R. Fry (Seeley, 1905), and A. Dobson (W.C., with the *Idler* papers). There is valuable editorial matter in L. Dimier's French translation (1909). Sir Joshua's letters have been collected and ed. F. W. Hilles (C.U.P., 1929). The standard biography is C. R. Leslie's *Life and Times of Sir J. R.*, completed by Tom Taylor (1865). F. W. Hilles has written a study of *The Literary Career of Sir J. R.* (C.U.P., 1936), in which he prints a more accurate text of Reynolds's interesting character of Johnson than that used by G. B. Hill in *Johnsonian Miscellanies*.

TOOKE, John Horne (1736–1812)

Horne Tooke was a radical politician and a critic not of letters but of language. His political and critical activities were closely connected, for he considered that he owed his conviction in the courts of law to an erroneous interpretation of words. He started to formulate his philosophy in prison and published a sketch of it in 1778 with the title *A Letter to John Dunning, Esq.* This was considerably expanded in subsequent years and published with the title *Epea Pteroenta, or the Diversions of Purley* (Part I, 1786; Part II, 1805). An ed. by R. Taylor, which also contains the *Letter to Dunning* was published in 2 vols in 1829. "The whole of his reasoning," in Hazlitt's words, "turns upon showing that the conjunction *That* is the pronoun *That*, which is itself the participle of a verb, and in like manner that all the other mystical and hitherto unintelligible parts of speech are derived from the only two intelligible ones, the Verb and Noun." *Memoirs of J. H. T.* by Alexander Stephens was published in 2 vols. in 1813. A study by M. C. Yarborough is published (1928) by the Columbia U.P. Hazlitt's character sketch of Tooke will be found in *The Spirit of the Age*.

WORDSWORTH, William

His chief critical writings are the preface to the second edition of *Lyrical Ballads* (1800), the preface to the collected poems published in 1815, and the essay supplementary to his preface. See p. 197.

COLERIDGE, Samuel Taylor. See p. 199.

SHELLEY, Percy Bysshe. See p. 204.

LAMB, Charles. See p. 270.

HAZLITT, William. See p. 270.

THE *EDINBURGH* AND *QUARTERLY* REVIEWERS, ETC. see pp. 271–2.

D'ISRAELI, Isaac (1766–1848)
Isaac D'Israeli's work is partly critical, partly historical, partly anecdotal. He spent his life amongst books and wrote a large number of short essays from the huge stores of miscellaneous information which he had collected. The first vol. of *Curiosities of Literature* was published in 1791 and the sixth in 1834. The popularity of the work may be estimated by the fact that twelve editions were published in D'Israeli's lifetime. In the meanwhile he had written *Calamities of Authors* (1812–13) and *Quarrels of Authors* (1814); *Amenities of Literature* was published in 3 vols. in 1841. D'Israeli's more specifically historical works are *An Inquiry into the Literary and Political Character of James I* (1816) and *Commentaries on the Life and Reign of Charles I*, 5 vols. (1828–31). A life written by his famous son, Benjamin Disraeli, was published as a preface to a 7-vol. ed. of his works (1858–9). A selection from *Curiosities of Literature* is edited by E. V. Mitchell (Appleton, 1932).

IV

THE NOVEL

THE following historical studies of the novel in this period may be recommended: Sir W. Raleigh's *The English Novel* (Murray, 1894); E. A. Baker's *The History of the English Novel*, vols. 3–6 (Witherby, 1929–35); J. M. S. Tompkins's *The Popular Novel in England, 1770–1800* (Constable, 1932).

DEFOE, Daniel. See p. 258.

HAYWOOD, Mrs. Eliza (1693–1756)

Mrs. Haywood's first novel, and the first of a series of passionate romances, was *Love in Excess*, published in 1720. Encouraged perhaps by the example of Mrs. Manley (see p. 279), she turned to the writing of scandalous chronicles and produced *Memoirs of a certain Island adjacent to Utopia* (1725) and *The Secret History of the Present Intrigues of the Court of Caramania* (1727). Her latest experiment was the domestic novel. Of this kind she published *The History of Mrs. Betsy Thoughtless* (1751) and *The History of Jemmy and Jenny Jessamy* (1753). Mrs. Haywood also published an imitation of *The Spectator* which appeared in monthly parts between 1744 and 1746, and was called *The Female Spectator*. G. F. Whicher's *The Life and Romances of Mrs. E. Haywood* was published by the Columbia U.P. in 1915.

RICHARDSON, Samuel (1689–1761)

Richardson was a printer who took to novel-writing late in life. His three novels, written in the form of letters, are *Pamela* (2 vols., 1740; *Part II*, 2 vols., 1741), *Clarissa Harlowe* (7 vols., 1747–8), and *Sir Charles Grandison* (7 vols., 1753–4), in all of which he made a minute and protracted examination of the workings of the human heart. Although he was not the first who, in Johnson's words, "taught the passions to move at the command of virtue", his blend of sentiment and morality became popular and was often reproduced both here and abroad. An ed. of the novels in 12 vols., introd. L. Stephen, was published in 1883, another 12-vol. ed. by W. L. Phelps (Heinemann) in 1902, and a third is published in 18 vols. by the Shakespeare Head Press (Blackwell). *Pamela* and *Clarissa* are rptd. in E.L. in 2 and 4 vols. respectively. An abridgement of *Clarissa* by Mrs. Humphrey Ward was published in 1868, and an abridgement of *Sir Charles Grandison* by G. Saintsbury in 1895. Richardson also prepared an aid to letter-writing called *Familiar Letters on Important Occasions*, 1741—it has been edited by B. W. Downs (Routledge, 1928)—and wrote the only paper in Johnson's *Rambler* (No. 97), which enjoyed a good sale. *The Correspondence of S. R.* (6 vols., 1804) was stigmatised by Jeffrey in the *Edinburgh Review* as a "melancholy farrago"; but the first vol. contains a life by Mrs. Barbauld which is still the principal authority. A study by B. W. Downs was published by Routledge in 1928, and another by J. W. Krutch in *Five Masters* (Cape, 1930).

FIELDING, Henry (1707–54)

An incompetent ed. of Fielding's works with an inadequate biography was prepared by Arthur Murphy (see p. 303) in 1762 (4 and 8 vol. issues). Subsequent editors have made slight improvements, but none is either complete or worthy of Fielding. These are A. Chalmers's (10 vols., 1806), L. Stephen's (10 vols., 1882), and W. E. Henley's (16 vols., Heinemann, 1903).

Dramatic Works.

Fielding started as a dramatist, and gained considerable popularity for several years. His most lively plays are his burlesques, or "dramatick satires", as he called them: *The Author's Farce* and *Tom Thumb* (1730); *Pasquin* (1736), whose political satire was largely responsible for the Licensing Act of 1737; *The Historical Register* (1737). *Tom Thumb* was revised and amplified in 1731, and renamed *The Tragedy of Tragedies*. Both versions are rptd. in J. T. Hillhouse's ed. (O.U.P., 1918).

Journalistic and Legal Works.

Fielding's first paper was *The Champion*, described by a recent critic as a cross between *The Tatler* and *The Grub Street Journal*. Its chief purpose was to attack Walpole's government. Fielding directed the frontal attacks, but preferred to use irony or allegory as his own weapons. He contributed about 70 essays and minor pieces to this paper between 1739 and 1741, and was the leading spirit in two more political journals, *The True Patriot* (1745-6), occasioned by the '45 rebellion, and *The Jacobite's Journal* (1747-8). In his last paper, *The Covent Garden Journal* (1751-2), Fielding was more exclusively critical of letters and society, and drew to some extent on his experience as a magistrate; an ed. by G. E. Jensen is published by O.U.P. (2 vols., 1915).

Fielding was called to the bar in 1740. He worked on the western circuit for some time and became a magistrate at Bow Street in 1748, where his aim was "to bring a rogue to the gallows" and reclaim the young from the contamination of prison life. His most important legal tract is *An Enquiry into the Causes of the Late Increase of Robbers* (1751).

Fiction.

Richardson's *Pamela* provoked a skit entitled *An Apology for the Life of Mrs. Shamela Andrews* (1741). This highly entertaining criticism of the morality of *Pamela* is almost certainly by Fielding. He followed it up with *The History of the Adventures of Joseph Andrews and his friend Mr. Abraham Adams* (1742), which only derives from Richardson in part. *The History of Tom Jones, a Foundling*, was commenced in 1746 and published in 6 vols. in 1749. *Amelia* was published in 4 vols. in 1751. Fielding later revised it, the revised version being first published in Murphy's ed. (1762).

In addition to these novels Fielding also wrote *A Journey from this World to the Next* and *The Life of Mr. Jonathan Wild the Great*, both published in his *Miscellanies* (1743). *Jonathan Wild*, in this early form, incorporated a good deal of allegorical satire at the expense of Walpole, which was blurred and generalised in Fielding's revised version (1754). Fielding's last work, published after his death, was *The Journal of a Voyage to Lisbon* (1755).

The novels have been frequently rptd., the best ed. being the Shakespeare Head (10 vols., Blackwell, 1926). E.L. rpts. all but *Shamela* and the *Journey* in 6 vols. There is an ed. of *Shamela* by R. B. Johnson (Golden Cockerel Press, 1926) and another by B. W. Downs (Gordon Fraser, 1930). The *Journey* has been rptd. by the Golden Cockerel Press, 1930.

Biography and Criticism.

All lives of Fielding previous to A. Dobson's (E.M.L.) suffer from errors and misapprehensions. The standard biography is W. L. Cross's *The History of H. F.* (Yale and O.U.P., 3 vols.,

1918). F. W. Bateson's *English Comic Drama, 1700-1750* (Cl. P., 1929) contains a good chapter on Fielding's plays. B. M. Jones has written a study of Fielding's legal work entitled *H. F., Novelist and Magistrate* (Allen and Unwin, 1933). A. Digeon's *The Novels of Fielding* (Routledge, 1925) can be recommended. F. T. Blanchard has conducted an elaborate examination of Fielding's contemporary and subsequent reputation, entitled *Fielding the Novelist* (Yale and O.U.P., 1926).

SMOLLETT, Tobias George (1721-71)

A collected ed. of Smollett's writings was published in 6 vols., in 1790, and another in 8 vols. with a brief but authoritative life by J. Moore in 1797. This was re-edited·in 1872. A 12-vol. ed., with an introduction by W.' E. Henley, was published in 1899-1901.

Smollett's novels are coarse-grained, without the subtlety of either Richardson's or Fielding's. They are rambling, boisterous stories of multifarious adventures, full of grotesque and "humorous" characters. The earliest is *Roderick Random*, for which Smollett drew upon his personal experiences; it was published in 2 vols. in 1748. *Peregrine Pickle* in 4 vols. followed in 1751. *Ferdinand Count Fathom*, 3 vols., 1753; *Sir Launcelot Greaves*, 2 vols., 1762; *The Adventures of an Atom*, 2 vols., 1769. The last, and best, is *Humphrey Clinker*, 3 vols., 1771, the story of a tour undertaken through England and Scotland, in which Smollett provides an interesting picture of social life in Bath, London and Edinburgh. In addition to these novels, Smollett wrote a *History of England* (4 vols., 1757-8; 2nd ed., 11 vols., 1758-60; continued in 5 vols., 1763-5), an account of his travels in France and Italy (2 vols., 1766), and was the first editor of *The Critical Review* (1756).

An ed. of the novels in 12 vols. was published by the Navarre Soc. in 1925, and another in 11 vols. was published by the Shakespeare Head Press (Blackwell). E.L. rpts. *Roderick Random* and *Peregrine Pickle* in 3 vols.; W.C. rpts. *R. R.*, the *Travels*, and *Humphrey Clinker* (with some useful notes by L. R. Oxley) in 3 vols. Smollett's letters have been edited by E. S. Noyes (Harvard and O.U.P., 1926).

The best life of Smollett is the article in D.N.B. H. S. Buck's *Study in Smollett* (Yale and O.U.P., 1925) is mainly concerned with *P. P.* and Smollett's quarrels.

STERNE, Laurence (1713-68)

A 10-vol. ed. of Sterne's works was published in 1780. They

were re-edited by W. L. Cross (Taylor, New York, 12 vols., 1904) and again, anonymously, for the Shakespeare Head Press (Blackwell, 7 vols., 1926–7).

The Life and Opinions of Tristram Shandy began to appear in 1760, and ceased with the ninth vol. in 1767. The book is incomplete, but probably Sterne had no conclusion in mind. At the same time he began to publish *The Sermons of Mr. Yorick* (7 vols., 1760–9), offering as a reason the favourable reception accorded to the specimen published in *Tristram Shandy*. In 1767 he fell violently in love with Mrs. Elizabeth Draper. On the lady's being summoned to return to her husband in India, she and Sterne promised to keep diaries for each other's consolation. Only the third part of Sterne's diary (April to August 1767) survives. It was first published in Cross's collected ed. (1904) with the title *Journal to Eliza*. While keeping this diary Sterne was also writing *A Sentimental Journey* (2 vols., 1768): "In the journal," writes W. L. Cross, "we have the crude expression of the maudlin sentiment . . . in the *Sentimental Journey*, we have the sentiment refined to an art." Sterne's letters present difficult problems in detecting which are spurious. Mrs. Draper authorised the publication of *Letters from Yorick to Eliza* (1773), and Sterne's daughter published a 3-vol. ed. of his letters in 1775. The standard ed., which also contains the *Journal to Eliza*, is by L. P. Curtis (Cl. P., 1935). A selection, ed. R. B. Johnson, was published by Lane in 1927. *Tristram Shandy* and *A Sentimental Journey* are rptd. in E.L. and W.C. The E.L. *Sentimental Journey* also includes the *Journal* and *Letters from Yorick to Eliza*; the W.C. vol. contains a good introduction by Virginia Woolf.

The best book about Sterne is W. L. Cross's *Life and Times of L. S.* (Yale and O.U.P., 3rd ed., 1929).

MACKENZIE, Henry (1745–1831)

In *The Man of Feeling*, 1771 (ed. H. Miles, Scholartis Press, 1928), Mackenzie affected the palpitating prose of *Tristram Shandy*, and held the sympathetic tear in even greater prestige than Sterne had done. It is as important as Beattie's *Minstrel* in indicating the taste and feeling of the time. Mackenzie also conducted two periodicals, worthy successors of *The Spectator*, *The Mirror* (1779) and *The Lounger* (1785), in both of which he wrote surprisingly severe criticisms of the cult of Sensibility. Both papers contain good critical essays, such as *Mirror*, no. 24 by W. Richardson, and *Lounger*, no. 97 (the first appreciation of Burns) by Mackenzie. A collected ed. of Mackenzie's works in 3 vols.

appeared in 1807, and an authorised ed. in 8 vols. in 1808. His *Anecdotes and Egotisms* were first published by H. W. Thompson (O.U.P., 1927), who has also written a life of Mackenzie entitled *A Scottish Man of Feeling* (O.U.P., 1931).

WALPOLE, Horace. See p. 294.

GOLDSMITH, Oliver. See p. 186.

BURNEY, Fanny (1752–1840)

It is generally agreed that Fanny Burney's four novels show a progressive deterioration from *Evelina* (1778) through *Cecilia* (1782) and *Camilla* (1796) to *The Wanderer* (1814). The same progress is also apparent in her diaries, whose original brightness is eventually dimmed. *Evelina*, which is a lively anticipation of Jane Austen's manner, has been excellently edited by Sir F. D. Mackinnon (Cl. P., 1930), and is also rptd. in E.L. *Cecilia* was ed. A. R. Ellis in 2 vols. (Bell, 1882; rptd. 1906). A few extracts from *Camilla* and part of the preface to *The Wanderer*, in which Fanny Burney expounds her views of novel-writing, are included in R. B. Johnson's *F.B. and the Burneys* (Stanley Paul, 1926) which also contains some hitherto unpublished extracts from the diaries and some selections from the writings of other members of the family (F.B.'s father was the historian of music). The diaries which contain some vivid minutes of Johnson's domestic behaviour, have been ed. A. R. Ellis (*Early Diary*, 1768–78, 2 vols., Bell, 1889; rptd. 1913) and A. Dobson (*Diary and Letters*, 1778–1840, 6 vols., Macmillan, 1904). A selection ed. M. Masefield was published by Routledge in 1931. Fanny Burney's life has been pleasantly written by C. Lloyd (Longmans, 1936). Macaulay's famous essay appeared in the *Edinburgh* as a review of the first ed. of her diary (1842).

BECKFORD, William. See p. 236.

RADCLIFFE, Ann (1764–1823)

Mrs. Radcliffe was the most successful purveyor of novels of terror, whose vogue had started with Horace Walpole's "gothic" *Castle of Otranto* (see p. 294). Her popularity was partly owing to her "sensibility", to her nature descriptions which foreshadow Scott's, and to the tact with which she allowed her readers the pleasures of anticipating a thrill without the shock of experiencing it. Her heroes and heroines are Men and Women of Feeling

THE NOVEL

holidaying in a more adventurous age. The novels by which her
fame was acquired are *The Romance of the Forest* (1791), *The
Mysteries of Udolpho* (1794), and *The Italian* (1797), of which only
The Mysteries is accessible in a modern rpt. (E.L.).

INCHBALD, Elizabeth. See p. 236.

GODWIN, William. See p. 236.

HOLCROFT, Thomas. See p. 306.

LEWIS, Matthew Gregory (1775–1818)
Lewis was incited to complete the abandoned manuscript of
The Monk (1795) by the success of Mrs. Radcliffe's *Mysteries of
Udolpho*. But it has none of the reticence of *The Mysteries*. Lewis
was unsparing in the supply of voluptuous thrills, and produced
what Coleridge well described as "a fever dream—horrible,
without point or terror". But Coleridge had nothing but praise
for his unaffected *Journal of a West Indian Proprietor* (1815–17),
first published in 1834, which shows much finer powers of mind.
Brentano issues a rpt. of *The Monk* (1924), and M. Wilson has
edited the *Journal* (Routledge, 1929). Lewis's *Life and Correspondence* was published by M. Baron-Wilson (2 vols., 1839).

EDGEWORTH, Maria (1767–1849)
A collected ed. of Maria Edgeworth's works in 14 vols. ap-
peared in 1825, and was revised and extended to 18 vols. in
1832. Her best novels are *Castle Rackrent, An Hibernian Tale* (1800)
Belinda (1801), and *Ormond*, published with *Harrington* in 1817.
In addition to these she wrote a number of short stories for
children and others: *The Parent's Assistant* (1796) and its sequel,
Moral Tales for Young People (1801), *Popular Tales* (1804), and
Tales of Fashionable Life (1809–12), of which the most distinguished is *The Absentee*. Scott confessed that he would never have
thought of a Scottish novel had he not read M. E.'s "exquisite
pieces of Irish character". A 12-vol. rpt. of the novels was published by Dent in 1893. *Castle Rackrent* is rptd. with *The Absentee*
in E.L. Macmillan published rpts. of *Belinda, Ormond*, and *The
Parent's Assistant* between 1895 and 1897. A vol. of selections, ed.
G. Griffin, was published by Fisher Unwin (now Benn) in 1918.
The most authoritative life of M. E. was written by her step-
mother (3 vols., 1867). Two vols. of "life and letters" were ed.
A. J. C. Hare in 1894, and a selection of letters was published

233

by Cape (introd. F. V. Barry) in 1931. *The Black Book of Edgeworthstown*, ed. H. J. and H. E. Butler (Faber, 1927) contains much information about her family. A useful "bibliographical tribute" by B. C. Slade was published by Constable in 1937.

BARRETT, Eaton Stannard. See p. 236.

AUSTEN, Jane (1775–1817)

Four of Jane Austen's novels were published during her life: *Sense and Sensibility* (1811), *Pride and Prejudice* (1813), *Mansfield Park* (1814), *Emma* (1816). Her last completed novel, *Persuasion*, was published with a revised version of an earlier novel, *Northanger Abbey*, in 1818. In 1871, Jane Austen's nephew, J. F. Austen-Leigh, published a second ed. of the *Memoir* of his aunt, to which he added a short tale, *Lady Susan*, a substantial fragment of a novel, which he called *The Watsons*, and a cancelled chapter of *Persuasion*. The fragment of another novel, at which she was working shortly before her death, was published by the Cl. P. in 1925; it is usually called *Sanditon*. In addition, 2 vols of juvenilia have appeared: *Love and Freindship* (Chatto, 1922; cheap rpt., 1929; introd. by G. K. Chesterton), and *Volume the First* (Cl. P., 1933). The best ed. of the novels is R. W. Chapman's (O.U.P., 5 vols., 3rd ed., 1933). This does not include *Lady Susan* and *The Watsons*, but these have been rptd. from the manuscripts by the Cl. P. (2 vols., 1925, 1927), which also publishes Jane Austen's letters (ed. R. W. Chapman; 2 vols., 1932).

The chief authorities for Jane Austen's life are J. F. Austen-Leigh's *Memoir* (1869; ed. R. W. Chapman, Cl. P., 1926), and W. and R. A. Austen-Leigh's *Jane Austen, Her Life and Letters* (Smith, Elder, 1913); C. L. Thomson's *Jane Austen* (Marshall, 1929) is a serviceable critical study, and M. Lascelles, who has written well on Jane Austen's style in E.S.M.E.A., xxii. (1937), has recently published a study of great importance called *Jane Austen and her Art* (O.U.P., 1939).

SCOTT, Sir Walter (1771–1832)

The Waverley Novels were one of the last of Scott's many literary ventures. He published some translations from the German in 1796, but he had already been collecting Border ballads for some four years, which he eventually published in 3 vols. in 1802–3 with the title *Minstrelsy of the Scottish Border*. From this work arose *The Lay of the Last Minstrel* (1805), whose success "at once decided that literature should form the main business of Scott's life" (Lockhart). His other long poems followed within a few years: *Marmion* (1808), *The Lady of the Lake* (1810), *Rokeby* (1812), *The Lord of the Isles* (1815). Their reputation is now low, and chiefly rests upon such lyrics as *Proud Maisie* and *Brignall Banks*. The long series of novels began with the anonymous *Waverley* in 1814. Those who have not yet read any should start with one of the Scottish tales, such as *Guy Mannering* (1815), or *The Heart of Midlothian* (1818), or *Redgauntlet* (1824). In addition to reviews for the *Edinburgh* and later for the *Quarterly*, Scott also edited Dryden (18 vols., 1808), and Swift (19 vols., 1814), editions which are still well worth possessing both for Scott's biographies and for his notes.

Collected editions of Scott's poems were prepared by Lockhart in 1833 and 1848, and Scott himself published a collected ed. of the Waverley Novels with notes in 1829–33. There are numerous modern editions. *The Minstrelsy of the Scottish Border* is ed. T. F. Henderson (revised ed. 4 vols., Oliver and Boyd, 1932; one vol., Harrap, 1931). The standard ed. of Scott's letters (which Lockhart manipulated for his biography) is in 12 vols., ed. H. J. C. Grierson (Constable, 1932–7). Scott's *Journal*, to which Lockhart had access, first appeared in 1890 and was rptd. by Douglas and Foulis in 1927; but no complete or satisfactory ed. exists.

Lockhart's *Life of Scott* (see p. 277) remains the standard biography much as Boswell's is the standard life of Johnson; but the recent centenary evoked a number of biographical studies, of which John Buchan's (Cassell, 1932) was generally praised. A new biography by Sir H. J. C. Grierson has recently been published (Constable, 1938). For further criticism, see Grierson's preface to the *Letters*, and the essays which he edited and entitled *Sir Walter Scott To-day* (Constable, 1932).

PEACOCK, Thomas Love. See vol. 4, p. 276.

GALT, John (1779–1839)
Galt's best novels are *Annals of the Parish*, written in 1813 and published in 1821, a Scottish *Vicar of Wakefield*; *The Ayrshire Legatees* (1820), the record of a Scottish family's visit to England; *The Provost* (1822); *The Entail* (1823). *The Annals* is rptd. in O.M., and with *The Ayrshire Legatees* in E.L.; *The Entail* is rptd. in W.C. An ed. of Galt's works in 10 vols. by D. S. Meldrum and W. Roughead is published by Grant (1936). There is

a good biographical and critical study by J. W. Aberdein (O.U.P., 1936).

In addition to these novels there are a number which are well worth reading either for their intrinsic merit, or for their interest in the history of Taste, or for both reasons. HORACE WALPOLE's *Castle of Otranto* (1764), has already been mentioned as the first "tale of terror". Other memorable tales are MRS. SHELLEY's *Frankenstein*, 1818 (rptd. in E.L.), and C. R. MATURIN's *Melmoth the Wanderer*, 1820 (rptd. 1892). WILLIAM BECKFORD's Oriental tale, *Vathek*, is more luxurious than "horrid". Beckford wrote it in French and published it in 1787, but an unauthorised translation had appeared in 1786. The French original, with its sequel *Episodes of Vathek* (first published 1912), was edited by G. Chapman (2 vols., Constable, 1929), who has also written Beckford's life (Cape, 1937) and ed. his *Travel Diaries* (Constable, 1928). The English translation is rptd. in one vol. of E.L. (*Shorter Novels*, vol. 3) with *The Castle of Otranto* and *Rasselas*. One of the most remarkable novels written at the end of the century was *Caleb Williams* (1794) by WILLIAM GODWIN, the author of *Political Justice* (see p. 250). It is a story in which the characters, the dilemma, and the purpose are all admirably contrived. The last ed. was published by Routledge in 1903. At least two more novels deserve mention, both of them rptd. in O.M.: E. A. BARRETT's *The Heroine* (1813) and MRS. INCHBALD's *A Simple Story* (1791).

V

PHILOSOPHY

SIR LESLIE STEPHEN'S *History of English Thought in the Eighteenth Century* (2 vols., Murray, 1876; rev. 1927) is the standard survey of the philosophy of this period. C. R. Morris's *Locke, Berkeley, and Hume* (Cl. P., 1931) contains essays on the most notable philosophers. L. A. Selby-Bigge's *British Moralists* (2 vols., Cl. P., 1897) contains selections from the works of Shaftesbury, Hutcheson, Butler, Price and others.

LOCKE, John (1632–1704)

The books by which Locke became famous appeared in his old age. An abstract of the *Essay concerning Humane Understanding* (started in 1671) was published in French in his friend Leclerc's *Bibliothéque Universelle* in 1688. The *Essay* itself, and the *Two Treatises of Government* were published in 1690 and Locke's final revision of the *Essay* in 1706. In 1667 Locke had written an *Essay concerning Toleration*, first published in Fox Bourne's *Life*, which almost completely anticipated his *Epistola de Tolerantia* (1689), of which an unauthorised English translation was speedily published. The *Second Letter* on the same subject appeared in 1690, and the *Third Letter* in 1692. On July 19, 1684, Locke wrote the first of a series of letters to his friend Edward Clarke, for the benefit of his son's education. These were revised and printed as a treatise called *Some Thoughts concerning Education* (1693). In 1695 his *Reasonableness of Christianity* was published anonymously. Locke also wrote several papers relating to money, interest and trade, which were collected in 1696. Some other writings were first published in the *Posthumous Works of Mr. J. L.* (1706), of which the most notable is a practical appendix to the *Essay*, originally intended as an additional chapter to it, entitled *Of the Conduct of the Understanding* (1697).

Locke's works were collected in 3 vols. in 1714. J. A. St. John's ed. of the philosophical works (1843) is rptd. in Bell's Bohn Library. The educational writings, ed. J. W. Adamson (1912) were rptd. by C.U.P. in 1922. Two drafts of the *Essay* have recently been published: what is probably the second draft, ed. R. I. Aaron and J. Gibb (Cl. P., 1936) and the third draft, ed. B. Rand (Harvard U.P., 1931). The final version, ed. A. C. Fraser, is published by Cl. P. (2 vols., 1894), who also publish a useful abridgement, ed. A. S. Pringle-Pattison (1924). The *Two Treatises of Government* are rptd. in E.L. The letters which formed the basis of *Some Thoughts concerning Education* were ed. B. Rand (O.U.P., 1927) and entitled *The Correspondence of J. L. and Edward Clarke*. This book also contains a biographical study. *The Conduct*, ed. T. Fowler, is published by Cl. P. (5th ed., 1901).

The standard biography is H. R. Fox Bourne's (2 vols., 1876) and there is a good life by T. Fowler in E.M.L. The best brief introduction to the study of Locke is S. Alexander's *Locke* (1908). R. I. Aaron's *John Locke* (O.U.P., 1937) contains a short biography , an exposition of his theory of knowledge, and of his teaching on moral philosophy, political theory, education and religion. More specialised studies are J. Gibson's *Locke's Theory of Knowledge and its Historical Relations* (C.U.P., 1917) and K. MacLean's *J. L. and English Literature of the Eighteenth Century* (Yale and O.U.P., 1936). A bibliography of Locke by H. O. Christophersen was published in Oslo in 1930.

HERETICAL LITERATURE

Locke's *Essay* acted as a stimulus to "deistical" or "free-thinking" speculations which were already becoming popular owing to the writings of CHARLES BLOUNT (1654–93). JOHN TOLAND (1670–1722), a professed pupil of Locke, stated the case against Revelation in a book called *Christianity not Mysterious* (1696), a treatise designed to show that there is nothing in the Gospel contrary to reason nor above it. Further attacks upon orthodoxy were made by ANTHONY COLLINS (1676–1729), who published *A Discourse of Freethinking* in 1713, to which many Anglican divines, including Swift and Bentley, made replies. Eleven years later, in 1724, Collins published *A Discourse of the Grounds and Reasons of the Christian Religion*, in which he examined biblical prophecies and showed that an allegorical, i.e. a strained, interpretation was alone possible. THOMAS WOOLSTON (1670–1733) was bolder still, for he wrote *Six Discourses on the Miracles of our*

Saviour (1727-9) in which he made the first direct assault upon their authenticity, and was fined and imprisoned for his presumption. The most notable of the deists was MATTHEW TINDAL (1657-1733), whose *Christianity as Old' as the Creation* (1730) was an attempt to show that a positive revelation is superfluous. This book, "The Deists' Bible" as it has been called, provoked more than thirty replies, of which by far the most distinguished was Bishop Butler's *Analogy of Religion* (see p. 242). More remotely deistical are the writings of SAMUEL CLARKE (1675-1729), who deduced the moral law from logical necessity in his Boyle lectures (1704-5), and was suspected of Arianism on account of his *Scripture Doctrine of the Trinity* (1712). Yet in spite of his doubtful orthodoxy, Dr. Johnson, one of his many admirers, said "I would recommend to every man whose faith is yet unsettled, Grotius,— Dr. Pearson,—and Dr. Clarke." Deistical literature is surveyed in Sir L. Stephen's *History of English Thought in the Eighteenth Century* (2 vols., Murray, 1876; revised, 1927), and in E. C. Mossner's *Bishop Butler and the Age of Reason* (Macmillan, 1936).

JOHN ASGILL (1659-1738) was the author of a pamphlet entitled *An Argument proving that according to the covenant of eternal life revealed in the Scriptures, man may be translated into that eternal life without passing through death* (1700). Asgill was persecuted in his lifetime, but he was to receive high praise from Coleridge, who considered his pamphlet "invaluable" and could "scarcely remember elsewhere such uncommon skill in logic, such lawyer-like acuteness, and yet such a grasp of common sense" (*Table Talk*, July 30, 1831),

The Bangorian Controversy may also be considered here. It was provoked by BENJAMIN HOADLY (1676-1761), Bishop of Bangor, the able leader of the Low Church party, who wrote a sermon on the Nature of the Kingdom, or Church, of Christ (1717). In this work he maintained an extreme protestant position, saying that Christ "is Sole Law-giver to his Subjects, and Sole Judge, in matters relating to Salvation. . . . All his subjects are equally his subjects; and, as such, equally without Authority to alter, to add to, or to interpret, his Laws so, as to claim the absolute Submission of Others to such Interpretation". A flood of controversial pamphlets ensued, William Law (see p. 240) being one of Hoadly's most distinguished opponents.

SHAFTESBURY, Anthony Ashley Cooper, Third Earl of (1671-1713)

Shaftesbury was a pupil of Locke, but was severely critical of Locke's philosophical tenets. His "optimistic" philosophy is expounded in a 3-vol. collection of treatises entitled *Characteristicks of Men, Manners, Opinions, Times* (1711), which consists of *A Letter concerning Enthusiasm* (1708), *An Essay on the Freedom of Wit and Humour* (1709), *Advice to an Author* (1710), *An Inquiry concerning Virtue or Merit* (1699), which is his most important contribution to Ethics, and *The Moralists* (1709), which contains his views on Religion and Theology. The third vol. contains *Miscellaneous Reflections on the preceding Treatises*. The best ed. of the *Characteristics* is by J. M. Robertson (2 vols., 1900), but it does not contain the aesthetic treatises printed in some later editions of the eighteenth century. These were *A Letter concerning Design* (1712) and *A Notion of the Historical Draught or Tablature of the Judgment of Hercules* (1713). They were intended for a new collection to be entitled *Second Characters*; but Shaftesbury did not live to complete his plan. It was ed. B. Rand (C.U.P., 1914) who included— besides the *Letter* and the *Notion*—a treatise called *Plastics*, published for the first time. B. Rand also published (1900) a vol. which contains a life of Shaftesbury written by his son, some hitherto unpublished letters, and the *Philosophical Regimen* ("a revelation both of the inmost purpose and of the outward procedure of his life"). An ed. of Shaftesbury's complete works is in preparation by W. A. Alderman. The best life of Shaftesbury and exposition of his philosophy is T. Fowler's *Shaftesbury and Hutcheson* (1882). An article by C. A. Moore on *Shaftesbury and the Ethical Poets in England* appeared in P.M.L.A., vol. 31 (1916).

MANDEVILLE, Bernard (1670–1733)

Mandeville's best work is *The Fable of the Bees* (1714; part 2, 1729), developed from *The Grumbling Hive*, a verse squib of 1705. In it he takes up a position diametrically opposed to Shaftesbury. He provides "a continual play of acute, original arresting criticism of life, put forth with a vivacity not to be found in any other serious essayist of that age" (J. M. Robertson, in *Pioneer Humanists*, Watts, 1907). The standard ed. is F. B. Kaye's (2 vols., Cl. P., 1924). An abridgement, ed. D. Garman, is published by Wishart (1934). There is a chapter on Mandeville in B. Dobrée's *Variety of Ways* (Cl. P., 1932).

LAW, William (1686–1761)

Law was a divine who had refused the oath of allegiance to George I. Much of his literary life was spent in controversy. He opposed the Bishop of Bangor's views on church government, he replied to the *Fable of the Bees* (1724), he wrote in belated support of Jeremy Collier's views (see p. 299) on *The Absolute Unlawfulness of the Stage Entertainment* (1726), and he attacked Warburton's *Divine Legation* (1757). But his most lasting works are his manuals of Christian behaviour, *A Practical Treatise on Christian Perfection* (1726), which greatly influenced the Wesleys, and more important, *A Serious Call to a Devout and Holy Life* (1728). His works were published in 9 vols. in 1753–76, and again in 9 vols., ed. G. Moreton in 1892–3.

The Serious Call is rptd. in E.L. It has also been edited by J. H. Overton (Macmillan, 1898) and by C. Bigg (Methuen, 1899). *The Christian Perfection*, ed. L. H. M. Soulsby, is published by Longmans (1901), who also published an ed. of his *Liberal and Mystical Writings* by W. S. Palmer and W. P. Du Bose (1908). An ed. of his *Selected Mystical Writings* by W. L. and S. H. Hobhouse, was published in 1938. J. H. Overton's standard biography was published by Longmans in 1881, and S. H. Hobhouse's *W. L. and Eighteenth-Century Quakerism* by Allen and Unwin in 1927.

HUTCHESON, Francis (1694–1746)

An Inquiry into the Original of our Ideas of Beauty and Virtue (1725) was written in avowed defence of Shaftesbury, with whose ethical position Hutcheson was in fundamental agreement. *An Inquiry concerning Moral Good and Evil* appeared the same year, and *An Essay on the Nature and Conduct of the Passions, with Illustrations upon the Moral Sense* in 1728. These are Hutcheson's most important writings, and were all published before his appointment as Professor of Moral Philosophy at Glasgow in 1729, where his life and teaching became more influential than his works. A biographical and critical study by W. R. Scott was published by C.U.P. in 1900.

BERKELEY, George (1685–1753)

Bishop Berkeley's principal writings are *An Essay towards a New Theory of Vision* (1709); *A Treatise concerning the Principles of Human Knowledge* (1710), ed. T. E. Jessop (Brown, 1937) and rptd. in Routledge's *New Universal Library; Three Dialogues between Hylas and Philonous* (1713); *Alciphron* (1732); *The Theory of Vision* (1733); *The Querist* (1735); *Siris* (1744).

A collected ed. was published in 2 vols. in 1784. The standard ed. is by A. C. Fraser (4 vols., Cl. P., 1871; rptd. 1901). Cl. P. also publishes a selection made by A. C. Fraser, and the *Essay*, the *Treatise*, and the *Three Dialogues* are contained in one vol. of E.L.

The standard life of Berkeley is by A. C. Fraser, published in the fourth vol. of the *Works*. A more recent study by J. Wild is published by O.U.P. (1936). Berkeley's correspondence with Percival was edited by B. Rand (C.U.P., 1914). A bibliography by T. E. Jessop is published by O.U.P. (1934).

BUTLER, Joseph (1692–1752)

Bishop Butler was the ablest and most orthodox champion of Christianity in the Deistic controversy. His *Fifteen Sermons Preached at the Rolls Chapel* were published in 1726 and his *Analogy of Religion*, in 1736. Cl. P. publishes an ed. of his works by W. E. Gladstone (2 vols., 1896–7), another ed. by J. H. Bernard was published by Macmillan in 1900. The *Analogy* is also rptd. in E.L. ed. R. Bayne, and the *Sermons*, ed. W. R. Matthews, in Bell's Bohn Library (1914). A study by E. C. Mossner entitled *Bishop Butler and the Age of Reason* was published by Macmillan in 1936.

WARBURTON, William (1698–1779)

Bishop Warburton was one of the most portentous figures of the time in the world of learning and controversy. He is mentioned here because his most famous book, *The Divine Legation of Moses* (1738; Part II, 1741) was a defence of orthodox religion against the deistic contention that though the doctrine of rewards and punishments in a future state is essential to the well-being of society, no such doctrine is found in the Mosaic dispensation. Warburton admitted this and contended, with vast display of erudition, that the Mosaic dispensation was therefore supported by Divine Providence. *The Divine Legation* was preceded by *The Alliance between Church and State* (1736), in which Warburton showed the need both of an established church and of some form of Test law. Warburton also wrote the preface to Richardson's *Clarissa* and edited the works of Shakespeare (8 vols., 1747) and of Pope (9 vols., 1751), whose friendship he gained by defending the *Essay on Man* from the attacks of Crousaz. His writings were edited by Bishop Hurd (see p. 224) in 7 vols., 1788. The best introduction to a study of Warburton is A. W. Evans's *Warburton and the Warburtonians* (O.U.P., 1932).

HUME, David (1711–76)

Hume's chief works are the *Treatise of Human Nature* (3 vols., 1739–40), *Essays Moral and Political* (2 vols., 1741–2), *An Enquiry concerning Human Understanding* (1748), *An Enquiry concerning the*

Principles of Morals (1751), of which he wrote, "This, in my opinion (who ought not to judge on that subject) is of all my writings . . . incomparably the best," *Political Discourses* (1752). His brief autobiography and his *Dialogues concerning Natural Religion* were published posthumously in 1777 and 1779 respectively. His letters have been edited by J. Y. T. Greig (2 vols., Cl. P., 1932) who rptd. *My own Life* with them from the manuscript. For Hume's *History*, see p. 255.

The standard ed. of the philosophical works is by T. H. Green and T. H. Grose (4 vols., Longmans, 1874-5). The *Treatise*, ed. L. A. Selby-Bigge, is published by the Cl. P., and is also available in E.L. (2 vols.). The *Essays* are rptd. in Routledge's *New Universal Library*. The two *Enquiries*, ed. L. A. Selby-Bigge, are published by the Cl. P., who also publishes the *Dialogues*, ed. N. Kemp Smith. See also T. H. Huxley's *Hume: with aids to the Study of Berkeley*.

The best life of Hume for many years was J. H. Burton's *Life and Correspondence of D. H.* (2 vols., 1846); but the work of J. Y. T. Greig, who has written a life (Cape, 1931) besides editing the letters, has now displaced it.

HARTLEY, David (1705-57)

Hartley's *Observations on Man* appeared in 1749, and was re-issued in an abridged form by Priestley (1775), who hoped to make clearer Hartley's theory of the human mind "as far as it relates to the *association* of ideas only, omitting even what relates to the doctrine of *vibrations*". But in Coleridge's opinion, who devotes chs. 5 and 6 of *Biographia Literaria* to the criticism of his old favourite, this was impossible, since "all other parts of his system . . . once removed from their mechanical basis, not only lose their main support, but the very motive which led to their adoption". Hartley's philosophy is discussed in G. S. Bower's *Hartley and James Mill* (1881).

REID, Thomas (1710-96)

Reid's *An Inquiry into the Human Mind* (1764) was written in reply to Hume's *Treatise*. His *Essays on the Intellectual Powers of Man* (1785) and *Essays on the Active Powers of Man* (1788), are fuller but, it is generally agreed, are less incisive accounts of his philosophy, which, like Kant's, contested those assumptions which Hume had taken from Locke and developed into a fuller scepticism. The standard ed. of his works by Sir W. Hamilton is in 2 vols. (1846-63). A brief life by A. C. Fraser appeared in 1898. An examination of his philosophy, its points of departure from Locke and Hume, and a comparison of it with that of Kant, was made by A. Seth (Pringle-Pattison) and entitled *Scottish Philosophy* (Blackwood, 1885).

VI

POLITICAL AND ECONOMIC THOUGHT

THE political thought of the period is surveyed in Sir
Leslie Stephen's *History of English Thought in the Eighteenth
Century* (2 vols., Murray, 1876; rptd. 1927) and in W.
Graham's *English Political Philosophy from Hobbes to Maine*
(Arnold, 1899).

BARBON, Nicholas (d. 1698)
 Barbon was the originator of fire insurance. His economic
writings were *A Discourse of Trade* (1690) and *A Discourse concerning
Coinage* (1696).

LOCKE, John. See p. 237.

DAVENANT, Charles (1656–1714)
 Davenant was the son of the poet, Sir William D'Avenant
(see vol. 2, pp. 331–2, 354–5), a commissioner of excise, and an
authority on economic questions. His *Political and Commercial
Works* were collected in 5 vols., ed. C. Whitworth, in 1771.
The most important are *An Essay upon Ways and Means of Supplying
the War* (1695), *An Essay on the East India Trade* (1696), *Discourses
on the Publick Revenues, and on the Trade of England* (1698), *An Essay
upon the Probable Methods of Making the People Gainers in the Ballance
of Trade* (1699), *Reflections upon the Constitution and Management
of the Trade to Africa* (1709), *An Essay upon the National Credit
of England* (1710), and *New Dialogues upon the Present Posture of
Affairs* (1710). Two studies of Davenant's work have been
published: Y. Ballière's *L'Œuvre Economique de C. D.* (Poitiers,
1913), and W. Casper's *C. D. Ein Beitrag zur Kenntnis des englischen
Merkantilismus* (Jena, 1930).

DEFOE, Daniel. See p. 258.

MANDEVILLE, Bernard. See p. 240.

BOLINGBROKE, Henry St. John, Viscount (1678–1751)

Bolingbroke's parliamentary career was cut short at Queen Anne's death. On his return from exile he became the inspiration of Walpole's political opponents. His works still read well enough, but it soon becomes obvious that it was his personality rather than his thought which influenced his friends. He contributed largely to the success of *The Craftsman* (see p. 264) in which appeared his *Dissertation upon Parties* (1735). His *Letter on the Spirit of Patriotism* and his most famous treatise, *The Idea of a Patriot King*, on which George III is wrongly said to have been reared, were published in 1749 (ed. A. Hassall, O.U.P., 1917), the *Letters on the Study and Use of History* in 1752 (Letters 6 and 8 in defence of the Treaty of Utrecht have been ed. G. M. Trevelyan, C.U.P. 1932) and *A Letter to Sir William Wyndham* in 1753. An ed. of his works in 5 vols. was published in 1754, two vols. of letters being added in 1798. A. Hassall's *Life* (Blackwell, 1915) is the best available.

TUCKER, Josiah (1713–99)

Tucker was Dean of Gloucester and the most interesting writer on economics between the death of Davenant and the publication of Adam Smith's *Wealth of Nations*. His first distinctly economic production was *A Brief Essay on . . . Trade* (1749). His best and most systematic work is his *Elements of Commerce* (1755), written for the instruction of the future king, printed, but never "published" until recent years. Much of his writings is concerned with the colonial problem, his view being that colonies are of no value to the mother country. He published *The Case of going to War for the sake of . . . Trade* (1763) and *The True Interest of Great Britain Set Forth in Regard to the Colonies* (1774), both rptd. in *Four Tracts Together with Two Sermons* (1774), *The Respective Pleas and Arguments of the Mother Country and of the Colonies* (1775) and *Cui Bono? An Enquiry What Benefit can arise to the English Or Americans . . . from . . . the present War* (1781). A copious selection from Tucker's economic and political writings, with an introduction by R. L. Schuyler, was published by the Columbia U.P. in 1931. An essay with a bibliography of Tucker by W. E. Clark was published in the Columbia Studies in History (vol. 19, no. 1), 1903.

SMITH, Adam (1723–90)

Smith's *Theory of Moral Sentiments* appeared in 1759, his *Inquiry into the Nature and Causes of the Wealth of Nations*, on which he had been working since 1749 or earlier, in 1776. *The Wealth of Nations* reached a fifth ed. in 1789; the best is by E. Cannan (2 vols., Methuen, 1904; rptd. 1920). It is also rptd. in 2 vols. of E.L. and W.C. The standard biography is by J. Rae (Macmillan, 1895), but it has been supplemented by W. R. Scott's *A. S. as Student and Professor* (Jackson, 1937), which contains an early draft of *The Wealth of Nations* (c. 1763), Smith's correspondence and other documents.

BURKE, Edmund (1729–97)

Burke's most important writings are as follows: *Thoughts on the Cause of the Present Discontents* (1770); the *Speech on American Taxation* (1774) and the companion speech on *Conciliation with the Colonies* (1776); *Reflections on the Revolution in France* (1790), with its continuation, *An Appeal from the New to the Old Whigs* (1791); *Thoughts on French Affairs* (1791); and *Letters on the Proposals for Peace with the Regicide Directory of France*, of which the first two appeared in 1796, the third in 1797, and fourth, though written as early as 1795, not until 1812; the *Letter to Sir Hercules Langrishe* (1792) on the electoral disability of Roman Catholics in Ireland; *A Letter to a Noble Lord* (1796), in which Burke replied to the Duke of Bedford's attack upon the grant of Burke's pension. To these might be added *A Vindication of Natural Society* (1756) and *A Philosophical Enquiry into the Origin of our Ideas of the Sublime and Beautiful* (1757), see p. 218. Burke's writings were first collected in 8 vols., ed. F. Laurence and W. King, 1792–1827. The best modern collection is edited by W. Willis and F. W. Raffety (6 vols., W.C.). Two vols. of writings on American and French affairs are published in E.L., and a 3-vol. selection, edited by E. J. Payne, by Cl. P., which also publishes a selection of extracts, edited by A. M. D. Hughes.

Sir J. Prior's life of Burke appeared in 1824, and reached a fifth ed. in 1854. Additional information is to be found in T. Macknight's *Life and Times of E. B.* (3 vols., 1858–60), and more especially in A. P. I. Samuels's *Early Life, Correspondence, and Writings of E. B.* (C.U.P., 1923). A new biography by R. H. Murray was published in 1931 by O.U.P., and another by Sir P. Magnus has just been published by Murray (1939). J. Morley's vol. in E.M.L. and his *E. B., A Historical Study* (Macmillan, 1867) are still recognised as authoritative.

PRICE, Richard (1723–91)

Dr. Price was a Unitarian Minister of considerable abilities and wide interests. He published in 1758 *A Review of the Principal Questions and Difficulties in Morals* (3rd ed. revised, 1787) in which he opposed what he conceived to be the teaching of Shaftesbury and Hutcheson about the "moral sense", maintaining that it is the "understanding" which distinguishes within us between right and wrong. His *Observations on Reversionary Payments* (1771) first established the practice of insurance upon a reliable mathematical basis. But it was Price's political pamphlets which made the greatest impression. His *Observations on the Nature of Civil Liberty* (1776) helped the cause of American Independence. *Additional Observations* were published in 1777 and re-issued in 1778 with the former work as *Two Tracts on Civil Liberty*. In 1789 Price delivered his famous sermon *On the Love of our Country* before the Revolution Society, which met to commemorate the work of 1688. His praise of the French Revolution provoked Burke's *Reflections*, and a study of the effect of the Revolution in England must therefore begin with Price. It ends with Shelley's *Hellas*.

There are some pleasing recollections of Price in Rogers's *Table Talk* and Clayden's *Early Life of Rogers* (see p. 193). There is no "standard" life, but R. Thomas's *Richard Price* (O.U.P., 1924) is helpful.

PAINE, Thomas (1737–1809)

When Paine replied to Burke's *Reflections* with his *Rights of Man* (2 parts, 1791–2) he was already well known. Two years after his emigration to America, he had addressed his *Common Sense* (1776) to the American people urging them to gain their freedom; and when they severed themselves from English domination, he kept up their courage with a series of pamphlets called *The Crisis*, which he issued between 1776 and 1783. The first *Crisis* begins with the famous words "These are the times that try men's souls." His last important work was the deistic *Age of Reason* (1794), much of it written while imprisoned in France. Paine's works, ed. M. D. Conway, were published in 4 vols. by Putnam (1894–6), his *Political Writings*, ed. H. B. Bonner, by Watts in 1909. The *Rights of Man* is rptd. in E.L. and ed. H. B. Bonner (Watts, 1906; rptd. 1937). The *Age of Reason*, ed. J. M. Robertson, was published by Watts in 1910. The standard life of Paine is by M. D. Conway (2 vols., Putnam, 1892; rptd. Watts, 1909).

WOLLSTONECRAFT, Mary (1759–97)

Another less momentous reply to Burke's *Reflections* was made by Mary Wollstonecraft, called *A Vindication of the Rights of Men* (1790), which her husband, William Godwin, considered "chargeable with a too contemptuous and intemperate treatment of the great man". Her most important book is the feminist *Vindication of the Rights of Woman* (1792). It is rptd. in E.L. Amongst other works, Mary Wollstonecraft also wrote a vol. of *Original Stories* (1788), which is an "improving" book for children and their teachers, calculated "to cure those faults by reason, which ought never to have taken root in the infant mind". A rpt. was published in O.M. Her *Letters written during a short residence in Sweden, Norway and Denmark* were published in 1796. In 1798 Godwin published 4 vols. of her *Posthumous Works*, which contain *Lessons* written for her child, much more pleasing than *Original Stories*, some *Hints* intended for a second part of the *Vindication of the Rights of Woman*, and those letters to her first lover, Imlay, which Godwin thought might "possibly be found to contain the finest examples of the language of sentiment and passion ever presented to the world". They have been rptd. with a good memoir by C. K. Paul (Kegan Paul, 1879), and by R. Ingpen (Hutchinson, 1908).

Godwin's *Memoirs of the Author of a Vindication of the Rights of Woman* was published in 1798, a corrected ed. appearing the same year. A text based on the first ed. was published by Constable in 1927. The editor, W. C. Durrant, has added a "supplement" which amounts to a new biography. A cheap rpt. of the text, without the supplement, was issued in 1928. There is a good chapter on her work in H. L. Brailsford's *Shelley, Godwin and their Circle* (H.U.L.) and there are studies by G. R. S. Taylor (Secker, 1911), and Mona Wilson (in *From Anne to Victoria*, ed. B. Dobrée, Cassell, 1937).

MACKINTOSH, Sir James (1765–1832)

Yet another reply to Burke's *Reflections* was written by Mackintosh and called *Vindiciae Gallicae* (1791). But after acquaintance with Burke, Mackintosh recanted in his *Discourse on the Study of the Law of Nature and Nations* (1799), the preliminary to a course of lectures on the same subject which he delivered at Lincoln's Inn. Mackintosh's retrospective *Dissertation on the Progress of Ethical Philosophy* (1830) is remembered, if at all, because it provoked (see p. 252) James Mill's severe *Fragment on Mackintosh* (1835), and his *History of the Revolution in England in 1688*

(1834), because it was reviewed by Macaulay in the *Edinburgh*. Hazlitt's *Sir James Mackintosh* is one of the best of his brilliant sketches in *The Spirit of the Age* (see p. 270). Coleridge's estimate appears in *Table Talk*, April 27, 1823.

GODWIN, William (1756–1836)

If Godwin's philosophical work is more often talked about than read, one reason is that his important books have never been rptd. *An Enquiry concerning Political Justice*, which inspired so many of the young revolutionaries was published in 1793. It was revised for a second ed. in 1796 and once again in 1798. A vol. of essays in which his radical position was restated and many other themes pursued, was published in 1797 entitled *The Enquirer*. His reflections on the triumph of anti-jacobinism are contained in a pamphlet published in 1801, *Thoughts occasioned by the Perusal of Dr. Parr's Spital Sermon*. His fine novel, *Caleb Williams*, and his *Memoirs* of Mary Wollstonecraft are mentioned elsewhere (pp. 236, 249).

C. Kegan Paul's *W. G., His Friends and Contemporaries* (2 vols., 1876) provides a biographical commentary upon a large number of letters from the Shelley papers, most of which were then printed for the first time. F. K. Brown's *Life of W. G.* (Dent, 1926) is a more readable presentation of the facts. For a contemporary estimate, the reader cannot do better than turn to Hazlitt's sketch in *The Spirit of the Age*, and for a modern estimate to H. N. Brailsford's *Shelley, Godwin, and their Circle* (H.U.L.).

BENTHAM, Jeremy (1748–1842)

Bentham's first work was an examination of Sir William Blackstone's *Commentaries on the Laws of England* called *A Comment on the Commentaries*. This was finished in 1776, but remained in manuscript until 1928, when it was edited by C. W. Everett (Cl. P.). An extract was published, however, entitled *A Fragment on Government* (1776). At the same time, Bentham was at work on a comprehensive treatise to be called *The Elements of Critical Jurisprudence*. The first part, *An Introduction to the Principles of Morals and Legislation*, was printed in 1780, but not published till 1789. A Swiss disciple named Dumont took this book with some further material in manuscript and produced in 1802 a 3-vol. précis called *Traités de Législation de M. Jérémie Bentham* which gave Bentham a European reputation. The book was translated into English in 1864 with the title *Theory of Legislation*. It was Bentham's custom to leave his manuscripts in an unfinished state and hand them over to his disciples who edited them for the press. Thus Dumont produced the *Théorie des Peines et des Recompenses* (written about 1775) in 1811, later translated as *The Rationale of Reward* (1825) and *The Rationale of Punishment* (1830), and the *Traité des Preuves judiciares* (1823). When Dumont had returned the manuscripts of the *Traité*, Bentham handed them to J. S. Mill who produced from them *The Rationale of Evidence* (1827), as he explains in his *Autobiography*, ch. 4. Similarly the elder Mill edited the philosophical *Table of the Springs of Action* (1817), and Bingham *The Book of Fallacies* (1824), summarised by Sydney Smith in the *Edinburgh Review*. Of Bentham's other legal writings, it is generally agreed that the most comprehensive and mature is his *Constitutional Code for the Use of all Nations Professing Liberal Opinions*, which contains the final statement of his political views. Vol. 1 was published in 1830 and the remainder in the posthumous *Works*. Bentham also published several economic works, of which the most important are the *Defence of Usury* (1787) and *A Protest against Law Taxes*, published with another tract, *Supply Without Burden*, in 1795. A collected ed. of his writings in 11 vols. was published by J. Bowring in 1838–43, which contains, besides what had already appeared, several more "editions" of his manuscripts. The last 2 vols. contain a biography. *A Fragment on Government* has been edited by F. C. Montague (O.U.P. 1891) and the *Introduction* is rptd. by Cl. P. Kegan Paul published an ed. of *The Theory of Legislation* by C. K. Ogden in 1931.

A definitive life of Bentham is in preparation by C. W. Everett. In the meanwhile, students may turn for biography and criticism to L. Stephen's *The English Utilitarians*, vol. 1 (Duckworth, 1900), A. V. Dicey's *Lectures on the Relation between Law and Public Opinion* (Macmillan, 1905; rptd. 1914), A. S. Pringle-Pattison's *The Philosophical Radicals* (Blackwood, 1907) and E. Halévy's *Growth of Philosophic Radicalism* (Faber, 1928) which contains a bibliography by C. W. Everett. Hazlitt included a character of Bentham in *The Spirit of the Age* (see p. 270).

MILL, James (1773–1836)

Mill was Jeremy Bentham's lieutenant. Before he became known as an economic and political philosopher, Mill had already published his *History of British India* (3 vols., 1817; 10 vols., ed. H. H. Wilson, 1858). Soon after, he set to work on a series of articles for the supplement to the fifth edition of the *Encyclopædia Britannica*. Of these the most important is an *Essay on Government*, which was finished in 1820 and rptd. separately. A rpt. with an introduction by Ernest Barker was published by C.U.P. in 1937. This work was attacked by Macaulay in the *Edinburgh Review* (1829), and also by Sir James Mackintosh (see p. 249). Mill's reply, *A Fragment on Mackintosh*, was not published till 1835. Mill also published *Elements of Political Economy* (1821; 3rd ed., 1826) and, what in the opinion of some is his greatest work, *An Analysis of the Phenomena of the Human Mind* (1829). Besides these, he contributed largely to the *Edinburgh Review* (1808–13), and to the *Westminster Review*, which he helped Bentham to found (see p. 272).

The standard life of Mill is by A. Bain (Longmans, 1882); see also J. S. Mill's *Autobiography* (1873), L. Stephen's *The English Utilitarians*, vol. 2 (Duckworth, 1900), and E. Halévy's *The Growth of Philosophic Radicalism* (Faber, 1928).

MALTHUS, Thomas Robert (1766–1834)

An Essay on the Principle of Population, as it affects the future Improvement of Society appeared in 1798. After a period of travel and further study, Malthus published "a new edition very much enlarged" in 1803. "He chose to stand or fall not by the First but by the Second . . . [yet] if the form of the first edition had been that of the second, it would have succeeded with the economists but failed with the general readers" (Bonar). The *Essay* reached a sixth ed. in 1826, which is the text chosen in G. T. Bettany's ed. (Ward Lock, 1890). A facsimile of the first ed. with notes by J. Bonar, is published by Macmillan (1926). The *Essay* is also rptd. in E.L. Malthus published three pamphlets during the Corn Law controversy: *Observations on the Effects of the Corn Laws* (1814), *The Grounds of an Opinion on the Policy of restricting the Importation of Foreign Corn* (1815), and, more important, *An Inquiry into the Nature and Progress of Rent* (1815). His *Principles of Political Economy* was published in 1820, and a revised ed. with a memoir by Bishop Otter in 1836.

The standard work on Malthus is J. Bonar's *Malthus and his Times* (1885; rptd. Allen and Unwin, 1924). L. Stephen's *English Utilitarians* (Duckworth, 1900) should also be consulted. Hazlitt's *Reply to Malthus* (1807) is a specimen of the criticism to which the *Essay* was subjected.

RICARDO, David (1772–1823)

Ricardo's first writings were pamphlets contributed to the bullion controversy in 1809, and a criticism of Malthus's *Inquiry* called an *Essay on the Influence of a low Price of Corn on the Profits of*

Stock (1815). His most important work—"the economic bible of the Utilitarians" (Stephen)—was *Principles of Political Economy and Taxation* (1817), which (in De Quincey's words) "constructed what hitherto was but a collection of tentative discussions into a science of regular proportions, now first standing upon an eternal basis" (*Confessions*). His pamphlet *On Protection to Agriculture* appeared in 1822.

Ricardo's works were ed. with a biography by J. R. McCulloch (Murray, 1846). E. C. K. Gonner has ed. the *Principles* (Bell's Bohn Library, 1891) and the *Economic Essays* (Bell, 1923). *Minor Papers on the Currency Question* have been edited by J. H. Hollander (Johns Hopkins U.P., 1932), who has also published a critical estimate and an ed. of Ricardo's letters to McCulloch (American Economic Ass., 1895). Ricardo's letters to Malthus (ed. J. Bonar, 1887) and to Hutches and others (ed. J. Bonar and J. H. Hollander, 1899) are published by Cl. P. The *Principles* are also available in E.L.

VII

HISTORIANS

THE writing of history in the eighteenth century is surveyed by A. W. Ward and W. Hunt in C.H.E.L., vol. ix, chs. 7, 8; vol. x, chs. 12, 13, and by T. P. Peardon in *The Transition in English Historical Writing, 1760–1830* (Columbia U.P., 1933). C. L. Becker, in *The Heavenly City of the Eighteenth Century Philosophers*, ch. iii (Yale and O.U.P., 1932), offers some reasons for the renewed interest in history in the latter part of the century. J. B. Black's *The Art of History* (Methuen, 1926) contains essays on Hume, Robertson and Gibbon.

Before concentrating on the eminent historians of the latter part of the eighteenth century, their predecessors must be briefly surveyed. The chief works of the two great historians of the seventeenth century were published during the eighteenth: Clarendon's *History of the Rebellion*, which had been finished in 1671, was published in 3 vols. in 1702–4, and Bishop Burnet's *History of His Own Time*, started in 1683 and finished in 1713, was published in 2 vols. bearing the dates 1724 and 1734. See further, vol. 2, pp. 306–7. Of the many histories of England written and compiled before the time of Hume, we may mention those of LAURENCE ECHARD (1670–1730), who published the first part of his narrative ending with James I's reign in 1707, and the second part ending with the accession of William III in 1718, and THOMAS CARTE (1686–1754), whose history was published in 4 vols. (1746–55). Carte also wrote a *Life of James, Duke of Ormonde* (2 vols., 1736). There is an appreciation of his work in Isaac D'Israeli's *Calamities of Authors* (1812–13). A notable History of Rome was written by

NATHANIEL HOOKE (d. 1763) and published in 4 vols. (1738–71).

RYMER, Thomas. See p. 214.

STRYPE, John (1643–1737)

Strype was a painstaking antiquary rather than an historian. His *Memorials of Thomas Cranmer, Archbishop of Canterbury*, was published in 1694 (3 vols., 1848–54). The lives of other Tudor archbishops followed: Grindal (1710), Parker (1711), and Whitgift (1718). Strype also edited and brought up to date Stowe's *Survey of London* (2 vols., 1720), a valuable piece of work. See vol. 2, pp. 197–8.

HUME, David (1711–76). See also p. 242.

Hume considered his *History* to be of smaller importance than his philosophical work, as indeed it is. But his philosophical treatment and his style maintained it as a standard work for many years. The first vol. dealing with the reigns of James I and Charles I was published in 1754. Vol. 2 brought the narrative down to 1688 and was published in 1756. Vols. 3 and 4 (House of Tudor) followed in 1759, and the last 2 vols. which treated the period from Julius Caesar to Henry VII appeared in 1761. Hume's final corrections were embodied in the 8-vol. ed. of 1778. The *History* in abridged form and with later additions continued to be published till 1888.

ROBERTSON, William (1721–93)

The best ed. of Robertson's works was published in 8 vols. in 1825. It contains *The History of Scotland during the reigns of Queen Mary and of King James VI* (1759), *The History of the Reign of the Emperor Charles V* (1769), *The History of America* (1777), *An Historical Disquisition concerning the Knowledge which the Ancients had of India* (1791).

GIBBON, Edward (1737–94)

The Decline and Fall of the Roman Empire was published in 6 vols. between 1776 and 1788. Two vols. of *Miscellaneous Works* (increased to 5 vols. in 1814) were edited by Lord Sheffield in 1796, the first of which contains his matchless autobiography. Of this work Gibbon had written six sketches, the version published in 1796 being Lord Sheffield's conflation of them. The six sketches were first published by John Murray in 1896. The best ed. which follows Sheffield but takes Murray's publication into account, is by G. Birkbeck Hill (Methuen, 1900). There are rpts. in W.C. and E.L. The best ed. of *The Decline and Fall* is J. B. Bury's (7 vols., Methuen, 1896; revised, 1909); but one of Milman's editions, first published 1838, will still be found serviceable, and there are rpts. in W.C. (7 vols.) and E.L. (6 vols.). There is no complete ed. of Gibbon's letters; the best is R. E. Prothero's (2 vols., Murray, 1896). The Journal which Gibbon kept from 1761 to 1763 gives "a picture of keen observations, indomitable industry, omnivorous reading, and the mastery of a powerful intellect amidst all the distractions of a busy life". It was first published by Chatto in 1929, ed. D. M. Low, who has also written an excellent life of Gibbon (Chatto, 1937). G. M. Young's briefer sketch (Davies, 1932) is heartily recommended.

LINGARD, John (1771–1851)

Lingard was a scholarly Roman Catholic historian whose aim was to provide Protestant readers with an inoffensive justification of the Church of Rome. His chief works are *The Antiquities of the Anglo-Saxon Church* (2 vols., 1806) and a *History of England* up to the year 1688 (8 vols., 1819–30). Abridgements of Lingard's narrative, with continuations until modern times, have been published by Bell in 1903 and 1912. His life and letters by M. Hailes and E. Bonney were published by Herbert and Daniel in 1911.

HALLAM, Henry (1777–1859)

Hallam's *View of the State of Europe during the Middle Ages* (2 vols., 1818) was the first great history to be published since Gibbon's. It continued to be rptd. till 1872. His next work was *The Constitutional History of England from the Accession of Henry VII to the Death of George II* (2 vols., 1827). This was the first important exposition of Whig views. It has been frequently rptd., and is available in E.L. (3 vols.). Macaulay's review appeared in the *Edinburgh* of Sept. 1828. Hallam's last work was an *Introduction to the Literature of Europe in the fifteenth, sixteenth and seventeenth centuries* (4 vols., 1837–9).

LOCAL HISTORIES

An increasing interest was taken during this period in local antiquities. The curious may observe that the majority of the county histories, which still remain as standard works on the open shelves of the Reading Room of the British Museum, were published between 1770 and 1840. Only a few of the earlier and more prominent can be mentioned here, such as, W. Maitland's *London* (2 vols., 1756), J. Nicholson and R. Burn's *Cumberland and Westmorland* (2 vols., 1777), E. Hasted's *Kent* (4 vols., 1778–99), T. Nash's *Worcestershire* (2 vols., 1781–2), J. Bridges and P. Whalley's *Northamptonshire* (2 vols., 1791), W. Hutchinson's *Durham* (3 vols., 1785–94), and his *Cumberland* (2 vols., 1794).

VIII

POLITICAL PAMPHLETEERS

DEFOE, Daniel (1660–1731)

When Defoe turned to writing the tales of adventure by which he is now remembered, he had already spent a lifetime of sixty years in political and religious controversy, which it is impossible to review in a work of this scope, and he had over three hundred publications to his name. When he published his first book, *An Essay on Projects*, in 1698 (written some five years earlier), he had already had experience of business life. In 1703 he had begun to publish his collected works of which the most remarkable are a satirical poem called *The True-born Englishman* (1701), *Legion's Memorial to the House of Commons* (1701), and *The Shortest Way with Dissenters* (1702). Throughout the greater part of Queen Anne's reign, Defoe was employed by Harley and Godolphin as a secret service agent, and it was in Harley's interests that he conducted the *Review* (1703–13), which appeared three times a week from 1704 onwards, at one period, with the *Little Review*, five times. At the close of the reign he published three pamphlets in favour of the Hanoverian succession written, like *The Shortest Way with Dissenters*, in ironic commendation of the opposite point of view: these were *Reasons against the Succession of the House of Hanover*, *And what if the Pretender should come?*, and *An Answer to a Question* (all 1713). His defence of his political career, *An Appeal to Honour and Justice*, was published in 1715. Of his other works written before he turned to fiction, mention must be made of *A True Relation of the Apparition of one Mrs. Veal* (1706), a realistic piece of reporting believed at one time to be Defoe's invention, and his bulky *History of the Union* (1709).

In 1719 Defoe started his tales of adventure with *Robinson Crusoe. Captain Singleton, Duncan Campbell*, and the *Memoirs of a Cavalier* were published in 1720; *Moll Flanders, Colonel Jack*, and *A Journal of the Plague Year* in 1722; and *Roxana* in 1724. That year he began to publish his *Tour through the whole Island of Great Britain*, of which vols. 2 and 3 appeared in 1725 and 1727.

Defoe's tales and a selection of his other writings are issued in Bell's Bohn Library (7 vols.) and by Blackwell (14 vols., 1927-8). Arber's *English Garner: Later Stuart Tracts* (ed. G. A. Aitken, 1903) contains rpts. of *Legion's Memorial, The True-Born Englishman, The Shortest Way*, extracts from the *Review*, and *An Appeal to Honour and Justice. The True-Born Englishman* is also rptd. in E.S.M.E.A. vol. 4, with notes by A. C. Guthkelch. *Robinson Crusoe, Captain Singleton, Memoirs of a Cavalier, Moll Flanders*, and the *Journal* are all rptd. in E.L. *Roxana* may be had in the Abbey Classics, and *Colonel Jack* was rptd. by Constable in 1923. *The Tour*, ed. G. D. H. Cole, is published by Davies (2 vols., 1927). A rpt., introduced by G. D. H. Cole, is in E.L. (2 vols.). A facsimile edition of *The Review* has been recently published by A. W. Secord, and an ed. of Defoe's letters is being prepared by H. C. Hutchins.

The best life of Defoe is by J. Sutherland (Methuen, 1937), and the best critical studies are P. Dottin's *Daniel De Foe et ses Romans* (3 vols., 1924), and A. W. Secord's *Studies in the Narrative Method of Defoe* (Univ. of Illinois Press, 1924). W. P. Trent's *Daniel Defoe. How to know him* (Bobbs-Merill, Indianapolis, 1916) is a good introductory vol. with plentiful quotation from Defoe's less accessible writings.

SWIFT, Jonathan (1667-1745)

The first attempt to collect Swift's writings was made by Faulkner, the Dublin publisher, who issued a 4-vol. ed. in 1735. Further vols. were added in subsequent years, the 20th vol. being published in 1772. Meanwhile an ed., the work of Hawksworth, Deane Swift, and Nichols, was published between 1755 and 1779. Sir Walter Scott's 19-vol. ed., based on Nichols's ed. of 1811, was published in 1814, and corrected in 1824. This ed. is still the best. Temple Scott's ed. of the prose works was published by Bell (12 vols., 1897-1908). The first 3 vols. of a new ed. by H. Davis in 14 vols. has been published by Blackwell (1939-40).

There are also numerous selections from Swift's works of which the best are Sir H. Craik's 2 vols. (O.U.P., 1892-3); 2 vols. in the O.S.A. series, the first containing *Gulliver's Travels, A Tale of a Tub*, and *The Battle of the Books*, the second (ed. W. A. Eddy) containing selections from *The Journal to Stella*, the poems, and the letters, as well as miscellaneous essays and satiric pieces; and

John Hayward's admirable one-vol. selection (Nonesuch Press, 1934).

Poems.

Swift's poems were not collected in his lifetime. The best ed. is by Harold Williams (3 vols., Cl. P., 1937). A study of them by F. Elrington Ball entitled *Swift's Verse* was published by Murray in 1929.

A Tale of a Tub, etc.

A Tale of a Tub was published with *The Battle of the Books* in 1704. The best ed. is by A. C. Guthkelch and D. Nichol Smith (Cl. P., 1920). An ed. of *The Battle of the Books*, with a good introduction by A. C. Guthkelch, is included in The King's Classics (1908). They are also included in a vol. of the O.S.A. series with *Gulliver's Travels*, and in E.L. with *A Meditation upon a Broomstick* (1710) and *Polite Conversations* (1738). The most recent (1939) is that by Herbert Davis, the first vol. of a complete ed. of the prose works. There is an important critical study of *A Tale of a Tub* by M. E. Pons entitled *Les Années de Jeunesse et le Conte du Tonneau* (University of Strasburg, 1925) which is also useful bibliographically.

Miscellaneous Writings before 1714.

In 1710 Swift started his career as a writer for the Tory party. He took over a weekly paper called *The Examiner* in November and conducted it in the Tory interests until June 1711. In 1711 he published *The Conduct of the Allies*, a pamphlet which succeeded in reconciling public opinion towards a peace with France. His last notable pamphlet for the ministry of Harley and Bolingbroke was *The Publick Spirit of the Whigs* (1714).

Two pamphlets, believed to have been written in 1708, show the measure of his interests in religious and ecclesiastical affairs at this time. These are *The Sentiments of a Church of England Man* and *An Argument to prove, that the Abolishing Christianity in England may . . . be attended with some inconveniences, and perhaps not produce many good Effects proposed thereby.*

Swift's three pronouncements upon the use of the English language are (i) a paper contributed to *The Tatler* (no. 230; Sept. 28, 1710), (ii) *A Proposal for Correcting, improving, and Ascertaining the English Tongue: in a Letter to the . . . Lord Treasurer* (1712), (iii) *A Letter to a Young Gentleman, Lately entered into Holy Orders* (1720).

Miscellaneous Writings after 1714.

In 1713 Swift was appointed to the Deanery of St. Patrick's, Dublin, a post which he held till his death. After the fall of the Tory ministry at Queen Anne's death in 1714, Swift returned to Ireland and devoted his time to philanthropy and Irish politics. His first Irish pamphlet was *A Proposal for the Universal Use of Irish Manufacture* (1720). Of much greater importance was the famous series of *Drapier's Letters to the People of Ireland against receiving Wood's halfpence* (1724). A standard ed. has been made by Herbert Davis for the Cl. P. (1935). Two more Irish pamphlets are specially notable, *A Short View of the State of Ireland* (1728) and *A Modest Proposal for preventing the Children of Poor People from being a Burthen to their Parents* (1729).

Amongst his non-political writings of these years must be mentioned *A Letter To a very Young Lady on Her Marriage*, published in the Pope-Swift *Miscellanies* (vol. 2, 1727), *Polite Conversations* (1738), rptd. by Elkin Mathews in 1927 (a selection is printed with *A Tale of a Tub* in E.L.) and *Directions to Servants* (1745).

Gulliver's Travels.

Gulliver's Travels first appeared in 1726 and has gone into countless editions. Of these the best is by Harold Williams (First Edition Club, 1926). A Cl. P. ed. by C. H. Firth and D. Nichol Smith is in preparation. Firth's *The Political Significance of "Gulliver's Travels"* (*Essays*, Cl. P., 1938) is indispensable for a detailed study. Since "Gulliver" has become a children's book, the text has frequently been modified; it is therefore important to secure an "adult" version such as the O.S.A. or the Nonesuch ed.

Letters.

The Journal to Stella was written to Esther Johnson and Rebecca Dingley between the years 1710 and 1713. It was first printed in the tenth vol. of Swift's *Works* in 1765. The best ed. is by G. A. Aitken (Methuen, 1901); there are also editions in the Bohn Library and in E.L. The standard ed. of Swift's letters is by F. Elrington Ball (6 vols., Bell, 1910–14), but it is not complete. *Vanessa and her correspondence with Jonathan Swift*, ed. A Martin Freeman (Selwyn and Blount, 1921) contains letters not published elsewhere, and Swift's letters to Ford were first collected and edited by D. Nichol Smith (Cl. P., 1935).

Biography.

The first life of Swift was written by his friend, Lord Orrery, with the title *Remarks on the Life and Writings of Dr. Jonathan Swift* (1752). Subsequent important biographies are Patrick Delany's *Observations upon Lord Orrery's Remarks* (1754), Deane Swift's *Essay upon the Life . . . of Dr. J. S.* (1755), Thomas Sheridan's *Life of Dr. Swift* (1784), and Sir Walter Scott's biography, prefixed to his ed. of the works (1814). Dr. Johnson's life in *The Lives of the Poets* is well worth reading though unsympathetic in tone. Of more recent biographies, none could be called "standard", unless it be H. Craik's (2 vols., 1882). The best short accounts are those by G. P. Moriarty, *Dean Swift and his Writings* (1893) and Leslie Stephen (E.M.L.). Of recent biographical-critical studies, R. Quintana's *The Mind and Art of Jonathan Swift* (O.U.P., 1936) may be recommended. This book contains a useful bibliographical list.

ARBUTHNOT, John (1667–1735)

Arbuthnot was Queen Anne's physician **and** an intimate friend of Swift and Pope. His principal literary work was a series of five allegorical pamphlets, published in 1712, maintaining the same political position as Swift's *Conduct of the Allies: Law is a Bottomless Pit, John Bull in his Senses, John Bull still in his Senses, An Appendix to John Bull Still in his Senses*, and *Lewis Baboon turned Honest*. The five were rptd. in the Pope-Swift *Miscellanies* (vol. 2, 1727) with the title *The History of John Bull*. The work was described by Macaulay in his *History* as "the most ingenious and humorous political satire extant in our language". It is rptd. with other writings in G. A. Aitken's *Life and Works of J. A.* (Cl. P., 1892), and Arber's *English Garner* (see under Defoe). In addition, Arbuthnot wrote several scientific treatises, contributed notes to *The Dunciad*, collaborated with Swift and Pope in the work of the Scriblerus Club, and with Pope and Gay in *Three Hours after Marriage* (1717).

Aitken's *Life* has been supplemented, but not displaced, by L. M. Beattie's more critical *J. A., Mathematician and Satirist* (Harvard and O.U.P., 1935).

THE CRAFTSMAN. See p. 264.

JOHNSON, Samuel. See p. 222.

JUNIUS. See p. 264.

COBBETT, William (1763–1835)

Cobbett had worked for many years as a ploughboy and as a soldier before he started political pamphleteering in America in the seventeen-nineties. He wrote so much that when he collected his American pamphlets in 1801 under the title of *Porcupine's Works*, they filled 12 vols. The most notable of these works is *The Life and Adventures of Peter Porcupine* (1796), an autobiography. Soon after his return to England in 1800, he started a journal called *The Political Register* (1802–1835), which he conducted till his death. His politics in America, and at his first return, had been Tory, but his conversion to Radicalism was more or less complete by 1806. This change did not alter the quality of his writing, which from first to last was independent, downright, and pugnacious. In 1819 Cobbett published *A Grammar of the English Language* in the form of letters to his son, an admirable work which might still serve its original purpose. It was impossible for Cobbett to be dull. *Cottage Economy* appeared in 1822; his popularisation of Lingard (see p. 256), *The History of the Protestant Reformation in England*, in 1824 and 1827; and in 1829 and 1830 his *Advice to Young Men*, instructions in the art of living, largely illustrated from his own life. His best known book is *Rural Rides*, the diaries of his expeditions through rural England, which first appeared in the *Register* and were afterwards collected in 1830. His *Tour in Scotland* was published in 1833, and his *Irish Tour* in 1834. It is to Cobbett we owe the plan of printing and publishing an account of proceedings in Parliament. He commenced this in 1804 and sold the enterprise to Hansard in 1812. Cobbett also undertook the publication of the available records of political proceedings from 1066 to 1803: *Cobbett's Parliamentary History of England*, as it was called, was published in 9 vols., 1806–12, and has not yet been completely superseded.

Peter Porcupine, ed. G. D. H. Cole, is published by the Nonesuch Press (1927). The *Grammar* and *Advice to Young Men* are rptd. in O.M., and *Cottage Economy* is rptd. by Davies (1926). *Rural Rides* is rptd. in E.L. (2 vols.) and elsewhere. By far the best ed. is that of G. D. H. and M. Cole (3 vols., Davies, 1930), in which the Scottish and Irish tours are rptd. for the first time. The Cl. P. publishes a vol. of extracts from Cobbett's writings, ed. A. M. D. Hughes.

Hazlitt's shrewd estimate of Cobbett appears in *The Spirit of the Age* (see p. 270). The best biography is by G. D. H. Cole (Collins, 1924).

IX

JOURNALISM

1. THE NEWSPAPER

A SKETCH of the development of the English Newspaper
is outside the scope of this book, but it should be borne
in mind that from the late seventeenth century onwards
space was allowed in newspapers for matter other than news
and advertisements. Two brilliant series of political essays
appeared in eighteenth-century newspapers; the attacks
which Bolingbroke and the Pulteneys made upon Walpole
in *The Craftsman* (1726 ff; rptd. in volume form), and the
even more famous *Letters of Junius* contributed to *The Public
Advertiser* between 1769 and 1772. The only recent ed., in
which the letters are (dubiously) attributed to the Earl of
Shelburne, is by C. W. Everett (Faber, 1927). The fullest
treatment of the authorship is by C. W. Dilke in *Papers of a
Critic* (1875, vol. 2).

The newspapers also contained essays on more general
themes, such as Dr. Johnson's series, *The Idler*, written for
The Universal Chronicle (1758–60), and the essays written by
Fielding, "the most gifted journalist of the middle of the
century", in his *Covent-Garden Journal* (1752). See pp. 222, 228.

Poems were printed in the newspapers from earliest times.
Pope's character of "Atticus" first appeared in *St. James's
Journal*, Cowper's *John Gilpin* in *The Public Advertiser*, Burns's
Tam o' Shanter in the *Edinburgh Herald*, and the *Morning
Chronicle* and the *Morning Post* published poems by Words-
worth, Coleridge, and others.

D. Nichol Smith's article on the Newspaper in *Johnson's
England* (Cl. P., 1933, vol. 2) is an admirable short account
and contains a bibliography for further reading. The best

bibliography is R. S. Crane's and F. B. Kaye's *A Census of British Newspapers and Periodicals, 1620–1800* (C.U.P., 1927).

2. THE PERIODICAL ESSAY

The periodical consisting of a single essay is a form of journalism peculiar to the eighteenth century. *The Tatler*, started by Steele in 1709, is the first of any literary quality, but Steele had been anticipated in all his devices by previous journalists. *The Tatler* was concluded in 1711, and *The Spectator*, in which Steele and Addison were partners, was started the same year. Addison also gave some help to Steele in *The Guardian* (1713). There were numerous imitators, of which Ambrose Philips's *Freethinker* (1718–21) is one of the best. Johnson's *Rambler* (1750–2) served as the inspiration, though not always as the model, for another group of periodicals, of which the best were Hawkesworth's *Adventurer* (1752–4), to which Johnson and Joseph Warton contributed; Moore's *World* (1753–6), perhaps the liveliest of all, to which Lord Chesterfield contributed 24 essays, including two on Johnson's *Dictionary*, and Horace Walpole nine; Colman's and Thornton's *Connoisseur* (1754 –6); and Henry Mackenzie's *Mirror* (1779–80), a Scottish periodical, containing some interesting critical articles by William Richardson. A 30-vol. ed. of *The British Essayists* was published by R. Lynam in 1827. The best historical surveys are W. Graham's *The Beginnings of English Literary Periodicals* (O.U.P., 1926), and his *English Literary Periodicals* (Nelson, 1930).

STEELE, Sir Richard (1672–1729)

Steele's pamphlet, *The Christian Hero; An Argument to Prove that no Principles but those of Religion are Sufficient to make a Great Man* (1701) was written, while he was an Ensign in the Coldstream Guards, "to fix upon his own mind a strong impression of virtue and religion". His reputation with his brother officers suffered so much that he decided to restore it with a comedy, *The Funeral* (1702). Two more plays followed: *The Lying Lover* (1704) intended to show that a comedy "might be no improper entertainment in a Christian community", and *The Tender Husband*

(1705). His last comedy, *The Conscious Lovers*, which Fielding's Parson Adams thought the only fit play for a Christian to see, was produced in 1722: it is rptd. in *Eighteenth Century Comedies* (W.C.). There is an ed. of Steele's plays by G. A. Aitken in the Mermaid Series (Benn), and of *The Christian Hero* by R. Blanchard (O.U.P., 1932). Passages from *The Christian Hero* were rptd. in *Spectators* 356 and 516.

The Tatler (1709–11) was another attempt to insinuate moral reforms by genial methods. The best ed. is by G. A. Aitken (4 vols., 1898). Steele had been helped by Addison, but in *The Spectator* (see under ADDISON) they were equal partners. Addison also helped with *The Guardian* (1713), but Steele was mainly responsible, and wholly responsible for its political successor, *The Englishman* (1713 and 1715), and two theatrical periodicals, *Town Talk* (1715) and. *The Theatre* (1720). These have not been rptd. in recent times.

The best of Steele's many political pamphlets is considered to be *Mr. Steele's Apology for Himself and his Writings* (1714). His *Epistolary Correspondence* was edited by J. Nichols (2 vols., 1809) and a selection, containing the famous letters to his wife, is published by Lane (1927). A new ed. is being prepared by R. Blanchard.

Readers may select a life of Steele according to their taste. If they quail before the severe monument of G. A. Aitken's 2 vols. (1889), they may prefer the more deliberately picturesque methods of Willard Connely (Cape, 1934), who adds some new facts. There is a good chapter on Steele's plays in F. W. Bateson's *English Comic Drama*, *1700–1750* (Cl. P., 1929) and a chapter on Steele generally in B. Dobrée's *Variety of Ways* (Cl. P., 1932).

ADDISON, Joseph (1672–1719)

Collected Works.

Addison's writings were collected and published in 4 vols. in 1721. The editor was Tickell (see p. 171), Addison's intimate friend, who contributed a memoir and some noble elegiac verses. The only complete ed. is the "Bohn" in 6 vols., 1856 (rptd. 1883).

Poems.

Addison was a poet before he was an essayist, and (according to Pope) valued himself more upon his poetry than upon his prose. His *Letter from Italy*, which Pope liked the most of all his poems, appeared in 1704; *The Campaign*, commissioned by the Government to celebrate the victory of Blenheim, in 1705. *Rosamund*, an opera intended to "give a more natural and reasonable entertainment" than its popular Italian rivals, was performed in 1706 but was poorly received. His poetical drama, *Cato* (1713), was a great political success—and its rhetorical vigour may still be appreciated. But the only poems which live to-day are four hymns from the religious meditations published on Saturdays in *The Spectator*, "The Lord my pasture shall prepare" (no. 441), "When all thy mercies" (no. 453), "The spacious firmament on high" (no. 465), and "How are thy servants blest, O Lord!" (no. 489). The best ed. of the poems is by A. C. Guthkelch (Bell, 1914).

Prose.

In *The Tatler*, 1709–11 (see under STEELE), Addison, who wrote about 60 papers, was Steele's most valued contributor. In *The Spectator*, which appeared daily between March 1, 1710–11 and December 6, 1712, and thrice weekly between June 18 and December 20, 1714, Addison and Steele were equal partners. Addison wrote 274 papers, which he distinguished by signing them with one of the letters, C, L, I, O. *The Spectator* was re-issued in 7 vols. in 1712–13, an eighth volume being added in 1715. The best modern editions are those of G. A. Aitken (8 vols., 1898) and G. Gregory Smith (E.L., 4 vols.). Addison also contributed 53 essays to Steele's *Guardian* (1713), and conducted his own *Freeholder*, a periodical essay like *The Spectator* and *The Guardian*, which he published twice a week from December 23, 1715, to June 29, 1716. A selection of essays from *The Tatler*, *Spectator*, and *Guardian* is published by O.U.P., ed. A. Dobson. A vol. of Addison's miscellaneous prose, containing his *Remarks on Italy* (1705) and his *Dialogues upon Ancient Medals* (1721), was edited by A. C. Guthkelch (Bell, 1914). An ed. of Addison's letters is in preparation by W. Graham.

Biography and Criticism.

Addison's life was written by Dr. Johnson for *The Lives of the Poets*, and by Lucy Aikin (1843), in reviewing which Macaulay wrote one of his best essays for the *Edinburgh Review*. A useful biography was written by W. J. Courthope for E.M.L., and another is in preparation by W. Graham. Addison is no longer so highly esteemed as he was during the eighteenth and nineteenth centuries; for a modern revaluation, see B. Dobrée, *Essays*

in Biography 1680-1726 (O.U.P., 1925). The extent of Addison's
contribution to *The Tatler* is discussed by F. W. Bateson in
R.E.S., April 1929. The best account of the journalistic background of *The Tatler* and *The Spectator* is W. Graham's *The Beginning of English Literary Periodicals* (O.U.P., 1926).

PHILIPS, Ambrose. See p. 169.

JOHNSON, Samuel. See p. 222.

GOLDSMITH, Oliver. See p. 187.

WARTON, Joseph. See p. 265.

CHESTERFIELD, Lord. See p. 265.

WALPOLE, Horace. See p. 294.

MACKENZIE, Henry. See p. 231.

3. THE MAGAZINE

By the word "magazine" an eighteenth-century journalist
meant a periodical purporting to reprint the best which had
already appeared in contemporary newspapers, and to add
poetry, registers of books, obituary articles, lists of births,
deaths, and marriages, essays, learned discussions, etc.
The most famous was *The Gentleman's Magazine* (1731–1907),
(see E. Blunden's *Votive Tablets*, Cobden-Sanderson, 1931),
whose first editor was Edward Cave. Johnson was employed
in its early years as a writer of prefaces and short biographies,
and as a reporter of parliamentary debates. To its rival, *The
London Magazine* (1732–85), Boswell contributed his "Hypochondriack" essays (see p. 276). Goldsmith's shortlived *Bee*
(1759) more nearly resembles the modern literary magazine
which developed in the next century. *Blackwood's*, founded in
1817 and still in publication, was maintained by John
Wilson ("Christopher North"), James Hogg, and J. G.
Lockhart. It published savage reviews of Coleridge and
Keats, but was rather more discerning in its treatment of
Shelley. Scott and De Quincey (*Murder, The English Mail*

Coach, etc.) were amongst its contributors. *The London Magazine* (1820–9) prospered under the editorship of John Scott and published De Quincey's *Confessions of an Opium Eater*, Lamb's *Essays of Elia*, Hazlitt's *Table Talk*, and some of the character sketches from his *Spirit of the Age*, besides contributions by H. F. Cary and Darley; but after Scott's death in a duel in 1821, the magazine declined. *The New Monthly* was started in 1814 and was edited from 1820 till 1830 by Thomas Campbell. Much of Hazlitt's and Lamb's work was published in it. But the best of all was Leigh Hunt's and Byron's *The Liberal* (1822–3), whose first number contained Byron's *Vision of Judgment*. Hazlitt and Shelley were also contributors. Leigh Hunt's earlier paper, *The Reflector* (1810), has some claims in this section, though its sub-title "a collection of essays" suggests affiliations with the periodicals. The best contributions were written by Lamb and Hunt.

For further information, see W. Graham's *English Literary Periodicals*, op. cit. Selections from *Blackwood's* reviews are included in R. Brimley Johnson's *Famous Reviews* (Pitman, 1914).

WILSON, John (1785–1854)

"Christopher North" was the mainstay of *Blackwood's* from its inception. His most famous contributions were a series of imaginary dialogues with "The Ettrick Shepherd" and others, entitled *Noctes Ambrosianæ* (1822–35), in which "the affairs of the world, the personages assembled, and things in general" were freely and wittily discussed. They were collected in 4 vols. in 1843 and a modern rpt. is published by Routledge. Wilson was appointed Professor of Moral Philosophy at Edinburgh University in 1820. After his appointment he set himself to read up his subject, but was forced to rely for the substance of his flamboyant lectures on the letters and personal instructions of his friend, Alexander Blair. This extraordinary story is well told by E. Swann in her *Christopher North* (Oliver and Boyd, 1934), which presents a vivid picture of Wilson's personality. The standard ed. of Wilson's works was published in 12 vols., 1855–8.

HOGG, James, "The Ettrick Shepherd". See p. 210.

LOCKHART, J. G. See p. 277.

LAMB, Charles (1775-1834)

Lamb's first publication was some verses published in Coleridge's first vol. (1796). In 1798 he collaborated with Charles Lloyd in another vol. of poems, *Blank Verse*, which contains "The Old Familiar Faces" (rptd. in O.B.R.V.). *Tales from Shakespeare*, written in collaboration with Mary, appeared in 1807. He was working at the same time on his *Specimens of English Dramatic Poets who Lived about the Time of Shakespeare* published in 1808. A collected ed. of his works in 2 vols. appeared in 1818, dedicated to Coleridge. The tone of the dedication suggests that his work was complete. But in 1820 he started writing the series of *Elia* essays for the *London Magazine* upon which both his modern and contemporary reputation—at any rate in the eyes of De Quincey and Hazlitt—was founded. They were collected in 2 vols. (1823, 1833).

The standard ed. of the works of Charles and Mary Lamb is by E. V. Lucas (Methuen, 6 vols., 1912). *Tales from Shakespeare* ed. W. Macdonald, is published by Dent (1903) and is also available in O.S.A. and E.L. W. Macdonald has also edited Lamb's critical essays (Dent, 1903), and his *Specimens* (Dent, 2 vols., 1903). *Essays of Elia* are rptd. in E.L. and W.C., and O.U.P. publishes an ed. of *The Last Essays of Elia* by E. Blunden and F. Page (1929). The best ed. of Lamb's letters is by E. V. Lucas (Dent and Methuen, 3 vols., 1935). An ed. by W. Macdonald is published in E.L. (2 vols.).

There is an excellent life of Lamb by E. V. Lucas (2 vols., Methuen; revised, 1921), a great deal of which is told in the words of Lamb himself and of his contemporaries.

HAZLITT, William (1778-1830)

A complete ed. of Hazlitt's works, by P. P. Howe, is published by Dent (21 vols., 1930-4). His famous works are easily available in cheap rpts.: *Characters of Shakespeare's Plays* (1817) in E.L. and W.C., *Lectures on the English Poets* (1818), ed. F. W. Baxter, O.U.P., 1929—and in W.C. and E.L.; *Lectures on the English Comic Writers* (1819) in W.C., and in E.L. with miscellaneous essays; *Liber Amoris* (1823) rptd. by Routledge, 1907; *Table Talk* (1821-4) in E.L. and W.C.; *The Spirit of the Age*, 1825 (character sketches of his contemporaries, and perhaps his best work) in W.C. and in E.L., with *Lectures on the English Poets*; *The Plain Speaker*, 1826 (a collection of essays rptd. from the *London* and *New Monthly* magazines) in E.L.

The best life of Hazlitt is by P. P. Howe (Secker, 1922).

DE QUINCEY, Thomas (1785–1859)

The only complete ed. of De Quincey's works is in 14 vols., ed. D. Masson (1889–90). Most of these writings were contributions to magazines. When starting to collect them in 1853, De Quincey suggested a classification in three divisions: (1) Papers written primarily to amuse; (2) Essays addressed purely to the understanding; (3) Works of impassioned prose. The first group contains *On Murder, considered as one of the Fine Arts* (*Blackwood's*, 1827), *Recollections of the Lakes and the Lake Poets* (*Tait's*, 1834–9, rptd. in E.L.), and the *Autobiographical Sketches* (*Tait's*, 1834–40). The second group contains his essay *On the Knocking at the Gate in Macbeth* (*London Mag.*, 1823), a translation of Lessing's *Laocoon* (*Blackwood's*, 1826), and *The Logic of Political Economy* (1844). The third group contains *The Confessions of an Opium Eater* (*London Mag.*, 1821–2; rptd. in W.C. and E.L.; ed. R. Garnett, Kegan Paul, 1885), the *Suspiria de Profundis* (*Blackwood's*, 1845), and the most remarkable of his writings, *The English Mail Coach* (*Blackwood's*, 1849; rptd. with *Murder* and other writings in E.L.). A vol. of his literary criticism, ed. H. Darbishire, is published in O.M. A. H. Japp's life of De Quincey (revised ed., 1890), a valuable source of information, has been displaced by H. A. Eaton's (O.U.P., 1936); but the best biographical and critical study is E. Sackville West's *A Flame in Sunlight* (Cassell, 1936).

4. THE REVIEW

The Monthly (1749–1845) and the *Critical* (1756–90) were the most famous reviews of the eighteenth century, and in their political rivalry faintly anticipated the *Edinburgh* and the *Quarterly*. For over thirty years the *Monthly* was content with publishing abstracts of books and only became more thoroughly critical after 1783. Its most famous reviewers were Hawkesworth, Porson, Holcroft, R. B. Sheridan, and Goldsmith. The *Critical*, which was conducted by Smollett for its first seven years, was considered by Johnson to be superior to the *Monthly*. Goldsmith and he were occasional reviewers. Both the *Monthly* and the *Critical* attempted to survey every publication. In this they were unlike the *Edinburgh* (1802–1929), which selected only such books as presented the reviewer with an opportunity of ample disquisition. Its founders were Sydney Smith, Horner, Jeffrey, and Brougham, Jeffrey being appointed editor after the first number. Scott was one of the reviewers in its early years, and later Mackintosh, Hazlitt, Malthus, Hallam, Thomas Arnold, Macaulay, and Carlyle were all employed. The *Quarterly* (1809 and still published) was started by Scott, Murray, and the two Cannings, to combat the Whiggism of the *Edinburgh*. The first editor was Gifford (see p.185), and Southey, Scott, Lamb, Lockhart, and Croker were some of the reviewers. The *Westminster* was started in 1824 by Jeremy Bentham to propagate the opinions of the third political party, the "philosophical radicals". Its principal supporters were James Mill (see p. 251), who castigated both the *Edinburgh* and the *Quarterly* in its pages, and his son J. S. Mill, subsequently its proprietor (see J. S. Mill's *Autobiography*, ch. 4).

JEFFREY, Francis (1773–1850)
Jeffrey published a 3-vol. selection of his reviews in 1844, which is still easy to obtain. A one-vol. selection ed. D. Nichol Smith, is published in O.M. Jeffrey was an advocate, and his criticism is judicial; his method was to expound with lavish quotation from the "documents" before him, and to temper blame with praise. His antagonism to Wordsworth is offset by his enthusiasm for Keats. Hazlitt's favourable sketch of Jeffrey in *The Spirit of the Age* pays tribute to his quick-wittedness. His life was well written by his friend Cockburn (2 vols., 1852).

SMITH, Sydney (1771–1845)
Smith had a wide reputation as a reformer, a wit, and a preacher. His works, a collection of which he published in 1839, include contributions to the *Edinburgh*; *Peter Plimley's Letters* (1807), a series of ten written in defence of Catholic emancipation (ed. G. C. Heseltine, Dent, 1929; with selections from his other writings); speeches in favour of the Reform Bill, in one of which he compared the attempt of the Lords to stop the progress of reform with Mrs. Partington's efforts to push away the Atlantic Ocean from her house with a mop; and letters on the Ecclesiastical Commissions of 1837. A pleasing memoir by his daughter, Lady Holland, gleans some of his wit—there is some more in Rogers's *Table Talk*—and displays his wholly admirable character. It was published with a selection of his letters in 2 vols.

(1855). G. W. E. Russell's *Life* in E.M.L. is packed with information, which corrects Lady Holland in points of detail.

BENTHAM, Jeremy. See p. 250.
  For J. S. Mill, see vol. 4, p. 212.

*   *   *   *   *

TOM BROWN (1663–1704) and NED WARD (1667–1731) fit awkwardly into any category. Their satirical commentaries and vivid reporting of the life they observed around them show their kinship with some of the periodical essayists. They were journalistic, even if they were not journalists. Ned Ward's *London Spy* began to appear in monthly parts in 1698, and a complete issue of the eighteen parts was published in 1703. There are two modern editions: one, with an introduction by Ralph Straus (Casanova Soc., 1924); and another (expurgated) ed. A. L. Hayward (Cassell, 1927). Tom Brown's *Amusements Serious and Comical* appeared in 1700. They have also been edited by A. L. Hayward (Routledge, 1927). Ward's *Miscellaneous Writings in Verse and Prose* were published in 6 vols. (1717–24). A collected ed. of Brown's writings was published in 3 vols. in 1707–8. A fourth ed. corrected and much enlarged, appeared in 1715.

X

BIOGRAPHY

THE traditions of seventeenth-century biographical collections, such as Fuller's *Worthies* and Wood's *Athenæ Oxonienses* (see vol. 2, pp. 308, 316) were maintained and improved during this period. In 1691, Gerard Langbaine published the authorised edition of his *Account of the English Dramatic Poets*, an invaluable work of reference, containing lives of the dramatists, appreciations of their work, and lists of their plays. A continuation was compiled in 1719, entitled *The Poetical Register* (2 vols.). It was the work of Giles Jacob—"the scourge of Grammar", according to Pope—who received help from Prior, and biographical details from many of his contemporaries. A further continuation was made by D. E. Baker, entitled *The Companion to the Playhouse* (1764). It was revised by Isaac Reed in 1782, and renamed *Biographia Dramatica*. The final revision by Stephen Jones (3 vols., 1812) is still a useful source of information. Other biographical collections are Theophilus Cibber's *Lives of the Poets of Great Britain and Ireland* (5 vols., 1753), mostly the work of Robert Shiels, an acquaintance of Dr. Johnson; Horace Walpole's *Royal and Noble Authors of England*, 1758 (see p. 204); John Nichols's *Literary Anecdotes of the Eighteenth Century* (9 vols., 1812–15), a vast heterogeneous collection of biographical details; and, most important of all, the *Biographia Britannica* (1747; second ed., 5 vols., 1778–93), which served the same purpose as our modern *Dictionary of National Biography*. These books are reference books with little artistic merit; but in the same category of biographical collections fall Johnson's *Lives of the Poets*, 1779 (see p. 222) and Sir Walter Scott's *Lives of the Novelists*, 1821.

In addition to these, several separate biographies were

written of men dead long ago. Rowe's slight life of Shakespeare, prefixed to the 1709 edition, deserves mention because it is the first life of Shakespeare. William Oldys's life of Raleigh, prefixed to his edition of Raleigh's *History* (1736) is a much more scholarly work. Conyers Middleton's *Life of Cicero* (2 vols., 1741) was much admired for its prose style. Scott's life of Dryden, prefixed to his edition (1808), is still the most readable account of Dryden's life, just as Malone's poorly-written life, prefixed to his edition of the prose works (1800), is still the most authoritative. And there is much entertainment in J. H. Monk's *Life of Bentley* (1830), notably reviewed by De Quincey in *Blackwood's*.

Progress was also made in the biography of contemporaries. Mason, in his life of Gray (1775), was the first to use a new technique. The value of letters as documentary evidence had been realised by Izaak Walton and others, but Mason's use of them was so much more copious that he could declare that he was making Gray tell the story of his own life. This technique was adopted by Hayley for his life of Cowper (1803), and by Forbes for his life of Beattie (1806); but much more important was the extension of the principle by Boswell, who used his minutes of Johnson's conversation, and Lockhart, who had access to Sir Walter Scott's journal.

Considerable interest was shown at the beginning of the period in details of the lives of the notorious. Defoe wrote lives of criminals such as Jack Sheppard (1725) and Jonathan Wild (1726), and Theophilus Lucas compiled the *Memoirs of the Lives of the Most Famous Gamesters* (1714). There were at least two similar compilations: Alexander Smith's *Complete History of the Lives of the most Notorious Highwaymen* (1718) and Charles Johnson's *General History of the Pirates* (1724), both of which have been ed. A. L. Hayward (Routledge, 1926).

The best general account of this subject is M. Longaker's *English Biography in the Eighteenth Century* (O.U.P., 1931). Another history is in preparation by D. A. Stauffer.

BOSWELL, James (1740–95)
Boswell wrote very much more than his two books about

Johnson, and had acquired European fame as a writer long before he had written them. But most of this work is no longer accessible. The most famous of his un-Johnsonian writings is *The Journal of a Tour to Corsica, and Memoirs of Pascal Paoli*, published with his *Account of Corsica* in 1768. It was rptd. by G. Birkbeck Hill in his ed. of *Letters between Erskine and Boswell* (1879; first published, 1763) and by S. C. Roberts (C.U.P., 1923). Seventy essays contributed to the *London Magazine* from 1777 to 1783 under the signature of *The Hypochondriack* have been ed. by M. Bailey (Stanford U.P., 1928), and three more essays *On the Profession of a Player*, contributed to the same magazine in 1770, have been rptd. (Elkin Mathews, 1929).

The Journal of a Tour to the Hebrides, with Samuel Johnson, LL.D., appeared in 1785. It was well edited by R. Carruthers (1852), and was included by G. Birkbeck Hill in his ed. of the *Life of Johnson* (see below) and will be included in L. F. Powell's revision. The best of the cheap editions is by R. W. Chapman, included in one vol. with Johnson's *Journey* (O.S.A., 1930; reduced from his more elaborate ed., 1924). The original manuscript was discovered in a croquet box at Malahide Castle (see below) in 1930, and was published by Heinemann (ed. F. A. Pottle and C. H. Bennett), in 1936.

The *Life of Johnson* appeared in 1791. The standard ed. (for reference only) is by G. Birkbeck Hill (Cl. P., 6 vols., 1887), revised and enlarged by L. F. Powell (4 vols., 1934). The best of the cheap editions is in the O.S.A. series.

Boswell's letters to his life-long and intimate friend Temple were first published in 1857. These and many other letters, 389 in all, were well edited by C. B. Tinker (Cl. P., 2 vols., 1924), but a large number have been discovered since.

It was generally supposed that Boswell's papers had been destroyed by his descendants. But in 1926 a large quantity of them was acquired from Lord Talbot de Malahide, Boswell's great-great-grandson, by Colonel Isham; and in 1930 some more were discovered at Malahide Castle, including the manuscript of the *Tour to the Hebrides* and 120 leaves of the manuscript of the *Life of Johnson*. These are also in Colonel Isham's possession. Publication of the papers in a limited ed. was started under the editorship of Geoffrey Scott in 1928, and completed by F. A. Pottle in 18 vols. in 1934. An index vol. is in preparation. This publication is of exceptional interest, but it is impossible to give more than the briefest summary of it here; readers are referred for more detailed accounts to F. A. and M. S. Pottle's

Private Papers of James Boswell . . . A Catalogue (O.U.P., 1931), or to R. W. Chapman's paper on *Boswell's Archives* in E.S.M.E.A., vol. 17, or to the relevant pages of *The Year's Work in English Studies*, vols. 10–15. The papers consist of correspondence, literary materials with drafts of published works, personal records, journals, notes and memoranda. Vol. 6 discusses the evidence presented by the papers of Boswell's methods as a biographer; vols. 7–18 present a text of the journals from 1765 to 1794 (with certain gaps), vols. 10, 11, and 13 being especially rich in Johnsonian entries. The discovery of further Boswell papers at Fettercairn House, Kincardineshire, was announced in *The Times* by C. C. Abbott on March 9, 1936, and was reviewed by him in the same paper on November 21, 1936. This collection is complementary to the Malahide collection. It largely consists of letters written to Boswell with drafts of his replies, and a few more journals. The catalogue of these papers, prepared by Professor Abbott, has been published by the Cl. P.

In view of the enormous wealth of this newly discovered material, previous biographies and studies of Boswell have become antiquated—even C. B. Tinker's *Young Boswell* (1922), itself based upon previously unused material. The first biographer to use the papers was C. E. Vulliamy, whose study (Bles, 1932) is not entirely sympathetic. The most valuable contributions towards a new biography are F. A. Pottle's *Literary Career of James Boswell* (Cl. P., 1929) and the same writer's and Geoffrey Scott's introductions to the vols. of the Malahide Papers. R. W. Chapman's account of Boswell's proof-sheets is rptd. in *Johnson and Boswell Revised*, essays by D. Nichol Smith, R. W. Chapman, and L. F. Powell (Cl. P., 1928).

LOCKHART, James Gibson (1794–1854)

Most of Lockhart's literary life was spent in the service of *Blackwood's* and the *Quarterly*. For *Blackwood's* he wrote a number of savage reviews in the rawness of youth, of which he repented in maturity; he was editor of the *Quarterly* from 1825 to 1853. A selection from his reviews, entitled *Lockhart's Literary Criticism*, ed. M. C. Hildyard, is published by Blackwell. In 1828 he completed the difficult task of writing a life of Burns (rptd. in E.L.). His life of Scott, a vivid but incomplete picture, was published in 7 vols. in 1836–8, and a narrative abridgement of it in 1843. A rpt. of the abridgement is published in E.L. Andrew Lang's *Life and Letters of J. G.* (2 vols., 1897) is a sympathetic work, and Harold Nicolson's *The Development of English Biography* (Hogarth Press,

1927) contains appreciative criticism of the *Life of Scott*. See also Sir H. Grierson's *Lang, Lockhart, and Biography* (O.U.P., 1934).

See also OLIVER GOLDSMITH (p. 186), THOMAS MOORE (p. 194), ROBERT SOUTHEY (p. 201).

For the early lives of Swift, see p. 262.

For Roger North's *Lives of the Norths* (1742-4), see vol. 2, p. 308.

XI

AUTOBIOGRAPHY AND MEMOIR

DUNTON, John (1659–1733)

Dunton was a bookseller and a journalist. His most famous publications were (1) *The Athenian Gazette, or Casuistical Mercury* (1691–6), a precursor of *Notes and Queries*, in which Dunton and his associates volunteered to resolve "all the most nice and curious questions proposed by the ingenious", and (2) *The Life and Errors of John Dunton* (1705). An "entire collection of all the valuable questions and answers" was published in 4 vols. in 1703 with the title *The Athenian Oracle* (3rd ed., 1728), and a selection from the *Oracle*, ed. J. Underhill, was published in 1892. *The Life and Errors* was edited by J. B. Nichols in 1818. A second vol. contains a selection from Dunton's miscellaneous works.

ELLWOOD, Thomas (1639–1713)

Ellwood was a Quaker, a friend of Milton and Penn, and the editor of Fox's Journal. His autobiography gives some impression of a Quaker's life during the seventeenth century. It was published in 1714 by Joseph Wyeth, who continued the story of Ellwood's life from 1693, the year in which the autobiography ceases. An ed. by C. G. Crump was published by Methuen in 1900.

MANLEY, Mrs. Mary de la Riviere (1663–1724)

If good faith and truthfulness are required from memoir writers, Mrs. Manley should have no place in this section, for she specialised in scandalous chronicles of the eminent, which she reported under feigned names. Sarah, Duchess of Marlborough's name is thinly disguised in the title *The Secret History of Queen Zarah and the Zarazians* (1705). More notorious was *Secret Memoirs and Manners of Several Persons of Quality, of both Sexes. From the New Atlantis* (1709). *Memoirs of Europe towards the Close of the Eighth Century* (1710) was later rptd. as the second and third parts of *New Atlantis*. *Court Intrigues* followed in 1711, and in 1714 appeared the autobiographical *The Adventures of Rivella, or the History of the Author of the Atlantis*.

Mrs. Manley also wrote several plays. *The Lost Lover*, a comedy, and *The Royal Mischief*, a tragedy, appeared in 1696. Another tragedy, *Almyra*, was published in 1707, and a third, *Lucius The First Christian King of Britain*, in 1717.

HERVEY, John, Baron (1696–1743)
Pope's "Sporus" was Vice-Chamberlain at the court of George II, and an intimate friend of Walpole and Queen Caroline. His brilliant *Memoirs of the Reign of King George II* provide an intimate record of palace life from 1733 till the Queen's death in 1737, and owe something of their freshness to Hervey's power of recording conversation, second only to Boswell's. They were first published in 1848. The best ed. is by R. Sedgwick (Eyre and Spottiswoode, 3 vols., 1931).

SPENCE, Joseph. See p. 176.

CIBBER, Colley. See p. 301.

HUME, David. See p. 242.

GIBBON, Edward. See p. 255.

FRANKLIN, Benjamin (1706–90)
Benjamin Franklin started to write an account of his life in 1771, and was able to complete the first twenty-four years. After several interruptions he finished his narrative in 1789. A French translation of the early life was published in 1791 and translated into English in 1793, but the account as Franklin wrote it was not published till 1818. Even this version lacked the conclusion of the narrative, and the complete autobiography was first published in 1868. There is a rpt. in W.C., and another, ed. N. C. Goodman, is published by Hamish Hamilton (1937).

LACKINGTON, James (1746–1815)
Lackington was a London bookseller who wrote entertaining accounts of the trade, and of his personal success in undercutting his rivals. His *Memoirs* were first published in 1791 and reached a thirteenth ed., "corrected and much enlarged" in 1810. His *Confessions* appeared in 1804. It is a pity that neither book has been reprinted in modern times.

HOLCROFT, Thomas (1745–1809)

Holcroft's importance no doubt lies in the history of the drama (see p. 306), but his autobiography is more frequently read than his plays. He started upon it only a few weeks before his death and had concluded no more than an account of his early vagabondage and his successful career as a stable boy at New-market. The book was finished by Hazlitt (1816) from Holcroft's diaries and papers, this part being specially interesting in its description of a strolling player's life. It forms vol. 3 of the complete ed. of Hazlitt's works and is rptd. in W.C. There is a 2-vol. ed. by E. Colby (Constable, 1925).

CARLYLE, Alexander (1722–1805)

"Jupiter" Carlyle was the leader of the Scottish "Broad Church" party, a man of wide acquaintance and generous sympathies. His autobiography, which he began to write in 1800, contains his eye-witness accounts of the Porteous riots and the battle of Prestonpans, and memorable sketches of Edinburgh society in the great days of Robertson, Hume, Fergusson and Blair. It was first published with a supplementary chapter by J. H. Burton in 1860. A new ed. was published by Foulis in 1910.

COCKBURN, Henry (1779–1854)

What Carlyle did for the Edinburgh of the 1760's, Cockburn, an eminent Scottish judge, did for the equally brilliant Edinburgh of Scott and Jeffrey, which was proudly called "The Modern Athens". Cockburn's *Memorials of His Time* was first published in 1856, and is specially rich in "characters" of the Scottish bench and bar. A new ed. was published by Foulis in 1909. A continuation known as the *Journal* was published in 2 vols. in 1872, and a vol. containing some of Cockburn's letters and pages omitted from the *Memorials* was ed. H. A. Cockburn (Grant and Murray, 1932). Cockburn also wrote the standard life of Jeffrey, see p. 272.

HAYDON, Benjamin Robert (1786–1846)

Haydon was a painter of vast conceptions but of incommensurate abilities. He managed to give more effective expression to his dramatic and strenuously active personality in his *Autobiography*, a book which contains, amongst other good things, vivid records of a dinner party with Wordsworth, Lamb and Keats, and of a private view of his "Christ's Entry into Jerusalem". Haydon brought his story down to 1820; it was

281

completed with edited extracts from his journal by Tom Taylor, who published it in 1853. An ed. with introd. by Aldous Huxley was published by Peter Davies (2 vols., 1926). The *Autobiography* alone is rptd. in W.C. with an introd. and epilogue by Edmund Blunden.

XII

TRAVEL

THIS is a period second only to the Elizabethan age in the richness of its travel literature and the geographical importance of the discoveries made. There is no collection of narratives which can compare with Hakluyt and Purchas, but the most important are to be found in vols. 2 and 3 of *Terra Australis Cognita* (3 vols., 1766–8), J. Harris's *Navigantium atque Itinerantium Bibliotheca* (2 vols., 1764), James Burney's *Chronological History of Voyages and Discoveries* (vols. 4 and 5, 1803–17), and J. Pinkerton's *General Collection of . . . Voyages and Travels* (16 vols., 1808–14).

A. TRAVELS IN DISTANT PARTS

DAMPIER, William (1652–1715)
  The popularity of voyage literature in the eighteenth century was started by the books of Dampier, a scientifically-minded buccaneer. These were *A New Voyage round the World* (1697), the value of which was recognised by the Royal Society, who issued a digest of it in their Proceedings; *Voyages and Descriptions* (1699); *A Voyage to New Holland* (1703). Dampier's last voyage was related by WOODES ROGERS in *A Cruising Voyage round the World* (1712). A collected ed. in 2 vols. was made by J. Masefield (Grant Richards, 1906). There is also a school ed. by A. E. M. Bayliss (Harrap, 1931) and separate editions of *A New Voyage* (ed. N. M. Penzer, Argonaut Press, 1927) and of *A Cruising Voyage* (ed. G. E. Manwaring, Cassell, 1928). Two studies have been published in recent years by Clennell Wilkinson (Lane, 1929) and W. H. Bonner (O.U.P., 1934).

ANSON, George (1697–1762)
  In 1740 Anson started upon a naval expedition against the Spanish colonies on the west coast of South America. He returned

to England in 1744 after circumnavigating the globe. Several accounts of the voyage exist, the most famous being *A Voyage round the World* (1748), compiled under Anson's directions by his chaplain, Richard Walter. It has been ed. G. S. L. Clowes (Hopkinson, 1928) and rptd. in E.L. with an excellent introd. by John Masefield. The story of the voyage has been retold by Vice-Admiral Boyle Somerville (Heinemann, 1934).

BYRON, John (1723–86)
Byron sailed in *The Wager* on Anson's expedition, and was wrecked off the coast of Chili in 1741. He published a lurid *Narrative* of his experiences in 1768, some of the incidents of which were used by his grandson for the second canto of *Don Juan*. The *Narrative* deserves reprinting.

FIELDING, Henry. See p. 228.

SMOLLETT, Tobias George. See p. 230.

COOK, James (1728–79)
Captain Cook made three famous voyages: (1) in which he discovered Australia (1768–71); (2) in which he crossed the Antarctic circle (1772–5); (3) in which he discovered the Sandwich Islands (1776–9). For a narrative of the first voyage, Cook's contemporaries had to rely on J. Hawkesworth's unsatisfactory *Account of the Voyages undertaken . . . for making Discoveries in the Southern Hemisphere* (3 vols., 1773) and S. Parkinson's *A Journal of a Voyage to the South Seas* (1773). Cook's own journal was first published by W. J. L. Wharton in 1893, and the journal of Sir Joseph Banks, the naturalist, who accompanied Cook, was first published by J. D. Hooker in 1896. The official account of the second voyage is Cook's *A Voyage towards the South Pole, and round the World* (2 vols., 1777). Cook also wrote the official account of the third voyage, entitled *A Voyage to the Pacific Ocean* (2 vols., 1784; a third vol. is the work of James King). The three voyages are represented in E.L. by Hawksworth's account of (1), and the official accounts of (2) and (3).

The standard biography of Cook is by A. Kitson (Murray, 1907) and there is also a good short life by R. T. Gould (Duckworth, 1935). The best modern account is said to be G. A. Wood's *Discovery of Australia* (Macmillan, 1922). M. Homes has compiled a useful bibliographical guide (Edwards, 1936). See also H. N. Fairchild's *The Noble Savage* (Columbia U.P., 1928).

BRUCE, James (1730–94)

Bruce's vivid accounts of his travels in Egypt and Abyssinia were published in 5 vols. in 1790 with the title *Travels to discover the source of the Nile in the years 1768, 1769, 1770, 1771, 1772, and 1773.* The 8-vol. editions of 1805 and 1813 are admirably prepared. "He will always remain the poet, and, his work the epic, of African travel" (Garnett).

YOUNG, Arthur (1741–1820)

Young was an agriculturalist who, during a very busy life, travelled up and down England, Ireland, Wales and France describing the conditions of the country. *A Six Weeks' Tour Through the Southern Counties of England and Wales* appeared in 1768, *A Six Months' Tour through the North of England* (4 vols.) in 1771, and *The Farmer's Tour through the East of England* (4 vols.) in 1770–1. In 1780 he published his *Tour in Ireland*, which Maria Edgeworth considered the most faithful picture to be had of the peasantry. It is rptd. in Bell's Bohn Library (2 vols.), ed. A. W. Hutton (1892) and selections ed. C. Maxwell are published by C.U.P. (1926). In 1784 Young started to compile his *Annals of Agriculture* which reached a 46th vol. in 1815. Amongst his own contributions are several tours in England and Wales, a selection from which is rptd. by the London School of Economics (Scarce Tract, No. 14). Most famous of all is his celebrated *Travels in France*, 1787–90, published in 2 vols. in 1792 and enlarged in 1794. The rpt. in E.L. omits most of Young's "General Observations"; C. Maxwell's ed. (C.U.P., 1929) abridges the observations. Of Young's other numerous works he himself considered his *Political Arithmetic* (1774) the best. His *Autobiography*, ed. M. Betham-Edwards, was published in 1898. There is a useful bibliography by G. D. Amery in the Journal of the Royal Society of Agriculture, vol. 85, 1924.

MACDONALD, John

Macdonald was a gentleman's servant who travelled with his masters in India, Spain, France, and Ireland, and published the entertaining account of his travels in 1790. He tells us that he was the first to popularise the umbrella in London, and relates the scene of Sterne's death at which he was present. His *Travels*, ed. J. Beresford, was rptd. in *The Broadway Travellers* (Routledge, 1927).

PARK, Mungo (1771–1806)

Park was the first European of modern times to find the Niger River. His *Travels into the Interior Districts of Africa* appeared soon after his return in 1799. It is rptd. in E.L.

FRANKLIN, Sir John (1786–1847)

Franklin was an Arctic explorer, who first discovered the North-West Passage. He published a *Narrative of a Journey to the Shores of the Polar Sea, in the years 1819, 1820, 1821, and 1822 and 1823*, and a *Narrative of a Second Expedition* in 1828. The earlier narrative is rptd. in E.L.

LEWIS, Matthew Gregory. See p. 233.

B. TRAVELS IN THE BRITISH ISLES

DEFOE, Daniel. See p. 258.

GILPIN, William (1724–1804)

Gilpin was a Hampshire parson who made his name by publishing a series of "picturesque tours", i.e., tours made with the object of "examining the face of a country by the rules of picturesque beauty". The first to appear was his *Observations on the River Wye relative chiefly to picturesque beauty* (1782). *The Mountains and Lakes of Cumberland and Westmorland* followed in 1786, *The Highlands of Scotland* in 1789, *The Western Parts of England* in 1798, *The Coasts of Hampshire, Sussex and Kent* in 1804, and finally the *Counties of Cambridge, Norfolk, Suffolk and Essex and several parts of North Wales* in 1809. They might well be read in conjunction with Gray's diary of his tour in the Lakes (*Letters*), Mrs. Radcliffe's *Observations during a Tour to the Lakes* (1795), and Wordsworth's *Guide to the Lakes*, to observe the differences of technique in describing scenery. The reader should afterwards turn to WILLIAM COMBE's (1741–1823) parody, *The Tour of Dr. Syntax in Search of the Picturesque*, 1812 (Part II, 1820; III, 1821), illustrated by Rowlandson. It was ed. J. C. Hotten (1868).

PENNANT, Thomas (1726–98)

Entirely different in kind are the historical, antiquarian, and biological observations of Pennant, the naturalist. He published his *Tour in Scotland* in 1771, with a Supplement in 1772, and the account of a second tour in 1774. Pennant remarked that the country was then "almost as little known to its southern brethren as *Kamtschatka*" but that ever since his tour it had been "*inondée* with visitants"; most famous of these was Dr. Johnson, who championed him on more than one occasion. The *Tour in Wales* appeared in 1778, and the *Journey from Chester to London* in 1782. Besides these tours Pennant wrote several zoological works, a book about London, and a complacent account of his *Literary Life* (1793). *The Tours of Thomas Pennant* is the subject of a paper by L. F. Powell, published in *The Library*, IV. xix. no. 2, 1938.

JOHNSON, Samuel. See p. 222.

BOSWELL, James. See p. 276.

YOUNG, Arthur. See p. 285.

TORRINGTON, John Byng, Viscount (1742–1813)
   Torrington's diaries of his tours through England and Wales during the years 1781 to 1794 convey a similar, but milder, criticism of agricultural life to what is found in Cobbett's *Rural Rides*. They are published in 4 vols. by Eyre and Spottiswoode (1934–8), ed. C. B. Andrews.

COBBETT, William. See p. 263.

XIII

DIARIES

EVELYN, John. See Vol. II, p. 309.

HEARNE, Thomas (1678–1735)

Hearne was an Oxford antiquary, who was for some years an assistant librarian in the Bodleian library. After publishing editions of Pliny and Livy, he turned his attention to English antiquities. An ed. of the *Itinerary* of John Leland, Henry VIII's antiquary was published in 1710–12, and an ed. of the *Collectanea* in 1715. The following year Hearne produced the first of a series of editions of the English Chroniclers, a task which he continued till the end of his life. His diary covers the years 1705 to 1735 and is a valuable, though politically prejudiced, record of Oxford personalities and Oxford gossip. It is published in 11 vols. (not consecutive) by the Oxford Historical Society, ed. C. E. Doble, D. W. Rannie, and H. E. Salter (1885–1921), with the general title *Remarks and Collections*. See D. C. Douglas, *English Scholars* (Cape, 1939).

SWIFT, Jonathan. See p. 261.

RYDER, Dudley (1691–1756)

Ryder was appointed Attorney General in 1737 and Lord Chief Justice of the King's Bench in 1754. The diary, which he kept as a young student of the Middle Temple (1715–16), has been transcribed and edited by W. Matthews (Methuen, 1939). It provides a valuable record of London life at the time of the '15 rebellion, and a self-portrait as intimately detailed as that of Pepys.

COWPER, Lady Mary (1685–1724)

Lady Cowper was a Lady in Waiting to the Princess of Wales, later Queen Caroline. Her diary, only a fragment of which survives, is a record of life at court between 1714 and 1720. It was first published in 1864.

EGMONT, John Percival, first Earl of (1683–1748)

The diarist was a staid and sober courtier. As a revelation of personality the book is dull, but as a record of political activity from day to day during the years 1730–47 it is of the very first importance. The diary was edited on behalf of the Historical Manuscripts Commissioners by R. A. Roberts (3 vols., 1920–3).

MARCHMONT, Earls of

A Selection from the Papers of the Earls of Marchmont, commonly known as the *Marchmont Papers* was edited by Sir G. H. Rose in 1831. They are extremely interesting politically, and give a vivid notion of political life in the reign of George II.

DODINGTON, George Bubb, Baron Melcombe (1691–1762)

Dodington was a small poet and a patron of poets, a wit, and a politician more powerful in influence than in principles. His diary, which covers the years 1749–61, allows a glimpse of political and court intrigues. It was first published in 1784. L. Sanders's study of Dodington, entitled *Patron and Place-Hunter*, was published in 1919 by Lane.

WESLEY, John (1703–91)

Wesley's journals of his ministries in Georgia and England cover the years 1735 to 1791. Extracts first appeared in 1739 and subsequent years. The standard ed. is by N. Curnock (8 vols., Culley, 1909–16), a one-vol. abridgement by the same editor being published by the Epworth Press. There is also a 4-vol. ed. in E.L. The standard ed. of Wesley's letters (ed. J. Telford) is published by the Epworth Press (8 vols., 1931). Hodder and Stoughton have published a selection (1915).

WOODFORDE, James (1740–1803)

Parson Woodforde was rector of Weston Longeville, Norfolk, from 1774 till 1803. His diary (ed. J. Beresford; O.U.P., 5 vols., 1924–31) describes every-day life, first in Oxford, then in the country districts of England, between 1758 and 1802. An abridgement amounting to about one-third of the diary was made by the same editor and published by O.U.P. (1935).

BURNEY, Fanny. See p. 232.

FARINGTON, Joseph (1747-1821)

Farington was a pupil of Richard Wilson, the landscape painter, and a Royal Academician, but his fame rests entirely upon the journal which he kept from 1793 to 1821. It is not only an important document for the history of the Academy and for the rise of Turner's reputation, but it also gives a valuable day to day account of the London society in which men of letters, artists, and statesmen lived. The diary was first published in the *Morning Post* in 1922–3. An ed. by J. Greig, in which captions and editorial comments are unpleasantly mingled with the text, is published by Hutchinson (8 vols., 1922–8).

WORDSWORTH, Dorothy. See p. 197.

ROBINSON, Henry Crabb (1775–1867)

Crabb Robinson's diary (1811–67) is the most valuable record we possess of the literary society of the Romantic age. H. C. R. was on terms of intimacy with Wordsworth, Coleridge, Lamb, Southey, Rogers and others, and made shrewd critical appreciations of them and their works, his accounts of Coleridge's lectures being specially interesting. Although his intellect was not of the first order, he was responsible for bringing German influence to bear upon English thought. His *Diary, Reminiscences, and Correspondence*, ed. T. Sadler, was published by Macmillan (3 vols., 1869; revised ed., 2 vols., 1872). A remarkable review by Walter Bagehot appeared in the *Fortnightly* and was rptd. by E. J. Morley in her admirable *Life and Times of H. C. R.* (Dent, 1935). A selection from H. C. R., ed. E. J. Morley, is published by Manchester U.P. and Longmans (1932) entitled *Blake, Coleridge, Wordsworth, Lamb, etc.* His letters are not yet all published: *The Correspondence of H. C. R. with the Wordsworth Circle, 1808–1866*, ed. E. J. Morley (Cl. P., 2 vols.) appeared in 1927, and extracts from his letters written from Germany between 1800 and 1805, ed. E. J. Morley (O.U.P.) in 1929.

GREVILLE, Charles Cavendish Fulke (1794–1865)

Greville was Clerk to the Privy Council from 1821 till 1859, a close associate of Wellington and Palmerston, and a peculiarly well-informed observer of the political struggles of his time. The diary, which he kept from 1818 to 1860, is an historical document of the first importance, while its lucid, courtly style and its sharply defined character-sketches appeal—in selection—to the General Reader. A copious but discreet selection was edited by H. Reeve and published in three instalments in 1875, 1885, and 1887. A 2-vol. selection by P. W. Wilson (Heinemann,

1927) contains passages hitherto unpublished, but the entries are shuffled to suit the editor's purpose. P. Morrell let Greville speak for himself in one vol. of *Leaves from the Greville Diary* (Nash and Grayson, 1929). A few copies of the only complete ed. (ed. L. Strachey and R. Fulford, 8 vols., 1938) are published at great price by Macmillan.

Greville's cousin, ROBERT FULKE GREVILLE (d. 1824) was an equerry to George III. His diaries for the years 1781, 1788–9, and 1794 provide an interesting impression of court life at Windsor and Weymouth, and a detailed account of George III's first mental breakdown. They were ed. F. M. Bladon (Lane, 1930).

CREEVEY, Thomas. See p. 295.

HAYDON, Benjamin Robert. See p. 281.

XIV

LETTERS

THE art of writing letters was cultivated during this period as never before. Several excellent collections have been published, abundantly varied in style, subject, and personality. They range from the studied politeness of Pope to the easy domestic trivialities of Cowper, from Lady Mary Wortley Montagu's observations of Turkey to Gilbert White's observations of the natural history of Selborne, and from Lord Chesterfield's instructions in good breeding and social decorum to Horace Walpole's brilliant sketches of what society was really like. Most of the bibliographical details will be found on other pages, but the names of the most famous letter-writers are mentioned here for the sake of emphasis. Only those whose letters are their best work are fully treated in this section.

SWIFT, Jonathan. See p. 261.

POPE, Alexander. See p. 175.

WENTWORTH, Thomas, Earl of Strafford (1672–1739)
A selection from the correspondence of Lord Strafford was made by J. J. Cartwright in 1883, entitled *The Wentworth Papers 1705–39*. The news and gossip of the day is chiefly recounted by Lord Wentworth's brother, Peter. The character and phonetic spelling of his mother, Lady Wentworth, can scarcely fail to please.

MONTAGU, Lady Mary Wortley (1689–1762)
Lady Mary (Pope's "Sappho") accompanied her husband to Constantinople on his appointment as ambassador in 1716. Her letters, which describe Turkish customs, and incidentally provide the earliest account of inoculation for small-pox, were

published in 1763. The remaining letters were published with some negligible essays and poems by J. Dalloway in 1803. The standard ed. is by W. M. Thomas (2 vols., 1893). A selection from the *Letters from Constantinople*, ed. H. Chatwin, is published by Methuen (1922), and there are further selections in E.L. and Cape's *Travellers' Library* (ed. A. W. Lawrence, 1930). The most authoritative biography is by G. Paston (Methuen, 1907).

SHENSTONE, William. See p. 180.

GRAY, Thomas. See p. 181.

HUME, David. See p. 243.

CHESTERFIELD, Philip Dormer Stanhope, Earl of (1694–1773)

Chesterfield's *Letters to his Son* were published by his son's widow in 1774. Two vols. of *Miscellaneous Works*, containing other letters, speeches, characters of eminent personages, his witty periodical essays on Johnson's *Dictionary* and other subjects, and a Memoir by Maty, followed in 1777. In 1817 there appeared *Letters from the Earl of Chesterfield to Arthur Charles Stanhope*. All these letters were gathered together by Lord Mahon in his 4-vol. ed. of 1845, to be followed by a fifth vol. of the miscellaneous works in 1853. In 1890, the Earl of Carnarvon published the *Letters . . . to his Godson*, even more important for an understanding of Chesterfield than the letters to his son. The best ed. of the letters alone is by B. Dobrée (Eyre and Spottiswoode, 6 vols., 1932), containing his political letters to Newcastle and others, and a valuable biographical preface. *Some Unpublished Letters of Lord Chesterfield* were edited by Sidney L. Gulick, Jr. (University of California Press, Berkeley, 1937). There are selections from the letters in E.L. and W.C. The best studies of Chesterfield are Roger Coxon's *C. and his Critics* (Routledge, 1925), S. Shellabarger's *Lord C.* (Macmillan, 1935) and W. Connely's (Cassel) 1939.

WHITE, Gilbert (1720–93)

The Natural History and Antiquities of Selborne is written in the form of letters, 44 addressed to the naturalist, Thomas Pennant, with whom White had been in correspondence since 1767, followed by 66 addressed to the Hon. Daines Barrington. The work was published in 1789. Of subsequent editions, the best is by T. Bell (2 vols., 1877). Lane publishes a charming ed., by. Grant Allen, with illustrations by E. H. New, in series with Le Gallienne's ed. of Walton's *Compleat Angler*. There are rpts. in E.L. and W.C.

WESLEY, John. See p. 289.

JOHNSON, Samuel. See p. 223.

BOSWELL, James. See p. 276.

COWPER, William. See p. 189.

WALPOLE, Horace (1717–97)

Besides his letters Walpole wrote several books still occasionally read or consulted. These are: several entertaining and mildly "improper" essays contributed to *The World* between 1753 and 1756—the reader is recommended to No. 28; *A Catalogue of the Royal and Noble Authors of England* (2 vols., 1758), which is a bibliography similar to this work in design, but briefer and more lively; *Anecdotes of Painting in England* (1762–71); *The Castle of Otranto* (1764), the progenitor of a brood of "Gothic" novels; *Historic Doubts on Richard III* (1768); and two posthumous collections of memoirs, (i) of the last ten years of the reign of George II (2 vols., 1822), (ii) of the reign of George III (4 vols., 1845). The best ed. of the *Royal and Noble Authors* is by T. Park (5 vols., 1806). The *Anecdotes of Painting* was edited by R. N. Wornum (3 vols., 1888). *The Memoirs of the Reign of George III* was edited by G. F. Russell Barker (4 vols., 1894). *The Castle of Otranto* which is available in E.L. with Beckford's *Vathek* and Johnson's *Rasselas* in one vol., has also been edited by C. F. E. Spurgeon (King's Classics, 1902) and O. Doughty (Scholartis Press, 1929).

Walpole's letters run well into the thousands. P. Cunningham's ed. in 9 vols. (1857–9), which contained 2,654 letters, was displaced by Mrs. Paget Toynbee's which contained 3,420 (Clarendon Press, 16 vols., 1903–5; 3 supplementary vols., 1918–25). This in its turn is being displaced by W. S. Lewis's which will contain 6,000 letters to and from Walpole. The first 2 vols., *Walpole's Correspondence with Cole*, are published by Yale Univ. Press and Milford, 1937. A selection is published in E.L. D.M. Stuart's biographical study (E.M.L.) may be recommended.

WOLLSTONECRAFT, Mary. See p. 249.

WORDSWORTH, William. See p. 197.

COLERIDGE, Samuel Taylor. See p. 200.

BYRON, George Gordon, Lord. See p. 203.

SHELLEY, Percy Bysshe. See p. 204.

KEATS, John. See p. 206.

LAMB, Charles. See p. 270.

CREEVEY, Thomas (1768–1838)

Creevey was a member of the Whig opposition in Parliament a man possessed of a large number of eminent acquaintances and the recipient of many confidences which he reconfided either to his diary or in letters to his step-daughter, Miss Ord. A selection from these was made by Sir Herbert Maxwell and called *The Creevey Papers* (2 vols., Murray, 1903; 1 vol. rpt., 1905). A further selection was made by J. Gore (*Creevey's Life and Times*; Murray, 1934), which contains nothing printed in *The Creevey Papers* and concentrates more upon the social than upon the political history.

XV

DRAMA

THE best collections of the plays of this period are the *British Theatres* of Bell (36 vols., 1791–1802) and Mrs. Inchbald (20 vols., 1824). There are representative selections in E.L., (i) *Restoration Plays* and (ii) *Eighteenth Century Plays*; and in W.C., (i) *Restoration Tragedies*, (ii) *Eighteenth Century Comedy*, and (iii) *Lesser Comedies of the Eighteenth Century*.

Of early accounts of plays and playwrights, mention must be made of D. E. Baker's *The Companion to the Playhouse* (see p. 274) and J. Genest's *Some Account of the English Stage, 1660–1830* (10 vols., 1832). The most comprehensive surveys are A. Nicoll's four works, *A History of Restoration Drama*, *A History of Early Eighteenth Century Drama*, *A History of Late Eighteenth Century Drama*, and *A History of Early Nineteenth Century Drama* (2 vols.), all published by C.U.P. (1923–30).

Certain aspects of the drama are treated in G. H. Nettleton's *English Drama of the Restoration and Eighteenth Century* (Macmillan, 1914), E. Bernbaum's *The Drama of Sensibility* (Ginn, 1915), J. W. Krutch's *Comedy and Conscience after the Restoration* (Columbia U.P., 1924), B. Dobrée's *Restoration Comedy* (Cl. P., 1924) and his *Restoration Tragedy* (Cl. P., 1929), and F. W. Bateson's *English Comic Drama 1700–1750* (Cl. P., 1929).

DRYDEN, John. See vol. 2, pp. 367–8.

SHADWELL, Thomas. See vol. 2, pp. 358–9.

SETTLE, Elkanah (1648–1724)
Most of Settle's work as a dramatist and as a Whig pamphleteer had been done in the Restoration period (see vol. 2, p. 361).

After some nine years' neglect of the stage, he returned to it and produced a series of plays, none of which was so famous as his *Empress of Morocco* (1673). These were *Distress'd Innocence* (1691), *The Ambitious Slave* (1694), *Philaster*, an adaptation of Beaumont and Fletcher's play (1695), *The Siege of Troy* (1707), a comedy called *The City Ramble* (1711), and *The Lady's Triumph: A Comi-Dramatic Opera* (1718). In 1691 Settle was appointed City Poet; that is, he was commissioned to prepare pageants for the Lord Mayor's show. He also produced numerous funeral poems and poems calculated to assist the Whig cause, such as *Eusebia Triumphans: The Hannover Succession to the Imperial Crown of England, An Heroick Poem* (1702, and frequently rptd.), *Augusta Triumphans* (1707) occasioned by Marlborough's successes, *Irene Triumphans* (1713) one of many poems inspired by the Treaty of Utrecht, and *Rebellion Display'd* (1715). It is of some interest to note that *Eusebia Triumphans* provoked Pope's earliest satire, *To the Author of a Poem entitled Successio*. The only biographical and critical study of Settle is F. C. Brown's *E. S. His Life and Works* (Chicago U.P. and C.U.P., 1910).

SOUTHERNE, Thomas (1660–1746)

See vol. 2, p. 363. Southerne's first play was a tragedy, *The Loyal Brother* (1682). After producing a few comedies, he returned to tragedy with *The Fatal Marriage* (1694) and *Oroonoko* (1696), the two plays upon which his reputation as a "pathetic" dramatist is based. Collected editions of Southerne's works were published in 1721 (2 vols.) and 1774 (3 vols.). A study by J. W. Dodds, *Thomas Southerne, Dramatist*, is published in the Yale Studies in English (1933).

CONGREVE, William (1670–1729)

See vol. 2, pp. 311, 362–3. Congreve's four comedies were all written before he reached the age of thirty. They are *The Old Batchelor* (1693), *The Double Dealer* (1694), *Love for Love* (1695), the most lively and stageable, and *The Way of the World* (1700), his masterpiece. A tragedy, *The Mourning Bride*, was published in 1697 and received with considerable applause; but though it is one of the best tragedies of that age, it is now remembered only by the famous opening line, "Music hath charms to soothe a savage breast", and by the description of a temple in Act II, scene i, which Dr. Johnson considered "the most poetical paragraph in the whole mass of English poetry". Congreve also published a novel, *Incognita* (1692; ed. H. F. B. Brett-Smith,

P.R., 1922), a reply to Jeremy Collier (see p. 299), a masque, *The Judgement of Paris* (1701), an adaptation from Molière, *Monsieur de Pourceaugnac, or Squire Trelooby* (1704), in which he collaborated with Vanbrugh and Walsh—it is doubtful whether the printed versions can be ascribed to Congreve and his fellows (see an article by J. C. Hodges in R.E.S., iv. 1928)—an opera, *Semele* (1710), which Handel set to music, and several poems. A collected ed. was published in 3 vols. in 1710.

The first complete ed. of Congreve's works was edited for the Nonesuch Press by M. Summers (4 vols., 1923). There is also an ed. by B. Dobrée (2 vols., W.C.). A separate ed. of *The Way of the World* by W. P. Barrett, is published in the Temple Dramatists (Dent, 1933); and another of exceptional merit, the work of G. R. Noyes, is published in C. M. Gayley's *Representative English Comedies*, vol. 4 (Macmillan, 1936).

Biographies of Congreve have been written by E. Gosse (revised ed., 1924) and D. Crane Taylor (O.U.P., 1931), but neither is completely satisfactory. The best criticism will be found in the introds. to editions mentioned above, in the books listed at the head of this section, and in Hazlitt's *Lectures on the English Comic Writers*.

VANBRUGH, Sir John (1664–1726)

See vol. 2, p. 362. Vanbrugh's best comedies are *The Relapse* (1697), *The Provok'd Wife* (1697), and *The Confederacy* (1705), all of which have been successfully revived in recent years. A collected ed. appeared in 1730.

A selection of Vanbrugh's plays, ed. A. E. H. Swaen, is published in the Mermaid series (Benn). The standard ed. of the complete works is the Nonesuch ed. (1929) in 4 vols., ed. B. Dobrée and G. Webb, with critical introductions and life. An excellent ed. of *The Provok'd Wife*, by A. Thaler, is published in C. M. Gayley's *Representative English Comedies*, vol. 4 (Macmillan, 1936).

A short life of Vanbrugh by B. Dobrée is published in his *Essays in Biography 1680–1726* (O.U.P., 1925). More elaborate, but no more informative, is L. Whistler's *Sir John Vanbrugh Architect and Dramatist* (Cobden-Sanderson, 1938). In addition to the criticism included in these works and in the books listed at the head of this section, readers should turn to *A Re-evaluation of Vanbrugh* by P. Mueschke and J. Fleisher (P.M.L.A., xlix, 1934) and to H. T. E. Perry's *The Comic Spirit in Restoration Comedy* (Yale U.P., 1925).

GRANVILLE, George, Lord Lansdowne. See p. 168.

COLLIER, Jeremy (1650–1726)

The immorality of Restoration drama has been discussed with varying animosity from that day to this. Wycherley had taken an early opportunity of saying the last word on the subject in *The Plain Dealer* (1677), Act II, sc. i., Dryden had exhibited the workings of his conscience in his ode *To the Pious Memory of . . . Mrs. Anne Killigrew* (1686), and Blackmore (see p. 166) had written in general terms of condemnation in the preface to *Prince Arthur* (1695). It was left for Jeremy Collier, a non-juring parson, to rouse the public with *A Short View of the Immorality and Profaneness of the English Stage* (1698). Collier was an experienced controversialist who had amassed an ample supply of material and indignation—too much, in fact; for he is indignant if a comic writer even uses such words as *inspiration* and *martyr*, or names a character *Samson*. Congreve, Vanbrugh, and others replied the same year. Vanbrugh's *Short Vindication* is lazy; Congreve's *Amendments* is weak and petulant. Each, among other defences, offered the excuse of youth, and Congreve even admitted that he had been recovering from an illness, which allowed Collier to inquire in *A Defence of the Short View* (1699), what kind of illness it could have been that was attended by such a convalescence.

There were several other attacks and replies. Collier himself, whose *Short View* reached a fourth ed. in 1699, produced two *Defences* in 1699 and 1700. An anonymous defender of Congreve (1698) scored one or two good debating points. Collier, he suggested, had evidently enjoyed making his smutty collection, from the relish he showed in retailing passages even from banned plays. The same criticism was made by Dryden in *Cymon and Iphigenia*, ll. 15–20; but apart from such a casual allusion, he offered no formal reply (see also the epilogue to *The Pilgrim*; the preface to the *Fables*, para. 13; lines to P. A. Motteux). In fact no convincing reply could be made by meeting Collier on the ground which he had chosen. The sensible reply was to argue, as Dennis did in his *Letters* (1721), that the immorality of the stage was a symptom of illness rather than an illness, that reforming the stage would not reform the town, though reforming the town would certainly reform the stage.

Collier continued his crusade by issuing (1703) a summary of the *Short View* with additions, called *Mr. Collier's Dissuasive from the Playhouse*, and his case was supported by at least three pamphlets in the following year. In 1707, *A Defence of Plays* was put out by a minor dramatist, Edward Filmer, who had already published two *Defences* in 1698. This was pounced upon by Collier for his final denunciation, *A Farther Vindication of the Short View* (1708).

After 1708 the spate of pamphlets began to subside. Of Collier's party the most prolific combatant was Arthur Bedford, who started with some *Serious Reflections* in 1705 and delivered *A Serious Remonstrance* as late as 1719. The dramatists' most able advocate was John Dennis (see p. 216), who published *The Usefulness of the Stage* in 1698, and replied to William Law's attack (see p. 240), *The Absolute Unlawfulness of the Stage-Entertainment* (1726), with *The Stage Defended* (1726).

An interest in the subject has never quite died out. The dramatists' case has been put by Hazlitt in *Lectures on the English Comic Writers* (no. 4, 1819), by Lamb in *On the Artificial Comedy of the Last Century* (*Essays of Elia*, 1823), and by Leigh Hunt in his ed. of Wycherley and others (1840). On Collier's side are ranged Macaulay (a review of Leigh Hunt to be found in his collected *Essays*) and William Archer (*The Old Drama and the New*, Heinemann, 1923). There are good detailed accounts of the controversy, with bibliographies, in A. O. Beljame's *Le Public et les Hommes de Lettres* (see p. 162) and in J. W. Krutch's *Comedy and Conscience after the Restoration* (Columbia U.P., 1924), chs. 5 and 6. See also R. Anthony's *The Jeremy Collier Stage Controversy* (Marquette U.P., 1937).

FARQUHAR, George (1677–1707)

Farquhar's most notable comedies are *The Constant Couple* (1699), *The Recruiting Officer* (1706), and, the best of all, *The Beaux Stratagem* (1707). These are rptd. in a vol. of the *Mermaid* series (Benn) with a good introd. by William Archer. The most elaborate ed. is by C. Stonehill (2 vols., Nonesuch Press, 1930). The introd. is the fullest biography up-to-date. B. Dobrée devotes one ch. to Farquhar in his *Restoration Comedy* (Cl. P., 1929). See also J. Palmer's *The Comedy of Manners* (Bell, 1913).

BURNABY, William (1672?–1706)

Burnaby's comedies were published in the following order: *The Reform'd Wife* (1700), *The Ladies Visiting-Day* (1701), *The Modish Husband* (1702), *Love Betray'd* (1703). A collection edited by F. E. Budd, was published by the Scholartis Press in 1931. Burnaby also translated Petronius's *Satyricon* with the title,

The Satyr of Titus Petronius Arbiter (1694). It was rptd. in the Abbey Classics in 1923.

CIBBER, Colley (1671–1757)
Cibber was the hero of Pope's revised *Dunciad*, an eminence which he scarcely deserved. His most successful plays were *Love's Last Shift* (1696), *She Wou'd, and she wou'd not* (1703), *The Careless Husband* (1705), praised even by Pope, *The Non-Juror* (1718), a political play, for which Cibber was rewarded with the laureateship, *The Provoked Husband* (1728). A collected ed. in 2 vols. appeared in 1721. In 1740 Cibber published his *Apology for the Life of Mr. Colley Cibber, Comedian*, which is interesting both as a self-portrait and as an account of stage conditions. He shows a remarkable power of describing his fellow actors at work. The best ed. is by R. W. Lowe (2 vols., 1889). It is also rptd. in E.L. F. D. Senior's *Life and Times of C. C.* (Constable, 1928), contains a rpt. of *The Careless Husband*. See also F. W. Bateson's *English Comic Drama, 1700–50* (Cl. P., 1929), and R. H. Barker's *Mr Cibber of Drury Lane* (Columbia U.P., 1939).

STEELE, Richard. See p. 265.

ROWE, Nicholas (1674–1718)
Rowe was the leading tragic dramatist during the early years of the century. His best plays, which were collected in 2 vols. in 1714, are *Tamerlane* (1702), *The Fair Penitent* (1703), and *Jane Shore* (1714). These were edited by J. R. Sutherland for the Scholartis Press (1929). Rowe was also the first editor and biographer of Shakespeare (see vol. 2, pp. 244, 254) and his version of Lucan's *Pharsalia* (1718) is one of the best translations of the century. A ch. is devoted to Rowe in Dobrée's *Restoration Tragedy* (Cl. P., 1929).

MANLEY, Mrs. Mary de la Riviere. See p. 280.

DENNIS, John. See p. 217.

CENTLIVRE, Mrs. Susannah (1667?–1723)
Mrs. Centlivre's best comedies (of intrigue) are generally admitted to be *The Busie Body* (1709) and *The Wonder* (1714), both of which held the stage for many years and were rptd. as "Standard plays" as late as 1883. At least two others of her many comedies were frequently performed, *The Gamester* (1705) and *A Bold Stroke for a Wife* (1718). A collected ed. was published in 3 vols. in 1760–1 and rptd. in 1872. Hazlitt's praise of Mrs.

Centlivre's work is to be found in his *Lectures on the English Comic Writers*. Mona Wilson has published a short appreciation in *These were Muses* (Sidgwick and Jackson, 1924), and there is a ch. devoted to her in F. W. Bateson's *English Comic Drama 1700—50* (Cl. P., 1929).

PHILIPS, Ambrose. See p. 169.

ADDISON, Joseph. See p. 267.

YOUNG, Edward. See p. 181.

HUGHES, John. See p. 171.

FENTON, Elijah. See p. 178.

GAY, John. See p. 170.

FIELDING, Henry. See p. 228.

LILLO, George (1693-1739)
Lillo's reputation rests upon his two tragedies of low life, *The London Merchant: or, The History of George Barnwell* (1731) and *Fatal Curiosity* (1737), usually acted with the title *Guilt its own Punishment or Fatal Curiosity*. These plays offered an escape (which was not accepted at the time) from the traditions of heroic and classical tragedy. There is an excellent ed. of them by A. W. Ward (Belles-Letters Series; Heath, 1906). *The London Merchant* is also rptd. in *Eighteenth-Century Plays* (E.L.).

THOMSON, James. See p. 178.

MALLET, David. See p. 179.

CAREY, Henry. See p. 169.

MILLER, James. See p. 177.

JOHNSON, Samuel. See p. 221.

MOORE, Edward (1712-57)
Moore's importance as a dramatist is that he followed the lead of Lillo in writing non-heroic tragedy. *The Gamester*, adapted from

the Elizabethan *A Yorkshire Tragedy*, was published in 1753. Moore had already written two comedies, *The Foundling* (1748) and *Gil Blas* (1751). His chief non-dramatic works are *Solomon: A Seranata* (1743), set to music by William Boyce, and *Fables for the Female Sex* (1744), in which he followed a lead set by Gay (see p. 170). A collected ed. of his *Poems, Fables, and Plays* was published in 1756. Moore was also the editor of *The World* (see p. 265), one of the liveliest of eighteenth-century periodicals. A biographical and critical study by J. H. Caskey was published by the Yale U.P. and O.U.P. in 1927.

MASON, William. See p. 182.

HOME, John (1722–1808)

Home was the author of a romantic tragedy called *Douglas*, whose first performance in Edinburgh (1756) caused what has been described as an uproar of exultation, one Scot going so far as to cry "Whaur's your Wullie Shakespeare noo?" Its reception is interestingly described in Alexander Carlyle's *Autobiography* (see p. 281), ch. 8.

MURPHY, Arthur (1727–1805)

One of the gayest comedies of the period is Murphy's *The Way to Keep him* (1760), rptd. in *Lesser Comedies of the Eighteenth Century* (W.C.). Amongst his other comedies may be mentioned *All in the Wrong* (1761) and *Know your own Mind* (1777). Murphy was also the editor and biographer of Fielding and Dr. Johnson (see pp. 228, 220).

COLMAN, George (1732–94)

Colman's first literary venture was his part-editorship of *The Connoisseur*, 1754–6 (see p. 265). At that time he had thoughts of a legal career and was called to the bar, but his interests were deflected to the theatre. He was a close associate of Garrick, became one of the most noted theatrical managers of the day, and was the author or adapter of some thirty plays, an ed. of which was published in 4 vols. in 1777. Of his original plays the most successful were *The Jealous Wife* (1761), rptd. in *Lesser Comedies of the Eighteenth Century* (W.C.), and *The Clandestine Marriage* (1766), which he wrote with Garrick. It is rptd. in *Eighteenth Century Plays* (E.L.). Colman also wrote a translation of Terence's comedies (1765) which, in Hazlitt's words, "has always been considered, by good judges, as an equal proof of the author's knowledge of the Latin language, and taste in his own". A biographical and critical study was written by E. R. Page (Columbia U.P., 1935).

GARRICK, David (1717–79)

Besides collaborating with Colman in *The Clandestine Marriage* (1766), Garrick adapted a large number of plays for the contemporary stage and wrote several, of which the best are considered to be *A Peep behind the Curtain* (1767), and *Bon Ton, or High Life above Stairs* (1775).

FOOTE, Samuel (1720–77)

Foote's talent lay in the caricature of contemporary figures; but it has also been said of his plays that "there is not a folly, a vice, a sham of the time which they do not expose". *The Minor* (1760) is generally agreed to be his best play; though *The Lyar* (produced, 1762; printed, 1764), which contains few portraits, had a longer career and was revived as recently as 1896. Amongst his other plays may be mentioned *The Mayor of Garret* (1763), *The Patron* (1764), *The Lame Lover* (1770), and *The Maid of Bath* (1771). An ed. of his works was published in 4 vols. in 1770–86, and 2-vol. editions were published in 1799 and 1809. W. Cooke's *Memoirs*, with a collection of his genuine bon-mots, was published in 3 vols. in 1805, and the bon-mots were rptd. in 1902. Two biographies have appeared in modern times, Percy Fitzgerald's *S. F., A Biography* (Chatto, 1910), and M. M. Belden's more scholarly *The Dramatic Work of S. F.* (Yale U.P. and O.U.P., 1929). See also J. Forster's *Historical and Biographical Essays* (1858).

GOLDSMITH, Oliver. See p. 187.

CUMBERLAND, Richard (1732–1811)

Cumberland was one of the most successful comic writers in the sentimental manner. *The Brothers* was well received on its production in 1769 (printed, 1770), and encouraged him to write *The West Indian* (1771), which proved a prodigious and lasting success. *The Fashionable Lover* followed in 1772; but the next ten years were filled with disappointments and failures. A domestic tragedy, *The Mysterious Husband* (1783), inspired by Walpole's *The Mysterious Mother* (1768, had a better reception; and another tragedy, *The Carmelite* (1784), was played with some success. Two more comedies, *The Natural Son* (1784; printed,

1785) and *The Imposters* (1789), were produced before Cumberland regained his early popularity with *The Jew* (1794) and *The Wheel of Fortune* (1795). There is no collected ed. of his plays, but *The Brothers*, *The West Indian*, *The Jew*, and *The Wheel of Fortune* are rptd. in Mrs. Inchbald's *British Theatre*, vol. 18 (1808). *The West Indian* is also rptd. in *Eighteenth-Century Plays* (E.L.).

Memoirs of Richard Cumberland, Written by Himself was published in 1806, and a supplement was added in 1807. A biographical and critical study by S. T. Williams, *R. C. His Life and Dramatic Works*, was published by Yale U.P. and O.U.P. in 1917. There is also an essay on Cumberland in F. Hitchman's *Eighteenth-Century Studies* (1881). But more famous than any of these is Goldsmith's character sketch in *Retaliation* (see p. 186).

MORE, Hannah (1745–1833)

Hannah More's most successful play was a tragedy called *Percy* (1777), which was given a most gratifying reception: "one tear," she wrote, after the second performance, "is worth a thousand hands, and I had the satisfaction to see even the men shed them in abundance". *Percy* and her next tragedy, *The Fatal Falsehood* (1779), had been produced with Garrick's assistance; but after his death in 1779, Hannah More ceased to write for the stage, though she published a vol. of *Sacred Dramas* in 1782. From this time onwards her mind was occupied with more serious reflections. *Thoughts on the Importance of the Manners of the Great to General Society* appeared in 1788, and numerous moral and religious works followed, such as *An Estimate of the Religion of the Fashionable World* (1790), *Strictures on the Modern System of Female Education* (1799), *Practical Piety* (1811), and *Christian Morals* (1813). Her most popular book proved to be *Cœlebs in Search of a Wife* (1809). An ed. of her writings in 19 vols. appeared in 1818–19, and another in 11 vols. in 1830. W. Roberts's *Memoirs of the Life and Correspondence of Mrs. H. M.* appeared in 4 vols. in 1830. There is also a not unpleasing life of Hannah More by Charlotte M. Young in the Eminent Women Series (1888).

SHERIDAN, Richard Brinsley (1751–1816)

Three of Sheridan's plays were first performed in 1775: *The Rivals*, *St. Patrick's Day*, printed in 1788, and a comic opera, *The Duenna*. At first *The Rivals* was a failure, but by revision Sheridan transformed it into a success. The extent of his revision may be seen in R. L. Purdy's ed. of the original version and the first ed. in parallel texts (Cl. P., 1935). Two more plays were performed in 1777: *A Trip to Scarborough* (1781), which is Sheridan's rehandling of Vanbrugh's *Relapse* (see vol. 2, p. 362), and *The School for Scandal*. This play was first printed in 1780, but the genuine text was not published till 1799. Sheridan's final revision was published in his collected works in 1821. *The Critic*, a brilliant dramatic burlesque, was performed in 1779 and published in 1781. The dramatic works are published in E.L., O.S.A., and W.C. A more elaborate ed. by R. C. Rhodes is published by Blackwell (3 vols., 1928). Mr. Rhodes has also written a biography entitled *Harlequin Sheridan* (Blackwell, 1933) which should be supplemented by the introductions in his ed. of the plays and poems.

In 1780 Sheridan entered parliament, where he gained a great reputation as an orator, his most famous speech being his indictment of Warren Hastings in 1787. His collected speeches were published in 5 vols. in 1816.

HOLCROFT, Thomas (1745–1809)

Holcroft produced a number of serious comedies, amongst which may be mentioned *The School for Arrogance* (1791), *The Road to Ruin* (1792), which was the most successful, *Love's Frailties* (1794), and *The Deserted Daughter* (1795). In 1785 he perpetrated a daring piracy of Beaumarchais's *Le Mariage de Figaro*. No copy was available, so Holcroft and a friend attended the theatre every night for some ten days. After the performance they transcribed what they could recollect, and constructed a text by collating their two versions. This text Holcroft translated and successfully produced with the title, *The Follies of a Day*. Holcroft also wrote several novels of which the best are claimed to be *Anna St. Ives* (1792) and the autobiographical *Hugh Trevor* (1794). His famous memoirs are treated separately; see p. 281. *A Bibliography of Thomas Holcroft* by E. Colby was published by the New York Public Library (1922). It contains a prefatory critical study.

REYNOLDS, Frederick (1764–1841)

Reynolds was a popular writer of sentimental comedies. His best plays are said to be *The Dramatist* (1789), rptd. in *Lesser Comedies of the Eighteenth Century* (W.C.), *How to Grow Rich* (1793), *The Rage* (1794), *Fortune's Fool* (1796); and *Cheap Living* (1797). *The Life and Times of Frederick Reynolds written by himself* was published in 1826.

INCHBALD, Mrs. Elizabeth (1753–1821)

Mrs. Inchbald's first success in sentimental comedy was *I'll Tell You What*, produced in 1785 and printed in 1786. The town was equally pleased by *Such Things Are* (1787; printed, 1788), a comedy in which the character of Howard the prison-reformer is introduced, *Every One has his Fault* (1793), rptd. in *Lesser Comedies of the Eighteenth Century* (W.C.), and *Wives as They were and Maids as They are* (1797). But, for extraneous reasons, her most famous play was an adaptation from the German of Kotzebue, *Lover's Vows* (1798), which was rehearsed but never performed at Sir Thomas Bertram's house in Jane Austen's *Mansfield Park*. Mrs. Inchbald also wrote two successful novels, *A Simple Story* (1791) and *Nature and Art* (1796)—see p. 236—and edited three collections of plays, *The British Theatre* (25 vols., 1806–9), *The Modern Theatre* (10 vols., 1811), and *A Collection of Farces and Afterpieces* (7 vols., 1809).

J. Bowden's *Memoirs of Mrs. Inchbald* (2 vols., 1883) is the standard biography. A centenary sketch largely derived from it was written by S. R. Littlewood and entitled *Elizabeth Inchbald and her Circle* (O'Connor, 1921). *An Inchbald Bibliography* by G. L. Joughlin is published in the University of Texas Studies in English (1934).

BAILLIE, Joanna (1762–1851)

Joanna Baillie published her first vol. of plays in 1798 with the title *A Series of Plays: in which it is attempted to delineate the stronger passions of the mind*. A second vol. followed in 1802, and a third in 1812. It was only after publication that one of them *De Montfort* was given the test of stage presentation in 1800. Besides her plays Joanna Baillie also published *Metrical Legends of Exalted Characters* (1821) and *Fugitive Verses* (1840). A collected ed. of her dramatic and poetical works appeared in 1851. *The Life and Work of J.B.* is the title of a study by M. S. Carhart (Yale U.P. and O.U.P., 1923).

COLERIDGE, Samuel Taylor. See p. 198.

MORTON, Thomas (1764–1838)

Morton's three best comedies are said, by historians of the drama, to be *A Cure for the Heart-Ache* (1797), *Speed the Plough* (1800), and *The School of Reform* (1805). *Speed the Plough*, which is rptd. in *Lesser Comedies of the Eighteenth Century* (W.C.), has some claim to attention for having added Mrs. Grundy to English mythology.

COLMAN, George, the younger (1762–1836)

Colman's first play, a musical farce called *The Female Dramatist*, was produced by his father in 1782 but never printed. Of the large number of plays which he wrote, the most successful were the three comedies, *Incle and Yarico* (1787), *The Heir at Law* (1797; authorised ed., 1808), and *John Bull* (1803; authorised ed., 1805). A 4-vol. ed. of his dramatic works was published in Paris in 1827. Colman also wrote a good deal of light verse, a collected ed. of which, by G. B. Buckstone, was published in 1872; it contains *My Nightgown and Slippers* (1797), *Poetical Vagaries* (1812), and *Eccentricities for Edinburgh* (1820). R. B. Peake's *Memoirs of the Colman Family* (2 vols., 1841) is the chief authority for his life.

BYRON, Lord. See p. 202.

SHELLEY, Percy Bysshe. See p. 204.

LANDOR, Walter Savage. See p. 207.

XVI

THE BLUE STOCKINGS

THE Blue Stockings were a group of ladies famous not so much for their writings as for their evening assemblies, where elevated conversation took the place of card-playing. The name is said to have arisen from the peculiarities of one member of the society, Benjamin Stillingfleet, who was remarkable alike for his conversation and for his blue stockings. "His absence," says Boswell, "was felt as so great a loss, that it used to be said, 'We can do nothing without the *blue-stockings*,' and thus by degrees the title was established." A selection from these ladies' letters was made by R. Brimley Johnson and published by Lane (1926) with the title *Bluestocking Letters*.

MONTAGU, Mrs. Elizabeth (1720–1800)

Mrs. Montagu was the leading member of this society. She began to hold her evening assemblies in the seventeen-fifties and continued them with greater brilliance in her magnificent house in Portman Square, to which she moved in 1782. Her writings include the last three of Lord Lyttelton's *Dialogues of the Dead* (see p. 185), and *An Essay on the Writings and Genius of Shakespeare* (1769), intended as an answer to Voltaire's strictures. This was her most elaborate performance. It is little read to-day. Her letters have been presented in what may be called the life-and-letters form: *Elizabeth Montagu. The Queen of the Blue-Stockings. Her Correspondence from 1720 to 1761*, ed. E. J. Climenson is published by Murray (2 vols., 1906), and *Mrs. Montagu. Queen of the Blues. Her Letters and Friendships from 1762 to 1800*, ed. R. Blunt, is published by Constable (2 vols., 1923). There is a good study by R. Huchon entitled *Mrs. Montagu, 1720–1800. An Essay* (Murray, 1907) and a shorter essay by J. Busse, *Mrs. Montagu Queen of the Blues* (Howe, 1928).

CARTER, Elizabeth (1717–1806)

Mrs. Carter—she was never married, but the title was frequently given to unmarried ladies—was famous for her knowledge of Greek. She acquired the language at the expense of many a sleepless night when she kept herself awake by taking snuff, chewing green tea, drinking coffee, and applying a cold towel to the pit of her stomach. Her reward was the production of the standard translation of Epictetus's *Moral Discourses* (1758; rptd. in E.L.) and Dr. Johnson's commendation of a certain scholar, that he understood Greek better than anyone whom he had ever known, except Elizabeth Carter. Mrs. Carter also contributed two papers to Johnson's *Rambler* (nos. 44 and 100) and wrote several poems, one of which, an *Ode to Wisdom*, was rptd. in Richardson's *Clarissa*. Collected editions of her poems appeared in 1738, 1762, and in the second vol. of M. Pennington's *Memoirs of the Life of Mrs. E. C.* (1807), a book which will repay casual inspection.

CHAPONE, Mrs. Hester (1727–1801)

The time is long past since Mrs. Chapone's *Letters on the Improvement of the Mind* (1773) were to be found in every library. Her memory is better preserved by her sprightly correspondence with Richardson and Mrs. Carter, collected in 2 vols. with the title *The Posthumous Works of Mrs. Chapone* (1807). *Rambler* no. 10 is hers, and she also contributed three papers to *The Adventurer* (nos. 77–9). A collected ed. of her works appeared in 1786 (2 vols.) and another in 1807 (4 vols.). There is a short study of Mrs. Chapone in Mona Wilson's *These were Muses* (Sidgwick and Jackson, 1924).

INDEX

311

316